container gardening
COMPLETE

First published in 2017 by Cool Springs Press, an imprint of The Quarto Group, 401 Second Avenue North, Suite 310, Minneapolis, MN 55401 USA. Telephone: (612) 344-8100 Fax: (612) 344-8692 www.QuartoKnows.com

Cool Springs Press titles are also available at discount for retail, wholesale, promotional, and bulk purchase. For details, contact the Special Sales Manager by email at specialsales@quarto.com or by mail at The Quarto Group, Attn: Special Sales Manager, 401 Second Avenue North, Suite 310, Minneapolis, MN 55401 USA.

10 9 8 7 6 5 4 3 2 1

ISBN: 978-1-59186-682-4

Library of Congress Cataloging-in-Publication Data

Names: Walliser, Jessica, author.
Title: Container gardening complete : creative projects for growing vegetables
   and flowers in small spaces / by Jessica Walliser.
Description: Minneapolis, MN : Cool Springs Press, 2017. | Includes index.
Identifiers: LCCN 2017011390 | ISBN 9781591866824 (hc)
Subjects: LCSH: Container gardening.
Classification: LCC SB418 .W355 2017 | DDC 635.9/86--dc23
LC record available at https://lccn.loc.gov/2017011390

Acquiring Editor: Todd R. Berger
Project Manager: Alyssa Lochner
Art Direction and Cover Design: Cindy Samargia Laun
Page Design and Layout: Ashley Prine, Tandem Books
Illustration: Christopher R. Mills

Front and back cover photos by Jessica Walliser

Printed in China

container gardening

COMPLETE

creative projects for growing vegetables and flowers

IN SMALL SPACES

jessica walliser

COOL SPRINGS PRESS

Contents

To my son Ty,
the most amazing thing
I've ever grown.

Acknowledgments

Container Gardening Complete has been one of the most ambitious projects of my career. I learned a lot along the way and had a heck of a good time designing, building, growing, and photographing all the fantastic projects. None of it would have been possible without the help of the great crew of professionals at Cool Springs Press, my supportive family, an amazing group of photogenic friends, and a rock-solid bunch of gardening compadres. To all of you, I give a gigantic, heart-felt thank you!

My editor, Todd Berger, deserves a big dose of gratitude for entrusting me with this project and handing me the reins to run with it. Thank you for answering my many questions and for everything you did to help this book come to fruition. It's been a pleasure working with you!

To my band of extremely gracious models/friends, Brad and Greta Severson, Bobby and Lisa Standish, Rebecca and Mike Berty, Ron Sims, Susan Washburn, Nora Pickell, Liza Thornton, Kelli Russo, Jackie Simpson, and Hannah Reiff, I raise a glass to you and thank you for your willingness to hold a prolonged pose and dig into a project with energy and enthusiasm—and for wearing long sleeves and pants on some very hot days!

Also, thank you to the good folks at Garden Dreams Urban Farm and Nursery in Wilkinsburg, Pennsylvania, for their contribution to one of the projects featured in this book, the Good Bug Wheelbarrow Garden. Randy and the crew at Soergel Orchards and Garden Center in Wexford, Pennsylvania, deserve the same appreciation for providing me with some of the plants and gorgeous containers found throughout these pages.

Ron Sims was gracious enough to design and build the two woodworking projects featured in the first chapter—the Cedar Planter Box and the Pot Dolly. Thank you, Ron, for your attention to detail, your creative work, your good nature, and for allowing me to feature your designs in these pages.

Thank you to my neighbors and friends, the Kennedys, the Normans, the Washburns, the Seversons, and the Bertys, for allowing me to stage some of the photographs at your homes. And, a big-time hats-off to the many wonderful gardeners who let me come to their gardens and take photographs, including Mary Odom, Anna Singer, Jessica Carson, Robyn Macerelli, Katie Casker, Seth and Sonja Finn, Zolina Cook, Joyce Bolanovich, Jamie Earl, Ilona Yerger (my awesome mom!), and the World's Best Kitty and Garden Sitter, Liza Thornton.

To Paul Wiegman: I'm going to thank you forever and ever for all you did way back when to help me develop this wonderful little career of mine. Had you not welcomed me into the world of radio all those years ago, things would not be as they are today.

My fabulous business partners at SavvyGardening.com, Niki Jabbour, Amy Andrychowicz, and Tara Nolan, have my utmost appreciation for their professionalism, humor, and friendship. When writing a book, there's nothing better than having the unfailing support and well-seasoned advice of other authors. You guys rock!

And most importantly, to my husband John and my amazing son Ty: your inspiration, support, and love mean the world to me. Without the two of you, life wouldn't be nearly as much fun. You're everything that matters.

Introduction

Container gardening is far from a new invention. Humans have been growing plants in vessels since soon after the Neolithic Revolution thousands of years ago. While the methods and materials we use have certainly changed over the years, our intent has not. We continue to grow plants in containers to provide food and beauty for ourselves and those we love.

At the beginning, humans who grew plants in pots may have done so to overcome adverse soil conditions, more carefully tend a highly treasured medicinal plant, or focus irrigation needs on a smaller area in places where water was scarce. Today's gardeners, however, have a far more diverse list of reasons for growing plants in containers. Yes, many of us still use containers to avoid having to garden in soil with poor drainage, contaminants, or lousy fertility, and we still use them to grow coveted plants. But we also grow plants in containers to save time and space, reduce weeding and other chores, beautify our living spaces, and show off our creativity and sense of personal style.

Container gardening allows us to grow our own fresh food, even in a very limited space, and it affords a level of flexibility not found when growing these plants in the ground. With container gardening, we can feed our families without ever having to turn the sod, spread wheelbarrows of mulch, or fire up even a single piece of gas-powered equipment. Heck, you don't even have to own a shovel to grow plants in containers.

We're also gardening in pots for purposes beyond ourselves. We're designing plantings to attract and support butterflies, bees, and other

Container gardens can be designed to provide habitat and food for pollinators, such as this great spangled fritillary butterfly.

◀ There are many reasons to grow plants in containers, including avoiding soil conditions that are less than ideal, saving space, reducing gardening chores, growing food, or perhaps just because you want to grow something beautiful.

Growing edible plants such tomatoes, peppers, eggplants, and many others in containers requires much less effort than building and maintaining an in-ground garden, especially if you utilize the advice offered in this book.

pollinators, and we're filling containers with nectar plants for hummingbirds and berries for songbirds. We've come to recognize that habitat container gardening is a wonderful way to help all sorts of wildlife, without requiring a lot of space or effort.

The point is, whether you're gardening in a suburban neighborhood, on the balcony of an urban high-rise, or at the end of a long country lane, you can grow a broad diversity of plants in pots. And truth be told, you can do it for whatever reasons you'd like.

But growing a thriving container garden requires more than simply filling a container with dirt and sticking a couple of plants in it. Paying careful attention to container choice, soil composition, plant selection, and maintenance needs always pays off in spades, increasing your chances of having a healthy, productive container

garden. That's where *Container Gardening Complete* comes in. The purpose of this book is to hand you all the tools you'll need to make smart choices and filter through the myriad options available to today's gardeners.

Within these pages, you'll first learn about the three pillars of successful container gardening and the critical role they play in ensuring your success. You'll learn how choosing the right container influences plant growth and how to blend the best mixture of potting soil to fill it. These basics are covered in depth in the first chapter, setting the stage for advice on properly siting your container garden to optimize growth.

▶ In these pages you'll discover dozens of plants perfectly suited to container culture, and you'll learn plenty of tips for arranging them in an aesthetically pleasing way.

Growing in containers isn't complicated, though it isn't completely trouble-free either. With a bit of care, however, you can learn how to properly prune, water, fertilize, and otherwise care for your container plants so they'll always be in tip-top shape.

With the advice found in this book, you'll be able to make hearty harvests from each container, extending your growing season and keeping your kitchen counter full of homegrown goodness.

Then, Chapter 2 will fill you in on how to design beautiful containers. This chapter is overflowing with lists, charts, and photographs of dozens of flower, herb, fruit, and vegetable varieties perfect for growing in containers. You'll also find design "recipes" you can use in your container garden, if you're a bit shy about making your own plant combinations. You'll learn how to plant properly, and how growing edible plants differs from growing ornamentals.

Subsequent chapters will teach you how to water, prune, fertilize, and otherwise care for your container garden, without requiring a ton of time,

money, or exertion. A chapter on troubleshooting includes a gallery of common container garden pests with advice on managing them without the use of synthetic chemical pesticides. The same chapter also includes a section on managing plant diseases and other ailments that may affect your containerized plants.

Toward the end of the book, you'll be introduced to a few useful harvesting methods and you'll learn what to do with your plants and containers when the growing season ends.

Throughout the pages of this book, I've included 21 DIY container-gardening projects.

Some are tailored to beginner gardeners, while others are a bit more involved. But regardless of their complexity, these projects are an excellent way to get your creative juices flowing. After all, one of the best reasons to grow your plants in containers is the opportunity to develop and exhibit your own sense of style. Use the projects as a jumping off point and build on them however you wish. Each project is designed with a particular purpose in mind. Whether it's growing backyard berries on a deck, building a raised planter to improve accessibility, creating a container trellis to grow vertically and save space, or using a repurposed item as a pot to cut down on costs, each project's purpose and construction is outlined via clear, step-by-step instructions and photographs.

In the final chapter of the book, you'll find a gallery of dozens of additional creative ideas you can include in your own container garden. I'm sure you'll find the sky's the limit when it comes to cool container gardening concepts and trends.

My hope is that *Container Gardening Complete* becomes your bible for growing anything and everything in containers. Once you see how fun and easy gardening in containers is, and how, with just a little forethought, you can harvest armloads of homegrown goodies from the smallest of spaces, you'll come to love growing in containers as much as I do. There's a whole new world of gardening right here at your fingertips. Let's get started.

There's an infinite number of unique ways to design and exhibit garden containers. Whether they're purely practical, simply lovely, or utterly whimsical, partner your imagination with guidance from this book to come up with containers you love.

chapter 1

Getting Started

The best thing about container gardening is that anyone can do it. You don't need a lot of space, money, or time to grow a few containers filled with gorgeous plants. All you really need is the desire to grow something, a little inspiration, a touch of creativity, and a couple of bucks (and heck, if you're willing to get *really* creative, you can even cross that last one off the list). All the information you need to grow flowers, vegetables, fruits, herbs, and more is right here at your fingertips, in this book. For newbies, container gardening is a great way to jump into the world of gardening without needing a plot of land. Or, for more experienced gardeners, it's an excellent way to take your existing outdoor living space to the next level, without having to invest a significant amount of time or money. If you put a little effort into planning your container garden before you get started, the payoff will extend way beyond growing a few pretty plants.

By carefully considering what you're going to grow and how you're going to grow it, you'll be able to harvest your own fresh, homegrown produce month after month, or enjoy the season-long color of ornamental flower- and foliage-filled

◀ It doesn't take much room to grow a container garden if you spend some time planning before you get started. Even a small window ledge will do.

containers while providing habitat for butterflies, bees, hummingbirds, and lots of other living creatures. There are many benefits of growing in containers, but to reap those benefits, you have to start with the basics, which brings us to the topic of this chapter: getting started.

THE THREE PILLARS OF SUCCESSFUL CONTAINER GARDENING

Whether you're growing edible plants, evergreen shrubs, or flowering tropicals in your container garden, good planning is essential. The first step in growing a successful container garden is putting some careful consideration into building a good foundation for your plants. Many failed container gardens are the result of poor planning and not understanding the importance of setting your plants up for success right from the very beginning. As gardeners, we get so jazzed for the actual planting process that we sometimes forget all the important details that need to be in place before we even think about sowing a single seed. We love traipsing through the garden center picking out the prettiest plants

The three foundational pillars to successful container gardening include selecting the right kind of container, filling it with the right potting mix, and placing it in the best growing conditions.

and pouring through the seed catalogs on a quest to find the perfect pepper variety, but we don't always take the time to pick out the right potting soil, for example. It's a lot of fun to select plants, tuck roots into the soil, and sink seeds down into a pot, but it's not as much fun to tend to the nitty-gritty details. But if you neglect the less-glamorous tasks that are the focus of this chapter, all those pretty plants and perfect seeds will be unhappy, and you'll be a disappointed and discouraged gardener.

There are three pillars that comprise the foundation of successful container gardening, and if they're not in place, your chances of having a productive container garden are greatly reduced. Without the **right kind of container**, the **right potting mix**, and the **right location**, things may not turn out the way you planned. The rest of this chapter carefully examines each of these three pillars and gives you the information needed to establish a strong foundation for your container garden.

Choosing a Container

A quick internet search on container gardening results in well over five million hits on the subject. Many of them begin by telling you that you can use just about any object capable of holding soil as a garden container. While this may be true, it isn't necessarily the best advice. It may lull a new gardener into thinking she can plant just about any type of plant into any type of container and have great success, which just isn't the case. Yes, you can use a tea kettle or a boot or a coffee mug as a container, but is using such a tiny vessel really setting your plants up for success?

The answer, of course, is maybe. If you're growing a tiny, drought-proof succulent plant, a small container such as a boot or a coffee mug is just fine. But if you're growing a watermelon vine, a tea kettle is clearly a bad idea. Rather than encouraging the use of the cutest or cleverest object as a container, the focus should be on selecting the best container for its particular purpose.

The following project proves you can still use clever objects for containers, you just have to select the right plants to grow in them. This gutter garden makes a great vertical container planting, but for it to be a successful project, you have to make smart decisions about what to grow in it.

Using cute and clever containers in your garden is fine, as long as you remember to partner them with the right plants. This toaster is a good fit for these tiny succulent plants, but it wouldn't work for a tomato or other larger plant.

GUTTER GARDEN

Gardeners with limited space are sure to appreciate this project. As long as you have a wall or a fence, there's a place to grow a gutter garden. There are many ways to adapt this concept by changing the length of the gutters, adding more layers of gutters, arranging them in some kind of pattern, or even painting them.

The most important thing to remember is to choose the right kinds of plants to fill it. Because the volume of soil in the gutter is so small, look for plants that only grow to a few inches in height and can handle having their roots in cramped conditions. A gutter garden is not the place to grow full-sized plants. Instead, go for a mix of mini-sized flowers, foliage plants, and edibles. For this project, we used the following plants:

- Spicy Globe Dwarf Basil (*Ocimum basilicum* 'Spicy Globe')
- Thyme (*Thymus vulgaris*)
- Sweet Marjoram (*Origanum majorana*)
- Tri-color Sage (*Salvia officinalis* 'Tricolor')
- Golden Creeping Jenny (*Lysimachia nummularia* 'Aurea')
- Portulaca (*Portulaca grandiflora*)
- Curly Juncus (*Juncus effusus* 'Spiralis')
- Dwarf Ivy (*Hedera helix* cultivar)
- Baby Swiss Chard (*Beta vulgaris* subsp. *vulgaris*)

Make sure the fence or wall where you plan to mount your gutter garden is stable and secure, because once the gutters are filled with wet dirt and grown plants, they will be heavy. Use only the mounting brackets designed for the type of gutter you purchase to ensure the most secure fit.

At season's end, there's no need to take down your gutter garden. The gutters themselves are completely weather-proof. Simply pull out any frost-nipped plants and discard the spent potting mix. When the following spring arrives, refill with new potting mix and replant with a fresh generation of plants.

MATERIALS NEEDED

Aluminum gutter (one length 6 ft. long, another length 4 ft. long)

Gutter end caps (4)

Gutter mounting brackets (7)

2-in. wood screws (7)

Silicon caulk

Enough 50/50 potting soil and compost blend to fill the gutters

Plants

TOOLS NEEDED

Hammer

Scratch awl

Drill with driver bits

Level

Tape measure

Marker or pencil

Safety glasses

Caulk gun

HOW TO MAKE A GUTTER GARDEN

STEP 1 Lay the sections of gutter on a soft surface and use the hammer and scratch awl to pierce several drainage holes in the bottom of each gutter.

STEP 2 Push the gutter end caps over the open ends of both pieces of gutter, being careful to line them up properly until they slide into place.

STEP 3 Apply a bead of silicon caulking around the inside seam of the gutter end caps to secure them in place. Let the caulking dry before mounting and planting the gutters.

STEP 4 Hold one piece of gutter against the mounting surface with its flat side to the back, using a level to ensure the gutter is level. Use a marker or pencil to mark the entire top edge of the gutter onto the mounting surface. Once the line is marked, set the gutter aside.

STEP 5 Use a tape measure to measure and mark off the locations for the mounting brackets. Place the outside brackets about 5 in. from the ends of the gutter, then mark two additional evenly spaced brackets for the 6-ft. length of gutter, and a single middle bracket for the 4-ft. gutter.

STEP 6 Screw the gutter mounting brackets to the surface. Because the upper edge of the gutter will sit slightly above the top edge of the brackets, position the brackets slightly lower than the marked line. The distance will vary, depending on the type of gutters you have. (Note: If you're mounting your gutter garden on a brick or concrete wall, see the note on page 20 for different bracket-mounting instructions).

5

6

Continued

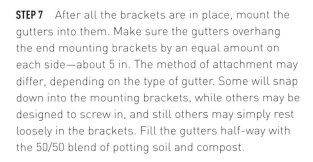

STEP 7   After all the brackets are in place, mount the gutters into them. Make sure the gutters overhang the end mounting brackets by an equal amount on each side—about 5 in. The method of attachment may differ, depending on the type of gutter. Some will snap down into the mounting brackets, while others may be designed to screw in, and still others may simply rest loosely in the brackets. Fill the gutters half-way with the 50/50 blend of potting soil and compost.

STEP 8   Take the plants out of their pots and position them in the gutters, taking your time to make sure you're happy with the layout. Then, fill in between the plants with more potting soil mixture until the gutters are almost filled. Be sure to leave a little headspace between the top of the soil and the gutter's edge to keep irrigation water from running off.

STEP 9   Water the plants well. If you included herbs or edible greens in your gutter garden, harvest them regularly to keep them from growing too large for the gutters. Keep your gutter garden well-watered throughout the growing season as the small volume of soil it holds will dry out more frequently than larger containers.

NOTE: If you're mounting your gutter garden on a brick or concrete wall, you'll need to adjust the bracket mounting hardware. Instead of wood screws, use 2-in. screws with masonry anchors. Drill a pilot hole for the screw anchors at each of the marked locations using a drill equipped with a masonry bit. Choose a bit that's appropriate for the size of the screw anchor you're using (this is often noted on the package they come in). Then, insert a masonry anchor into each pre-drilled pilot hole. Gently tap it with a hammer until the lip is flush with the wall. Position a bracket over each of the masonry anchors, lining the holes up, and use a drill with a driving bit to screw the bracket into place.

There are many qualities to consider when deciding what type of pots to use in your container garden. And, while physical appearance is certainly a big part of the decision, there are other, more important, factors to think about. Let's discuss each of them in turn.

Size

I'll skip using the obvious cliché to stress the importance of size when it comes to container gardening, and instead, point out the reasons *why* it matters so much. First, larger containers hold more potting mix, and the greater the volume of potting mix a particular container can hold, the more root growth it's able to support. A happy, healthy containerized plant is one whose roots reach deep to access nutrients and water, spreading through the whole container with plenty of room to spare. Plants with ample root systems are less prone to stress and have better overall health, making them less inviting to pests and better able to fight off pathogens.

Plants whose roots are crowded and circling around inside of the pot are called "pot-bound," and they're more prone to suffer the ill effects of root competition, drought, and nutritional deficiencies. In other words, pot-bound plants are under a lot of stress. Much like people, stressed plants have weaker immune systems, making them more susceptible to attacks from plant-eating pests and disease-causing pathogens. Choosing a container that holds enough soil to support a year's worth of root growth is the easiest way to encourage healthy, productive plants, no matter what you're growing. Plants grown in small containers often don't reach their full potential, but instead "max out" at a certain height because their puny root system simply can't support any more top growth. In most cases,

The larger a container is, the more potting mix it can hold and the more root growth it can support. Large-statured plants require big containers.

vegetable yields are significantly reduced when the plants are stuffed into pots that are too small. There's no doubt that containerized plants grown in enough soil to fully support their root systems perform the best.

Another big bonus of large containers is the reduced need to water. Because bigger containers hold more potting mix, they can also absorb and hold a greater volume of water. This

Because large containers hold a bigger volume of moisture-holding potting soil, they generally require less frequent irrigation than smaller containers.

is especially true if you use a high-quality potting mix like the ones introduced later in this chapter. All of this translates into a basic equation: bigger containers = greater soil volume = less watering. Of course there are other factors that influence this equation too, including how "thirsty" a particular plant is, how much sun the pot receives, whether or not the container is made of a porous material, and if the pot is subjected to drying winds. But, generally speaking, the larger the pot, the less frequently it needs to be

watered. I'll cover all the details on watering your container garden in Chapter 3, but this basic rule of thumb is an important one to remember when choosing a container.

The best size for a container is also obviously closely tied to the mature size of the plant itself. If you're growing a small lettuce plant (*Lactuca sativa*), for example, a container that holds one or two gallons of potting mix is more than enough room for the plant's roots. But, if you're growing a large tropical hibiscus (*Hibiscus rosa-sinensis*) or a fig tree (*Ficus carica*), you'll need a far larger container. Though some trial and error is required to figure out the ideal container size for each specific plant (or collection of plants) it's always better to have a pot that is too big rather than too small.

I recommend using the plant-specific guidelines found on the next page when selecting plants for your container. The container sizes found in this list hold the minimum soil volume needed by that particular plant. If you plan to combine different plants together into the same pot, then you'll need to add these measurements together to ensure there's enough room to produce an ample root system. For example, if you want to combine a tomato plant (*Solanum lycopersicum*) with a pepper plant (*Capsicum spp.*) and a few herbs, you'll need a container that holds at least 20 to 28 gallons of potting mix.

Obviously, the specific variety of any given vegetable is also closely tied to the size container it will need, so these are guidelines, not rules; there's no doubt you'll need a far bigger pot for a standard-sized tomato than you will for a determinate or dwarf-type tomato, but it's still best to err on the side of a larger container. Because

of the great amount of variation among specific varieties of plants, the next chapter delves deeper into the subject of pot size by introducing you to specific varieties of fruits and vegetables that were purposefully bred to be grown in containers. These selections are smaller in stature and have more compact growth, making them perfect choices for container gardeners who want to save space by using smaller pots or by growing more plants in each container. Combining the information below with the varietal information in the next chapter provides you with everything you'll need to make an informed decision about the best selection of plants to include in any particular pot.

The best container to use for any particular plant is also dependent on the eventual size of the mature plant. Small-statured plants, such as these Bonsai Japanese Maples (*Acer palmatum*), only require small-statured containers.

Minimum Soil Volume Needed for Specific Plants:

- **30 gallons minimum for each dwarf or columnar fruit tree,** evergreen, or small shade tree.

- **20 to 30 gallons minimum for each shrub or other large plant,** including figs, blueberries (*Vaccinium* spp.), goji berries (*Lycium* spp.), hydrangeas (*Hydrangea spp.*), tropical flowering plants, and many others.

- **10 to 15 gallons minimum for each extra-large vegetable,** such as full-sized tomatoes, winter squash (*Cucurbita spp.*), pumpkins (*Cucurbita* spp.), melons (*Cucumis melo*), and artichokes (*Cynara cardunculus* var. *scolymus*).

- **8 to 10 gallons minimum for each large fruit or vegetable plant,** including peppers, eggplants (*Solanum melongena*), tomatillos (*Physalis philadelphica*), dwarf blueberry bushes, cucumbers (*Cucumis sativus*), summer squash/zucchini (*Cucurbita pepo*), and bush-type winter squash varieties.

- **5 to 8 gallons minimum for each medium-sized vegetable or flowering plant,** including cabbage (*Brassica oleracea* var. *capitata*), broccoli (*Brassica oleracea* var. *italica*), cauliflower (*Brassica oleracea* var. *botrytis*), Brussels sprouts (*Brassica oleracea* var. *gemmifera*), bush-type cucumbers, and okra (*Abelmoschus esculentus*). This is also the suggested minimum soil volume for each flowering or foliage perennial or ornamental grass included in a container.

- **1 to 2 gallons minimum for each small-statured vegetable or flowering plant,** including many flowering or foliage annuals, kohlrabi (*Brassica oleracea* var. *gongylodes*), lettuce, kale (*Brassica oleracea* var. *sabellica*), chard, collards (*Brassica oleracea* var. *medullosa*), spinach (*Spinacia oleracea*), and other greens. Individual herb plants fit into this category as well.

- **Plants that are usually grown in a group,** such as strawberries (*Fragaria* x *ananassa*), corn (*Zea mays*), bush beans (*Phaseolus vulgaris*), peas (*Pisum sativum*), and roots and tubers such as potatoes (*Solanum tuberosum*), carrots (*Daucus carota* subsp. *sativus*), beets (*Beta vulgaris*), radish (*Raphanus sativus*), onions (*Allium cepa*), and turnips (*Brassica rapa* subsp. *rapa*) can be planted in almost any size container, as long as the seeds or plants are spaced at the appropriate distance for optimum growth (as noted on the plant tag or seed packet) and the pot is deep enough for the roots to have ample room to grow. The smaller the pot is, though, the fewer seeds or plants it can house.

Large shrubs and other plants, such as this Red Abyssinian Banana tree (*Ensente ventricosum* 'Maurelii'), need between 20 and 30 gallons of soil volume.

Select a container that holds at least 10 to 15 gallons of soil for each extra-large vegetable, including containerized melons like these growing in a fabric planter bag.

Large fruits and vegetables such as this eggplant need a minimum of 8 to 10 gallons of soil to perform their best; more if they're combined with other plants.

Flowering and foliage annuals, herbs, and small vegetables such as these lettuce plants only require 1 or 2 gallons of soil for each plant.

Each medium-sized veggie, such as these cabbage and broccoli plants, needs at least 5 to 8 gallons of growing mix.

◀ Strawberry plants can be grown in almost any size container, just remember that smaller containers will support a smaller number of plants.

Drainage

Another necessary quality to look for in a container is ample drainage. Most commercially made garden pots have a pre-drilled drainage hole in the bottom so excess irrigation water can escape out the bottom of the pot rather than saturate the soil and cause root rot and other issues. If you have a container that does not have a pre-made drainage hole present, you'll have to make one yourself.

- If the container is made of terracotta or concrete, use a drill fitted with a masonry bit to make a drainage hole.
- If the container is made from glazed ceramic or glass, use a drill fitted with a tile bit.
- If the container is made of wood, fit your drill with a spade or twist bit.
- If the container is made of metal, either punch holes through it using a scratch awl and a hammer, or drill holes with a high-speed steel (HSS) drill bit.
- If the container is made of plastic or resin, use a spur-point bit or plastics drill bit.

Use a slow speed and steady, soft pressure to drill through the bottom of the pot. To avoid damaging the container, do not push hard or use the wrong bit. It's best to make one or two large, ½- to 1-in.-diameter drainage holes in the bottom of a pot rather than many tiny holes that can easily become clogged. If you're using a scratch awl and hammer to make holes in the bottom of a metal container, rotate the awl around inside of each hole to make it larger.

There is no more important trait in a container than a place for excess water to drain out. Not only does a proper drainage hole keep the roots from sitting in water, but it allows excess

If you're repurposing an item such as a stock tank for use as a garden container, make sure it has drainage holes in the bottom. If none are present, you'll have to make your own.

fertilizer salts to be flushed out of the soil via the drainage water. Without proper drainage, the root and shoot tips of your plants could suffer from fertilizer salt burn.

If you're using a saucer beneath your container to catch the drainage water that exits through the hole, empty the saucer soon after watering. Leaving a saucer full of water sitting under the plant is not much better than a pot with no drainage hole at all.

The only time you don't want a drainage hole in the bottom of a container is when growing aquatic or bog plants. These carnivorous pitcher plants (*Sarracenia purpurea*) love saturated soil, so there's no drainage hole in the bottom of their container. You'll find more about growing carnivorous plants in containers in Chapter 6.

Contrary to a long-held popular belief, adding broken pot chards, rocks, or other materials in the bottom of a pot with no drainage hole does not "add drainage," nor does it improve it. Quite the contrary, in fact. Adding bulky materials to the bottom of the pot only serves to raise the water table inside the container, which floods the roots even more quickly. Pot shards and rocks are *not* a substitute for a proper drainage hole.

Materials

The next factor to consider when selecting pots for your container garden is the type of material. There are a nearly infinite number of commercially made garden pots on the market and an equal number of repurposed items that can be made into a growing container. Each material has its pros and cons, and thought should be given to each factor before deciding which kinds of pots are worth the investment. Here are some of the most popular materials for garden containers and a list of factors to consider before making any decisions.

Terracotta/clay. Though it's inexpensive, terracotta is heavy, breakable, and not weather resistant. Clay pots can also develop white salt stains on their exterior and turn green with moss

Terracotta or clay pots are inexpensive, but they easily turn green with moss or show white salt stains. If you don't like that kind of weathered look, select a different material for your containers.

growth (which may or may not be a good thing, depending on your sense of aesthetics). Terracotta containers are available in a large range of styles, shapes, and sizes, and those that are fired and/or glazed are less prone to flaking and cracking. Clay is porous, which means it dries out more quickly than other materials, but it allows for good air exchange for roots. Clay absorbs heat, too—a definite plus in the spring, but not so good in the summer when soil temperatures in the pot can get overly warm.

Glazed ceramic. Made from fine-textured clay that's been glazed and kiln-fired, glazed ceramic garden pots are available in many colors, styles, and sizes. They're beautiful, but they're also breakable, expensive, and very heavy. Though they're less porous than bare terra cotta, these containers may

still crack or flake in freeze-thaw cycles. The glaze can easily chip, but these containers hold moisture well and are very decorative.

Plastic. Plastic garden pots have come a long way in the last few decades. Manufacturers now use decorative colors and styles to make the pots look more like other materials. Lightweight and inexpensive, plastic containers are very durable and are much less likely to crack than terracotta or ceramic pots. With a variety of different finishes, some plastic containers are prone to fading, chipping, and cracking if dropped or left outdoors during the winter. Others are more resilient. Double-walled plastic pots have good insulation properties, and all plastic pots do a good job of retaining soil moisture. Plastic pots that have faded can be

Glazed ceramic pots come in a broad range of colors and styles. They're very decorative but will crack or flake if left outdoors in the winter.

Wooden containers such as these raised planter beds can be painted, if desired. They won't last forever, but using naturally rot-resistant wood, such as redwood, cedar, and locust, definitely improves their lifespan.

Plastic containers can come in some pretty wild colors. They're lightweight and durable, but less expensive models are prone to cracking if left outdoors in the winter.

Resin pots are made from a polyethylene composite that's molded and baked. They're easy to lift and resist cracking.

Fiberglass pots are molded into different styles and can be made to look like other materials.

painted with a good-quality exterior paint to restore their appearance.

Wood. Half whiskey barrels have been among the most ubiquitous garden containers for many years, but they aren't the only wood planters you can have in your garden. Wood planter boxes are very affordable, especially if you're willing to build your own. The informal, natural appearance of wood lends itself nicely to both cottage-style gardens and suburban landscapes. Naturally rot-resistant woods, such as redwood, cedar, or locust, make the best planters, though pressure treated lumber is also useful for planters where no edibles will be grown. Wood planters will eventually have to be replaced, but you'll get many years out of them before they do. Wood is an excellent insulator, protecting roots from fluctuations in temperatures during the heat of summer as well as in winter. An upcoming project will show you how to build a wooden planter box of your own.

Resin. Most high-quality resin garden pots are made from a low-density polyethylene composite that's poured into a mold and "baked." They can be made to look like granite, stone, or other materials that give them a contemporary look. Resin is maintenance free, very lightweight, and crack resistant. Poor-quality resin planters may fade with ultraviolet exposure. Containers made of resin handle temperature fluctuations well and some brands are made from recycled materials.

Fiberglass. Often molded into different styles and patterns to look like concrete, stone, or glazed ceramic, fiberglass garden pots are durable and lightweight. But, because of their thin walls, they can crack if dropped. They also tend to be fairly expensive. Fiberglass is made from a plastic embedded with glass fibers.

Fiberstone. This material is made from a combination of crushed limestone and fiberglass mixed with a composite. Fiberstone containers look like stone, but they're far lighter and easier to move. Weather-resistant and thicker-walled than regular fiberglass planters, fiberstone pots can be left outdoors year-round and are not likely to crack or flake. The biggest downside is their expensive price.

Metal. Metal containers can be made of copper, galvanized metal, stainless steel, steel, cast iron, aluminum, and many other metals. Though they're attractive, some types may rust if not painted, particularly steel and cast iron. Thinner metals such as aluminum are lightweight, but they'll easily dent. Others, such as cast iron, are not likely to crack or dent, but they're extremely heavy. Rust-proof metal containers include aluminum, galvanized metal, copper, and stainless steel. Some brands of steel and aluminum containers are powder-coated to provide a colorful, fade-resistant finish.

Polystyrene foam. High-quality polystyrene foam containers can be quite expensive, but they're made to look like heavier materials, such as terracotta, stone, concrete, ceramic, or metal. Foam planters insulate plant roots very well and protect them from excessive heat and cold. These containers are lightweight, which is a definite plus, but they're not as strong as some other materials. Polystyrene foam containers with raised, embossed designs may chip and dent. These containers can be left outside year-round and used for many years.

Fiberstone pots look like stone, but they're much lighter and can be left outdoors year-round.

There are many different types of garden containers made from metal, including cast iron, aluminum, and stainless steel.

Polystyrene foam containers can be expensive, but if you're looking for lightweight containers, they fit the bill. They can be left outdoors year-round but may be more prone to fading and denting if they are.

Fabric pots, such as the one housing this eggplant, are inexpensive and very useful. The geo-textile fabric they're made of promotes good air exchange and prevents root circling.

Metal hayracks, planters, and baskets lined with coconut fiber are attractive garden containers. They dry out very quickly, though, unless they're lined with plastic.

Fabric pots/grow bags. These extremely lightweight containers are made from a fibrous, geo-textile fabric that's portable and very easy to work with. Some brands even come with handles. Fabric pots are inexpensive, and the best brands to look for if you're growing food are those that are BPA-free. One of the biggest pluses of fabric bags is their ability to prevent root circling and pot-bound plants. When a growing root hits the fabric, instead of starting to circle around inside the pot, the root branches, creating a fibrous network of roots instead of a pot-bound plant. The roots stay within the fabric, and the containers last for many years, even when left outdoors during the winter. Fabric pots allow for good gas exchange, too, enabling the roots to breathe and stabilizing soil temperatures. They come in a broad range of colors and sizes; some are so big you can even grow good-sized trees in them.

Fiber-lined. Porch planters, hanging baskets, hayracks, deck railing planters, and lots of other containers are made in this style, which consists of a metal frame lined with coconut fiber (known as coir) or a similar-looking synthetic substitute. Pretty and fairly inexpensive, fiber-lined containers are lightweight, but they dry out very quickly unless you put a thin sheet of plastic with a few drainage holes in between the fiber and the potting soil. The liners need to be replaced every few years, but the natural look of fiber-lined planters is worth it.

▲ Hypertufa is a great replacement for heavy concrete. It's a fraction of the weight of concrete and is easy to make yourself.

▼ Concrete is extremely durable, but it's also extremely heavy. Large concrete planters like these urns are meant to stay put.

Concrete. Though concrete is very durable and weather-proof, it's also extremely heavy, making big concrete planters practically immovable. The cost varies greatly, based on the size of the container and the design, but concrete is generally considered to be fairly inexpensive. Over time, concrete pots develop a nice patina. Concrete is a great insulator and will protect roots from extreme temperatures.

Hypertufa. An excellent alternative to concrete, this durable, frost-proof material is far lighter than concrete but with a similar appearance. Hypertufa is made by combining Portland cement (a specific type of cement used to make concrete and stucco), peat moss, and perlite (a natural volcanic glass that's heated until it expands into smooth particles), and it's very easy to make. See the project described later in the text to build a hypertufa planter of your own.

CEDAR PLANTER BOX

MATERIALS NEEDED

1x6 cedar planks,
8 ft. long (9)

1¼ in. exterior decking
screws (1 box)

6d finishing nails
(1 small box)

TOOLS NEEDED

Miter saw

Straightedges

4 hand screw clamps

2 long bar clamps

Tape measure

Pencil

Circular saw

Speed square

Framing square

Drill with driver bits
and twist bits

Eye protection

Work gloves

Cedar is a wonderful rot-resistant wood. It's also lightweight and very easy to work with. This cedar planter box, designed by my friend Ron Sims, looks great on a patio or deck, and it can be made in an afternoon. It's one of the more complex projects in this book, but as long as you have the right tools and a little ambition, you'll be able to make this beautiful planter.

One of my favorite things about cedar is that it's typically sold in boards that have a rough texture on one side and a smooth texture on the other side. This means you can opt for a more rustic feel by putting the rough-textured side on the exterior, or choose a more sleek look by having the smooth side on the outside. For this demonstration, we made the box with the smooth side on its exterior.

Continued

HOW TO MAKE A CEDAR PLANTER BOX

CUT PLAN

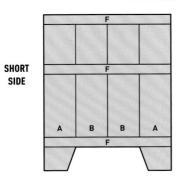

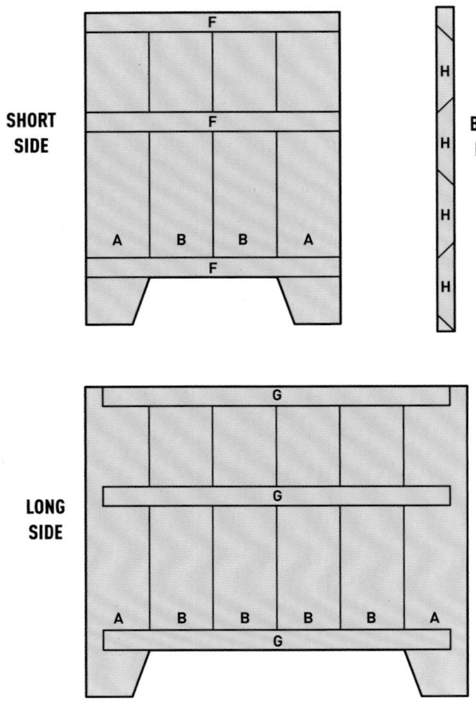

SHORT SIDE

BOTTOM BRACE

LONG SIDE

Preliminary Cutting List

PART	NAME	# NEEDED	DIMENSION
(A)	Legs	8	28 in.
(B)	Sides	12	23¾ in.
(C)	Pot shelf	4	31 in. (cut to fit after assembly)
(D)	Top frame (short)	1	20 in. (will be finished to 19¼ x 2⅝ in Step 3)
(E)	Top frame (long)	1	34 in. (will be finished to 33 x 2⅝ in Step 3)
(F)	Supports (short)	2	22 in. (will be finished to 21½ x 1¾ in Step 3—need 6)
(G)	Supports (long)	2	30 in. (will be finished to 29¼ x 1¾ in Step 3—need 6)
(H)	Bottom braces	1	30 in. (will be finished to 8 x 1½ in Step 4—need 4)
(I)	Vertical supports	1	17½ in. (will be finished to 6 x ⅞—need 4) and (finish to 11 x ⅞—need 4) in Step 5

ASSEMBLY

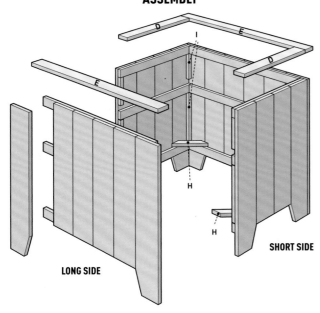

SHORT SIDE

LONG SIDE

STEP 1 Cut the pieces as follows, using a miter saw:

Board #1: cut four **(B)** Sides at 23¾ in.

Board #2: cut four **(B)** Sides at 23¾ in.

Board #3: cut four **(B)** Sides at 23¾ in.

Board #4: cut three **(A)** Legs at 28 in.

Board #5: cut three **(A)** Legs at 28 in.

Board #6: cut two **(A)** Legs at 28 in. and 1 **(C)** Pot shelf at 31 in.

Board #7: cut three **(C)** Pot shelves at 31 in.

Board #8: cut two **(G)** Supports (long) at 30 in. and 1 **(E)** Top frame (long) at 34 in.

Board #9: cut one **(D)** Top Frame (short) at 20 in. and two **(F)** Supports (short) at 22 in. Remainder of Board #9 will be used to cut parts **(H)** and **(I)**

STEP 2 Use a miter saw to cut a 20° angle on all eight legs **(A)**, removing a corner that is 4½ in. tall and 1½ in. wide. Remember, if you're using cedar that's smooth on one side and rough on the other, you'll want to cut four boards with the smooth side up and four boards with the rough side up.

STEP 3 Use a circular saw to rip the following pieces:
- Cut two of the short supports **(F)** in thirds, creating six strips, each 21½ x 1¾ in.
- Cut two of the long supports **(G)** in thirds, creating six strips, each 29¼ x 1¾ in.
- Cut one long top frame **(D)** in half, creating two strips, each 19¼ x 2⅝ in.
- Cut one short top frame **(E)** in half, creating two strips at 33 x 2⅝ in.

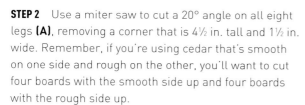

STEP 4 With the wood leftover from Board #9, create the **(H)** bottom braces. To do so, first use the circular saw to rip a 1½-in-wide strip from Board #9. Then measure and mark the bottom braces that are 8 x 1½ in. with 45° corners onto the strip, and cut them with a miter saw.

Continued

STEP 5 The remaining leftover wood from Board #9 can now be used to make the vertical supports **(I)**. Use the circular saw to rip two strips, each ⅞ in. wide, from the leftover board. Then, crosscut the strips to make four pieces at 6 in. long and four pieces at 11 in. long.

STEP 6 Begin building the side panels by attaching straightedges to your work table with four hand screw clamps. Use a speed square to make sure the corner is at a perfect 90° angle. Assemble the short side panels first by laying two legs **(A)** to the outside and two sides **(B)** in between them, making sure they sit squarely in the corner of your straight edges. If your cedar is rough-cut on one side and smooth on the other, make sure the side you want facing the outside of your planter box is facing down. Scribe a line across all four boards, 9 in. down from their top edges. This line will mark the edge of the support strip.

STEP 7 Position one short support **(F)** so its top edge is on the marked line. Set a second short support so its top edge is flush with the top edges of the side boards. Position a third short support so its bottom edge is flush with the bottom of the side boards. Drill pilot holes and attach the short supports to the side boards with two 1¼ in. exterior decking screws drilled into each side board.

STEP 8   Repeat Steps 6 and 7 to build the second short side panel, again being careful to keep either the smooth or rough side of the boards to the exterior. Then build two long side panels using the same process, except with four side boards between the legs. Also, the support strips on these long sides will be set in from the edges of the legs by ¾ in. on each side. This will allow the short side panels to be overlapped by the long side panels.

STEP 9   Cut and position the vertical supports **(I)** flush with the edges of the first side panel. The 6-in.-long vertical supports go between the top and the middle supports, and the 11-in.-long verticals go between the middle and the bottom supports. For the top vertical supports, make sure there is a gap of 1½ in. above the middle support (see inset). This gap will allow the pot shelf boards to be inserted once the box is assembled. Drill pilot holes and attach the vertical supports to the leg boards, using 1¼-in. deck screws spaced about 1½ in. apart. Now drill horizontal pilot holes through the adjoining face of each vertical support, spaced in between the vertical screws. These pilot holes will be used to secure the short side panels to the long side panels.

STEP 10   Stand one short side panel and one long side panel upright and join the corner together, using a framing square to make sure the angle is a perfect 90°. Then, join the two panels together by driving decking screws through the pilot holes on the vertical supports and into the leg boards on the long side panel.

Continued

STEP 11 Attach the third and fourth sides in the same fashion, again using the framing square to make sure the angles are 90°.

STEP 12 Once the box is assembled, attach a bottom brace **(H)** to the inside bottom of each of the four corners by drilling pilot holes then driving deck screws down through the brace and into the bottom supports.

STEP 13 Insert the four pot shelf pieces **(C)**, resting the ends on the middle supports on each short side panel. If necessary, you can cut them down slightly to fit.

STEP 14 To attach the top frame, lay the two long top frame pieces **(E)** and the two short top frame pieces **(D)** in place on the top edge of the box. Secure them with two long bar clamps. Attach the four pieces to the top of the planting box with 6d finishing nails. Sand any rough edges, and, if you'd like, you can finish the box with paint, stain, or sealant prior to planting. If left unfinished, cedar weathers to a silvery gray.

HYPERTUFA PLANTER

MATERIALS NEEDED

1 bag perlite

1 bale peat moss

1 bag Portland cement (not concrete mix, but pure Portland cement, commonly available in 47- and 94-pound bags).

Non-stick cooking spray

Water

TOOLS NEEDED

1-gallon bucket

Mixing tub or wheelbarrow

Mold or form (see Step 1 for options)

Plastic painter's tarp

Drywall saw

Drill

½-in. masonry bit

Dust mask or respirator

Thick rubber gloves

Eye protection

While concrete pots are gorgeous, they're also incredibly heavy. Hypertufa is an excellent alternative to concrete, since it's far lighter but just as weather-proof. Once you see how beautiful these planters are, making them becomes addictive. One word of caution about this project: mixing hypertufa is very messy! Spread protective plastic sheeting over your work surface, and wear old clothes to do the mixing. You'll also want to wear thick rubber gloves, a dust mask or respirator, and a pair of safety goggles. As you mix the hypertufa, small particles of the ingredients become airborne; it's important to protect your eyes and lungs.

Continued

HOW TO MAKE A HYPERTUFA PLANTER

STEP 1   Start by gathering your ingredients and selecting a mold or form to make your planter. The most popular mold for hypertufa planters is probably a box-in-box system, in which a smaller cardboard box is nestled inside of a larger one and the wet hypertufa is packed in between the two boxes to form the walls of the planter. While this is a great way to make a square, trough-like planter, using a single object and molding the hypertufa over it is an easier project for beginners and creates a more attractive planter. For this project, we used a half-sphere exercise ball to make a very large hypertufa planter. But if you want to make a smaller version, use an inverted salad bowl, shallow garden pot, or other hemispherical object.

STEP 2   Cover your work surface with the plastic sheeting and lay another piece of plastic over your mold. If you're working with cardboard or another mold you don't mind ruining, you can skip this step. Spray the plastic with a heavy layer of non-stick cooking spray, which will make separating the planter from the mold much easier.

STEP 3   Use the 1-gallon bucket as a "measuring cup" to combine two parts Portland cement with three parts perlite and three parts peat moss in a large cement bin or wheelbarrow.

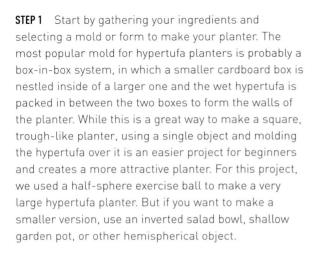

STEP 4 Sift the larger chunks and twigs out of the peat moss as you mix the dry ingredients together with your gloved hands. The amount of dry mix you'll need depends on the size of the project. For this large hypertufa bowl, we used 4 gallons of Portland cement, 6 gallons of perlite, and 6 gallons of peat moss.

STEP 5 Once the dry ingredients are well-blended, slowly add water in small increments, mixing it as you go. You'll need approximately two parts water for each batch of the ingredients listed in Step 3. The real amount of water needed, though, could be more or less, depending on how dry the peat moss is and the humidity level of the air. Add just a little water at a time, and use your gloved hands to work the water through the mixture after each addition of water. The final mix should form a ball when it's squeezed, and only a few drops of water should come out of it.

STEP 6 When your mix is the right consistency, let it rest for 5 to 10 minutes. Then, handful by handful, pack the wet mix around the outside of your mold. Start at the ground, and slowly work your way up to the top of the mold, packing the hypertufa mix in a layer 1 to 2 in. thick over the entire surface. We formed a wide lip around the edge of our pot by extending the layer of hypertufa out over the ground around the half-sphere exercise ball, but this isn't necessary if you want a planter without the lip.

Continued

7

8

9

STEP 7   After the mold is completely covered with mix, flatten the top. This will become the base of the planter after the dried hypertufa is lifted off the mold and flipped over, helping the planter sit level on the ground. Cover the entire planter with a sheet of clean plastic and allow the planter to dry. Lift the plastic a few times a day and squirt the planter with a mist of water, covering all surfaces—this will slow the curing and strengthen the planter. Small planters will be ready to remove from the mold in just a day or two, but large planters like this one can take up to a week.

STEP 8   You'll know your planter is ready to separate from the mold when the outer surface cannot be scratched with a screwdriver or scratch awl. Don't rush this initial stage. It's better to wait too long than it is to risk cracking the planter by taking it off the mold too early. Once your planter is ready, carefully lift it off

the mold. If you used enough non-stick cooking spray, it should separate from the plastic very easily. As soon as your planter is off the mold, cut away any uneven edges with a drywall saw. This is your only chance to do this because once the hypertufa fully cures, it will be too hard. Carefully move the planter to a shady area, flip it over, and leave it undisturbed for 3 to 6 weeks (or longer, if it's a larger planter).

STEP 9   When the planter is fully cured, it will be light gray and weigh much less than it did before. To leach out the alkaline lime found in the Portland cement, fill the cured planter with water and let it sit. Empty and refill the pot every few days for about two weeks. Once the leaching process is complete, use a drill fitted with a 1/2-in. masonry bit to drill a drainage hole in the base of the container. Your new hypertufa container is now ready to be planted!

As you decide which containers are best for your garden, remember, you don't have to stick to just one type of material. Find what works best for your budget, your landscape, and your sense of aesthetics. If you don't feel the need for every container to be the same, mixing different container materials can add interest and texture to your container garden. Experiment with different materials to find the ones that work best for you.

New Containers vs. Repurposed Items

In addition to considering what types of materials are best for the containers in your garden, you should also spend some time considering whether you'd like to purchase new (or gently used) garden containers, or create your garden with repurposed items. Or perhaps you'd like to have a container garden that combines both. As long as an object meets the important requirement of holding an ample volume of soil and it's made of an appropriate material, there's no reason why you can't turn it into a garden container.

The biggest plus of using repurposed items as growing containers is the cost. If you already have appropriate items on hand or find them from a garage sale, flea market, or someone else's trash pile, it will cost you little to nothing to get your container garden started. But before adding a repurposed object to your container garden, keep these considerations in mind:

- Make sure the object isn't something valuable. Before using an inverted glass lampshade or old beer stein to hold plants, make sure they are not valuable antiques.
- Be careful about using items that may have been painted prior to the late 1970s, because until 1978, many paints were lead-based—a well-known health hazard.

▲ Many household items (including old tool boxes) can be repurposed into garden containers. Just make sure they're made of an appropriate material and hold enough soil for the plants you want to grow in them.

▶ Old cast-iron bathtubs make great garden containers, but they may be contaminated with lead-based paints. Use caution when considering them for the garden.

- Make sure the object was not used to store chemicals of any kind. Solvents, synthetic pesticides, and other chemicals may leach into wood or other materials. This is of particular importance if you're using the container to grow food.
- If the object is made of plastic, you may want to skip using it to grow food. Newer plastic containers can be checked for the presence of BPA (bisphenol A), a chemical that has been shown to cause possible negative health effects. But with older plastic containers, it's harder to rule out the presence of BPA.
- Be careful about repurposing items that may contain asbestos. Prior to the early 1980s, asbestos was used in thousands of different household items, including hair dryers, toasters, crock pots, and coffee pots, to name just a few. Disturbing and handling asbestos has been shown to increase your chances of respiratory diseases and other ailments.

In general, modern, commercially made garden containers have a much smaller risk of including

When repurposing items for your container garden, be careful about using appliances made before the 1980s as they may contain asbestos.

a hazardous material than older objects do, but if you're growing edible plants in any type of container, it's worth the time to investigate its properties, regardless of whether it's old or new.

For added inspiration, here's a gallery of a few more cool container plantings, each made with a repurposed item.

There's nothing wrong with using different styles of containers in your garden and adding some whimsy, as long as it reflects the lifestyle and personality of the homeowner.

Matching Your Style

One final factor to consider when choosing containers for your garden is your personal style. No matter what types of containers you select, they should partner well with your home, your landscape, and your life. If your home is formal, wooden whiskey barrels might not be the best fit, nor would they match the vibe of a balcony outside of a sleek, urban flat. But they'd look great sitting on the front steps of a country cottage or on a rural deck. That urban balcony, on the other hand, would be a great place for a modern, powder-coated metal planter box. And a formal home's landscape would be nicely accented by using traditional terracotta containers or cast iron urns.

That's not to say you can't stir things up and go for a whimsical or purposefully funky vibe. Quite the opposite, in fact: if your personal style is a little offbeat, then you should have an offbeat container garden, even if you live in a more formal home.

If you have a bigger yard where you have room to experiment, feel free to make multiple container gardens, each with its own style. Use repurposed items as containers in the vegetable garden, but have more traditional containers flanking the front porch. There's nothing wrong with having a hodgepodge collection of containers, as long as you can take care of them properly and you remember that smaller containers dry out faster and need more frequent irrigation.

A Word on
Self-Watering Planters

For gardeners who want extremely low maintenance, or whose lives are so busy they're afraid they won't have time to water their plants, self-watering containers are an excellent option. Self-watering containers, also called subirrigated planters, have a water reservoir beneath the planting area. Water is drawn out of the reservoir and into the potting soil through capillary action. As the plants suck water up out of the soil, more water is drawn up from the reservoir to keep the soil moisture levels optimum without letting the roots sit in water.

There are several brands of self-watering containers on today's market, with the EarthBox® being among the most popular. Irrigating plants via this underground wicking action, rather than by watering from the top, helps keep foliage dry and can suppress certain fungal diseases. Though they aren't truly self-watering (you still have to keep the reservoir full), using self-watering containers does indeed significantly cut down on irrigation chores. The only downside to these containers is their cost. In Chapter 3, you'll find step-by-step plans for making an inexpensive DIY self-watering planter.

POTTING MIX FOR YOUR CONTAINERS

The second pillar comprising the foundation of a successful container garden is the growing medium that fills the containers and supports the plants. Potting mix, also called potting soil, is a soilless blend of ingredients used to grow plants. Often containing a combination of peat moss, coir fiber, vermiculite, sand, perlite, pine bark, compost, and other ingredients (but no "real" soil), there are dozens of brands of commercial potting mix on the market.

All good-quality potting mixes share the following characteristics: they're well-draining, lightweight, and easy to handle. But each potting mix definitely has its own distinct traits. There is a wide variation in texture, nutritional content, density, and water-holding capacity among different potting mixtures, and some mixes are better than others.

Which Potting Mix is Right for You?

Before selecting a particular potting mix, spend some time reading labels. Look first for an indication that the soil mix was created for a specific purpose. For example, lighter, finer-textured mixes are best for use in seed starting; mixes containing a high percentage of coarse sand or pine bark are best for potted trees and shrubs; and mixes with a sandy or gravely texture are formulated for cactus growing. There are dozens of specialized potting soil mixes like these, each tailored to the needs of a particular group of

The EarthBox® is one brand of self-watering planters designed to cut down on watering chores. As long as there's water in the reservoir in the bottom of the pot, the soil moisture level stays at the optimum level.

plants, but for most container gardeners, the best fit is a general, all-purpose potting mix.

Once you've read the label and made sure a particular potting mix isn't overly specialized, delve a little deeper into the ingredient list. Commercial potting mixes can be excellent, but sometimes they are quite poor. You may open the bag to discover the mix is too dense or too light; or that the bag is filled with chunks of bark, or that it's a wet, smelly mess. Each brand has its own formula, but most consist of a blend of the following ingredients.

Sphagnum peat moss. The primary ingredient in most commercial potting soils is sphagnum peat moss. A very stable material, peat takes a long time to break down and is widely available and inexpensive. It bulks up potting mixes without adding a lot of weight, and once wet it holds water fairly well. Before blending it with other ingredients, peat is typically treated with a wetting agent to help it absorb water. Sphagnum peat moss is well-draining and well-aerated, but it's very low in available nutrients and it has an acidic pH, typically ranging between 3.5 and 4.5. Limestone is often added to peat-based potting mixes to help balance the pH. The environmental impact of peat harvesting is a factor that may influence some gardeners when they're looking for a potting mix. There is much debate about whether or not peat harvesting is a sustainable practice; if this worries you, use a potting mix that replaces peat with coir fiber.

Coir fiber. A byproduct of the coconut industry, coir looks and acts a lot like sphagnum peat, only it's much easier to wet. It has more nutrients than peat moss and lasts even longer, but it's more expensive to purchase. Coir fiber's pH is close to neutral. Coir fiber is also sold in compressed bricks. Container gardeners may have to look

There are many different types of potting soil and some are tailored to the specific growing needs of a particular group of plants. Read the label carefully to make sure the mix is right for your plants.

harder to find coir-based potting soils, but they're worth seeking out.

Perlite. A mined, volcanic glass, when perlite is heated, it expands, making it look like small white balls of Styrofoam. Perlite is a lightweight, sterile addition to potting mixes. It holds three to four times its weight in water, increases pore space, and improves drainage. With a neutral pH, perlite is used in many different brands of potting mix.

Vermiculite. Vermiculite is a mined mineral that is conditioned by heating until it expands into light particles. It's used to increase the porosity of potting soil mixes, but it can also be found in everything from acoustic tiles and brake linings to insulation and plaster. In potting soil, vermiculite also adds calcium and magnesium, and increases the mix's water-holding capacity. Although asbestos contamination was once a concern with vermiculite, mines are now regulated and regularly tested.

Sand. Coarse sand improves drainage and adds weight to potting mixes. Mixes formulated for cacti and other succulents tend to have a higher percentage of coarse sand in their composition to ensure ample drainage.

Limestone. Pulverized calcitic or dolomitic limestone is often added to peat-based potting mixes to neutralize their pH. These minerals are mined from natural deposits and are readily available and inexpensive.

Fertilizers. Additional nutrient sources are often added to peat-based potting soils, as they don't naturally contain enough nutrients to support optimum plant growth. Ideally, the potting mix you select should contain a natural fertilizer derived from a combination of mined minerals, animal byproducts, plant materials, or manures—not synthetic chemical fertilizer. Natural fertilizers provide a long-term, stable and eco-friendly source of nutrients for your containerized plants. Check the ingredient list for items such as alfalfa meal, blood meal, bone meal, cottonseed meal, crab meal, feather meal, fish meal, greensand, kelp meal, dehydrated manures, and rock phosphate, among others. Synthetic fertilizers present in potting soils may or may not be included on the bag's ingredient list, but they'll often be announced on the front of the bag by phrases such as "feeds plants for 6 months" or "includes slow-release fertilizer."

Composted pine bark. Composted pine bark lightens up potting mixes by increasing the size of the pores between the particles, allowing air and water to travel freely in the mix. It's slow to break down but may rob nitrogen from the soil as it does, so the addition of a small amount of nitrogen fertilizer is necessary when using composted pine bark as an ingredient. Composted pine bark is most commonly found in potting mixes designed for potted perennials and shrubs.

Compost. Containing billions of beneficial microbes, and with superior water-holding capacity and nutrient content, compost is an

The primary ingredient in most commercial potting soils is sphagnum peat moss, a well-draining and well-aerated material that's harvested from bogs.

Perlite is a mined, volcanic glass that's heated until it expands. Its lightweight nature improves the drainage of potting mixes.

excellent addition to potting mixes, though it isn't found in very many commercial brands. Because it plays such a huge role in promoting healthy plant growth, I suggest mixing it with potting soil to create the ideal mixture for container gardening (more on this in the next section).

When selecting a particular brand of potting soil for your container garden, don't be afraid to ask the garden center if you can open a bag and check it out. Good-quality potting soil should be light and fluffy, with a well-blended mixture of ingredients. It should not shrink significantly or pull away from the sides of the container when it's dried out.

Avoid the following things when choosing a potting soil for your container garden:

- Do not purchase bags of potting soil if they're very heavy. The mix is likely to be too dense for good container performance. Plus, it may contain a high percentage of sand or be saturated with water.
- Do not use mixes that contain topsoil or garden soil. Often poorly draining and not sterile, these mixes may contain weed seeds or plant pathogens.

- Do not use mixes that smell bad. Potting soil with excessive amounts of nitrogen may smell like urine. Foul-smelling mixes could also be a sign of the presence of harmful pathogens or it may indicate that the mix is fermenting in the bag.
- Don't purchase bags of potting soil that contain sprouting seeds, moss, or mold. Commercial potting soil should be free of such items.

After using a particular brand of potting soil, it's important to evaluate its performance. At the end of the growing season, make note of which brands worked best for you and plan to use them again next year. It may take a few seasons to find your favorites, but once you have the chance to test and evaluate a few different brands, the differences between them will be clear.

It's also worth noting that potting soil is *not* the same as "garden soil," "topsoil," "peat mix," "manure soil," "mushroom manure," or several other bagged products you may find at your garden center. These items are best used as soil amendments, not as a growing medium to fill your containers.

Vermiculite increases the water holding capacity of potting soil. It's a mined mineral that expands when heated.

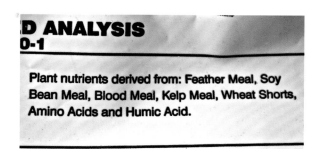

Some potting mixes come with fertilizer already added. Choose brands with natural fertilizers, rather than synthetic chemicals, for a more stable and eco-friendly source of plant nutrients.

Creating the Perfect Potting Soil Blend for Container Gardening

After deciding which potting mix makes the best base for your containers, it's time to kick it up a notch. Though you certainly can use straight commercial potting mix, you'll be missing an excellent opportunity to make your life easier and grow even healthier plants.

As you probably already know, compost is "black gold" to gardeners. It's made of decomposed organic materials, and it's filled with nutrients and alive with beneficial soil microbes. Compost also has an incredible moisture-holding capacity, and containerized plants grown in potting mixes containing at least 20 to 30% compost have been shown to have a lower rate of foliar disease. Adding compost to your containers introduces beneficial organisms that help your plants acquire nutrients, and it helps your containers retain moisture. Compost also helps add bulk to light potting soil mixes and improves their structure.

To make the ideal potting blend for container gardening, mix a high-quality commercial potting soil with compost that's been sifted to remove any large particles at a 50/50 ratio. Blend them together in a wheelbarrow or large bin before adding the mix to your containers. (Wear a respirator or dusk mask anytime you're working with potting soil.) Using this 50/50 mix means you'll cut down on expenses (compost is cheaper than potting soil, especially if it's homemade), reduce watering, and foster healthy plant growth. The only time I don't recommend adding compost to a potting mix is when you're growing succulents or cacti—these plants prefer a well-drained, coarse growing medium.

If you don't have a compost pile of your own, you can purchase compost by the truck load or

Adding compost to your containers introduces beneficial soil organisms and nutrients that help plants grow. It also aids in moisture retention to cut down on watering chores. Filling your containers with a 50/50 mix of compost and potting soil results in happier and healthier plants.

by the bag, but be warned that not all composts are created equal. Look for one that's comprised of a blend of decomposed ingredients and not just a single ingredient, such as composted cow manure or shredded wood. High-quality compost smells wonderful, has a fine texture, and has decomposed enough so that the original ingredients are no longer recognizable.

Making Your Own Potting Soil from Scratch

Making your own potting soil is an excellent way to save money, and it allows you to tailor a potting soil mix to suit your needs. Large volumes can be mixed in a cement mixer or a compost tumbler; for smaller quantities, blend the ingredients in a wheelbarrow, mortar mixing tub, or large bucket. Be sure to mix everything thoroughly to ensure a consistent result. And remember, if the recipe doesn't have compost already added, you'll need to mix the final product with compost until you have a 50/50 mixture of both.

General Soilless Container Gardening Mix (With Compost Already Added)

- 6 gallons sphagnum peat moss or coir fiber
- ¼ cup pulverized lime (if using peat moss)
- 4½ gallons vermiculite or perlite
- 6 gallons compost

Mix together: 2 cups rock phosphate, 2 cups greensand, ½ cup bone meal, and ¼ cup kelp meal. Add 1½ cups of this fertilizer blend to the finished mix. Or, add 1½ cups of any granular, organic, complete fertilizer instead.

Soilless Container Gardening Mix (Without Compost)

- 6 gallons sphagnum peat moss or coir fiber
- 6 gallons vermiculite or perlite
- 4 tablespoons pulverized dolomitic limestone
- ¼ cup bone meal
- 2 tablespoons blood meal

Potted Perennial and Shrub Mix

- 1 part compost
- 1 part coarse sand
- 1 part sphagnum peat moss
- 1 part composted pine bark
- 1 part perlite
  Add 1 tablespoon lime for each gallon of peat moss

Cacti and Succulent Potting Mix

- 3 gallons potting soil (either a commercial brand or the homemade mix above, without compost)
- 2 gallons coarse sand
- 1 gallon perlite

When making your own potting soil, use the batch as quickly as possible. But if storage is necessary, place the mix in plastic garbage bags in a cool, dry place, or pile it on a tarp in a shed or garage and cover the pile loosely with a sheet of plastic.

The following project uses the cacti and succulent potting mix mentioned above to grow a repurposed planter full of unique, drought-tolerant succulent plants.

To save money on the expense of potting soil, mix up your own instead of purchasing commercial brands. The ingredients are widely available at most garden centers and nurseries.

CEMENT BIN SUCCULENTS

Succulent plants have become very popular in the last few years, and deservedly so. They're low-maintenance, drought-tolerant, heat-tolerant, and absolutely gorgeous. Succulents are plants that store water in their thick, fleshy leaves. These plants thrive in dry conditions and can survive extended periods without water, making them perfect for gardeners in dry climates or for those who sometimes "forget" to water. But because these plants evolved in areas where moisture levels are low, they don't do as well in very humid climates or in gardening zones with a lot of rainfall.

Most succulents are not winter hardy, and in some climates they'll need to be moved indoors in the autumn before frost arrives. This project uses the specialized cacti and succulent potting mix described earlier to grow a variety of succulent plants in a repurposed cement mixing bin.

In addition to this project, you'll find many other ways to use succulent plants in your container garden in the final chapter of this book (Chapter 6).

Some popular plant candidates for a cement bin succulent planter include:

- *Adromischus* spp.
- *Aeonium* spp.
- *Agave* spp.
- *Aloe* spp.
- *Crassula* spp.
- *Dudleya* spp.
- *Echeveria* spp.
- *Euphorbia* spp.
- Flapjacks (*Kalanchoe thyrsiflora* 'Flapjack')
- *Graptopetalum* spp.
- *Haworthia* spp.
- Jade plants (*Crassula ovata*)
- Ox Tongue (*Gasteria liliputana*)
- *Portulaca* spp.
- *Sedum* spp.
- *Sempervivum* spp.
- *Senecio mandraliscae, S. serpens,* and others

HOW TO MAKE A SUCCULENT CEMENT BIN

STEP 1　Begin by placing the empty bin in a location that receives a minimum of 6 hours of full sun per day. Remember, most succulents like it hot. Once the bin is in place, use a hammer to pierce the bottom of the cement bin with the scratch awl in several places. Pivot the awl around in the holes to enlarge them to ½-in. diameter. Make at least five or six drainage holes in the bin.

STEP 2　Fill the bin to within 2 in. of the top edge with the well-draining cactus and succulent specific soil mix outlined in the previous section of the book. The mix consists of 3 gallons of potting soil, 2 gallons of coarse sand, and 1 gallon of perlite.

STEP 3:　Plant the succulents in the bin, using extra caution when planting anything with sharp spikes or thorns. Arrange the plants in a way that allows for maximum air circulation—wet succulents are prone to rot. If the plants have roots circling around inside their pot, be sure to gently loosen them before planting them. Be careful not to plant succulents too deeply. They should be planted to the exact soil depth they are inside their nursery containers. If you plant them too deeply, it could cause their fleshy stems to rot.

STEP 4　After all the plants are in place, top the soil with some decorative rocks, seashells, and other accents, if desired. Water the bin in well and enjoy your new succulent planter.

NOTE: If you want to enjoy more succulent plants in the future, know that most of these plants are easy to propagate. Many naturally spread; young plants develop off the side of the mother plant and can be dug out, separated, and replanted into a new location. Succulents are also easy to propagate via stem or leaf cuttings. See Chapter 5 to learn how to propagate plants via stem cuttings.

Filling Your Containers

Use a soil scoop, shovel, or trowel to fill your containers with the 50/50 compost and potting soil blend. With larger plants, you may find it easier to fill the pot three-quarters of the way, then slip the plants out of their containers, position them in the pot, and fill in around them. After planting, the soil level should be about 1 inch below the pot's upper rim. Even high-quality potting soil blends tend to settle a little after watering and throughout the course of the growing season, so take that into account when filling your pots. The extra head-space at the top of the pot keeps irrigation water from running off and encourages it to slowly percolate down through the soil to the plants' roots.

While big containers that hold a large volume of potting mix allow for more substantial plant root systems, they can also be very expensive to fill. If you're looking to manage your gardening budget, create a false bottom in larger pots by filling the bottom of the pot with large, lightweight, chunky materials. I've used empty soda cans and plastic bottles, inverted buckets or plastic flower pots, plastic zipper-top bags full of Styrofoam packing peanuts, or drained milk cartons or jugs.

Make sure the objects do not block the drainage holes in the bottom of the pot, and they shouldn't take up more than ¼ of the total volume of space in the container. You'll find that the roots of most plants will grow around and in between these materials quite easily. Obviously, this is not a necessary practice when using small and medium-sized pots. Use this type of false bottom only when growing annual flowers, vegetables, single-season tropicals, or other short-lived plants.

To help fill the volume of larger containers used to grow annual flowers, vegetables, and other short-lived plants, the bottom quarter of the pot can be filled with lightweight, chunky materials, such as empty plastic bottles and jugs. This cuts down on the amount of potting mix needed without impeding root growth.

SITING YOUR CONTAINERS

The third and final pillar of the foundation of successful container gardening involves finding the perfect location for your container garden to thrive. Though there are many factors to consider, sun exposure is the probably the most important. Start by spending some time watching your property carefully to see how much sun each part of it receives throughout the day. Though the sun tracks differently in the spring than it does in the summer or fall, a bit of observation can tell you a lot about the conditions of any particular site. You can also consult a website or smart phone sun tracking app, such as SunCalc.net, to confirm the light levels and sun exposure at various times of the year. The trick, of course, is to match the sun exposure of whatever site you choose with the perfect mixture of plants.

Site selection is best approached in one of two ways. Either decide which plants you want to grow first, then site your containers in a location that's well-suited to the light requirements of those plants; or find a home for your containers first, and then pick plants for them based on whatever light levels are present.

For example, if you'd like to grow sun-loving vegetables or varieties of flowering plants that perform best with maximum sun exposure, pick a site that receives a minimum of six to eight hours of full sun per day. If you don't have that kind of light, switch to flowering or foliage plants that prefer partial shade conditions, or move your containers from one location to another throughout the day to maximize their sunlight exposure. One excellent benefit of growing in containers is that lightweight, portable pots, a wheeled planter, or containers on pot dollies are easy to move around to take advantage of light. I know several gardeners who roll containers of tomatoes and peppers from one side of the deck to the other as the day progresses, just to give the plants a few more hours of light.

Aside from sun exposure, there's another important factor to consider when choosing a site for your container garden: its proximity to irrigation water. There are few bigger inconveniences in gardening than having to haul watering cans, buckets, or tubs full of water to

Continued on page 59

If you have minimal sunlight but want to grow vegetables or other sun-loving plants, consider putting the containers on pot dollies so they can be wheeled around a patio, driveway, or deck to follow the movement of the sun.

If you want to avoid staining patio or deck surfaces and encourage better drainage, elevate your containers on pot feet.

CEDAR POT DOLLY

MATERIALS NEEDED

1x3 cedar board,
  6-ft. long [1] (Note:
  real size is approx.
  ¾ x 2½ in. x 6 ft.)

1¼-in. exterior wood
  screws (1 box)

Caster wheels [4]

TOOLS NEEDED

Handsaw or
  power saw

Framing square

Cordless drill with twist
  bits and driver bits

Spring clamps (4)

Pencil

Tape measure

Eye protection

Work gloves

Carrying heavy garden pots or even houseplants from one location to another requires a lot of effort. This rugged but attractive cedar plant dolly, designed by my friend Ron Sims, makes it easy to move containers of almost any size across a porch, patio, deck, or other flooring surface. The caster wheels swivel, allowing you to easily change the direction of movement. This dolly is easy to build, even for those with minimal carpentry skills, and you can make it for a fraction of the cost of commercial pot dollies.

HOW TO MAKE A CEDAR POT DOLLY

STEP 1 Cut the piece of 6-ft. cedar board into six equal pieces, 12 in. long. Four pieces will make the top of the pot dolly and two will be used to create the bottom. Lay two of the boards down parallel to each other and approximately 12 in. apart. Lay two more boards on top of them with the corners overlapping to form a square. Place a spring clamp on each of the four corners to hold the boards in place. Lay the final two boards in between the outer two boards on one side. Use a tape measure to ensure there's an equal distance between each of the boards. The exact amount of space between each of the boards will depend on how dry the lumber is, the weather conditions, and how the lumber was milled.

STEP 2 Once the boards are equally spaced, use a pencil to mark their edges on the bottom two boards.

STEP 3 Remove the outer boards, then attach the crossmembers to the middle boards by drilling pilot holes then driving a pair of exterior screws into each board. Make sure to carefully align the boards to the pencil lines, which will ensure the boards are square.

Continued

5

6

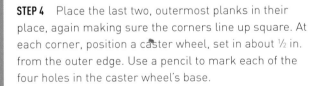

4

STEP 4 Place the last two, outermost planks in their place, again making sure the corners line up square. At each corner, position a caster wheel, set in about ½ in. from the outer edge. Use a pencil to mark each of the four holes in the caster wheel's base.

STEP 5 Drill pilot holes where each of the four caster wheel screws will go, holding the bottom board carefully in place. Make sure you don't drill all the way down through the bottom board.

STEP 6 Put the caster wheel back in place, and attach it with 4 screws driven down into the pilot holes. Repeat the process with the other three caster wheels, making sure each corner remains square as the wheels are installed.

NOTE: Your pot dolly is now ready to roll! If you'll be handling it quite a bit, you might want to sand down any rough edges. You can also paint, stain, or seal the cedar, if you wish.

Now that you've created a solid foundation for your container garden, it's time to choose the right combinations of plants and start planting!

Continued from page 55
irrigate container plantings that are too far away from the spigot. Save yourself a lot of trouble and locate your container garden within striking distance of a hose.

Once you've done this dirty work and built a secure foundation for your container garden by choosing the right kind of containers, filling them with the best potting mix and picking the perfect home for them, it's time to switch gears and put the spotlight on selecting the best plants for your pots and arranging them into beautiful, productive plantings (which, as it so happens, are the very topics of the next chapter).

chapter 2

Designing and Planting Your Containers

Now that the foundation of your container garden is in order, it's time for the most fun aspect of container gardening: plant selection and design. This is where you can express yourself through color, form, and texture, and where you can make colorful combinations to wow the eye or stick with monochromatic combos for high-impact plantings. With a little finesse, your container garden becomes a place to exhibit flair along with providing utility and productivity (especially if you're growing veggies!).

This chapter dives head-first into container design by first discussing useful tips for combining different plant structures and sizes together into asingle planting. You'll learn how to organize a variety of different plants into a cohesive arrangement using a few standard design formulas.

Next, the chapter will introduce you to some of the best plants for container gardening. With tables and lists full of varieties tailored to container culture and varied growing conditions, you'll be armed with everything you need to design and plant flower, veggie, fruit, herb, and foliage containers. The chapter concludes with a gallery of foolproof container photos and "recipes" you can copy plant-for-plant or modify for your own needs.

◀ Good container design involves partnering different plant structures, sizes, and colors with the container itself to create a cohesive arrangement.

CONTAINER DESIGN 101

Much like decorating your home, good container design is a matter of personal aesthetics. There will be color combinations that appeal to you and others that won't. The trick is to find what you love. But good design clearly extends way beyond color choice. It's also about partnering foliage and floral forms and textures in a pleasing manner,

Containers with edible plants, such as fruits, vegetables, and herbs, should also be designed in a pleasing manner.

61

and pairing vegetables, fruits, and herbs in a way that yields a good harvest. And, it's not just about combining the right plants with each other, but also with the right container.

When it comes to planting beautiful containers, there are three primary concepts to keep in mind as you create your designs.

Proportion

Plantings that aren't in the correct proportion with their container look off-kilter, top heavy, too dense, or flat, depending on which direction the designer erred. Even if your aim is to create a naturalistic container planting rather than one that looks planned, proportion is important.

The rule of thirds is an excellent guide to maintaining proportion in both container gardening and floral design. Begin by looking at the height of your container. For good proportion, your container should comprise either ⅓ or ⅔ of the total height of the plants and container combined, with the height of the plantings taking up the remainder. In other words, you should strive for a container-to-plantings height ratio of 1:2 or 2:1. The container won't be in perfect proportion until the plants reach their mature height, but most container plants grow quickly, and it won't be long before the correct pot-to-plant proportion is achieved.

Not every color combination is going to work for every gardener. Find what suits your personal aesthetics first and foremost.

This container at Chanticleer Garden near Philadelphia, Pennsylvania is a great example of the rule of thirds. In this case, the container is ⅓ of the total height of the plants and the pot combined.

Guard against having too many eye-catching plants in the same container. Instead, focus on having a single focal point to keep the design from becoming too busy.

Focal Point

Another goal for container garden design is having a single focal point. A focal point can be very direct and obvious, or more subtle. Often the largest plant in your design becomes a natural focal point by virtue of its size alone, but fun focal points can also be based on a jazzy color, bold leaf textures, variegated foliage, or a narrow, vertical element. No matter what you choose, use only one primary focal point for each container. Multiple focal points can be very distracting.

Balance

Well-conceived designs always have good balance, too, both vertically and horizontally. Proper balance keeps a container planting from looking lopsided or top-heavy. A tall, narrow container planted with a tree will always look like it's ready to topple over because the top-to-bottom visual balance is off. Or, if you're planting a window box or another long container, keep the tallest plant toward the center or have two or three of them spread out through the entire length of the pot. However, remember that balance *does not* necessarily mean symmetry. You don't have to use identical plants to have good balance; just select ones that balance each other in terms of visual weight.

Here are five simple design principles to help you create well-designed plant combinations for your containers, using a combination of proportion, focal point, and balance.

Thriller, Filler, and Spiller Style

There's an expression that's frequently used among container gardeners: "Every container needs a thriller, a filler, and a spiller." This concept advises that three heights of plants should be used to fill out a container on every available plane, while still maintaining balance and a proper pot-to-plant proportion. This is a particularly valuable design plan for containers that are meant to be viewed from all sides. By using this principle, you ensure there are no "bald spots" in your design and that it will look good from any direction.

First, a single "thriller" plant is selected for the center of the pot—typically, a large plant with bold foliage, interesting flowers, or some other eye-catching feature to serve as a focal point. Its mature height should fit within the parameters of the rule of thirds mentioned above to keep the design well proportioned. Nurseries are filled with many options for a thriller plant; look for unique plants that draw your eye and stand out from the crowd.

Once you've selected your thriller plant, look for "filler" plants to accent it. These plants are positioned around the thriller, filling in the space around it. Their mature height should be between ½ and ¾ of the height of the thriller feature. Depending on the size of the pot, use anywhere from three to seven filler plants. They can all be the same species, or you can mix two or three different plants into this layer. But avoid falling into the "I-must-have-one-of-everything" trap, because this layer becomes distracting if you include too many different plants. Filler

Containers designed in the thriller, filler, and spiller style utilize three different sizes of plants to create a container that can be viewed from all sides.

Surround the thriller plant in your container with mid-height filler plants, such as the golden shrimp plant (*Pachystachys lutea*) and purple Angelonia (*Angelonia angustifolia*) in this pot.

Spiller plants are those that cascade over the edge of the pot to soften the edge. Here, silver falls (*Dichondra argentea* 'Silver Falls'), creeps over the top edge of a glazed ceramic container.

plants can be flowering or foliage plants, or a mixture of the two. There are hundreds of plants that make good fillers for container plantings for both sun and shade.

Finally, the spiller plants are placed around the outer edge of the container. These plants cascade over the edge of the pot, draping it with colorful flowers or interesting foliage. Spillers soften the container and give it a sense of lushness. I often use three different spiller plants for each container—two flowering and one selected for its

interesting foliage. Avoid selecting too many, or the arrangement becomes distracting.

No matter which types of plants you choose to fill each layer, keep the scale appropriate to the size of the container, and keep the plants balanced vertically and horizontally. Fill the container with a mixture of color, texture, and form, without going overboard. Remember, don't just select plants for their flowers—foliage texture and plant form play an important role in good container garden design.

Flat-backed style containers like this one are ideal for places where they'll only be viewed from one side. Layer the plants so the tallest ones are toward the back and the plants in the foreground are low or cascading.

Flat-backed Style

This design technique is perfect for containers that are tucked against a building, fence, or pillar and are meant to be viewed only from one side. Rather than using horizontal layers, flat-backed style adds layers from back-to-front. This is one of my favorite container design techniques, because if you combine the right plants, it creates a very stylized planting.

Begin by selecting a tall, upright, narrow plant for the back of the container—one whose mature height fits the rule of thirds. Position it a little off center in the very back of the pot. If you're designing two symmetrical, flat-backed planters to flank your front door, for example, put this tall, narrow plant slightly to the left of center in the back of one of the pots and then slightly to the right of center in the back of the other pot.

Once you've planted this backdrop plant, select a slightly shorter plant to create the other half of the back layer. This plant should be more branched and less upright than the first plant. It adds density to the back layer but also keeps some height. If you have a very large container, choose two of these plants to finish your back layer.

After the back layer is selected, create a second layer of plants just to the front of it. The plants in this layer are slightly shorter than those comprising the backdrop; they should be between one-half and three-quarters of the height of the back layer. This mid-layer is where I love to use plants with interesting foliage colors and textures. My favorite flat-backed containers combine three foliage plants in this mid-layer, each with complementing foliage colors but with varying textures. I often pick one with soft, fine foliage, another with big and bold foliage to serve as the container's focal point, and one with narrow, upright foliage. But, there's lots of room for flexibility here; this mid-layer is also a great place to include flowers, too.

The third and final layer of a flat-backed design is at the front edge of the container. It consists of one to three plants that are small-statured and may cascade over the lip of the container, if desired. I try to stick to just one type of plant for this layer to prevent the design from looking

This autumn container is in a flat-backed style. Rather than using a plant as a focal point, it uses a collection of interesting gourds.

In this container, the featured specimen is a red-leaved banana (*Ensete ventricosum* 'Maurelii'). Its bold foliage is highlighted by a "skirt" of bronze-leaved oxalis (*Oxalis vulcanicola* 'Zinfandel'™).

too busy, especially if you used multiple types of plants in the mid-layer.

When planting a flat-backed design, don't keep the plants in three perfect rows. Instead, stagger the plants in each layer, stepping some slightly forward or backward. Doing so adds depth and dimension to the planting while still maintaining good balance.

For small containers planted in this style, each of the three layers might only consist of one plant. But even with just three plants, this style creates a beautiful effect.

Featured-specimen Style

This design technique is the perfect way to feature a single, unique, large-statured specimen plant, such as a big tropical banana, plumeria (*Plumeria* spp.), hibiscus tree, or perhaps a small shade tree. What I like to do is place the large-statured plant smack in the center of the container, then I put the icing on the cake by surrounding it with a skirt of plants that complement it without distracting from its beauty. These plants keep my vertical balance in check by making the container look more visually weighted.

This "icing" layer is comprised of low and cascading plants that form a ring around the base of the featured star and flow over the edge of the container. The best plants for this layer have a fine texture, whether they're foliage-based or flowering. I like to use plants with a light, frothy texture around the bold plant that takes center stage.

Monoculture Style

This style of container planting involves using just a single plant to fill a container. Whether it's one plant, or three to five plants of the same variety, the container is filled with only one species.

I love using this style with groups of containers of differing heights: each container is filled with a different plant, but all the plants complement each other, offering a singular or complementary color theme, a balance of textures, or some other unifying element. I think the monoculture style works particularly well when you have three or more sizes of the exact same container. Each container houses a different plant, but together, they make a cohesive collection

When using monoculture style for your container plantings, pay careful attention to the height of the plant you're using. It becomes very noticeable if the pot-to-plant proportion is off because everything *in* the pot will have the exact same height.

Pot-hugging Style

The final container garden design style takes the rule of thirds and good pot-to-plant proportion and tosses them both out the window. Pot-hugging style involves using only extremely low or cascading plants in a container. Though it isn't for everyone, this design technique makes for some visually stunning displays. Perhaps it's a big bowl of moss; a tall, rectangular planter filled with creeping ivy; or a planter box filled with ground-covering succulents—whatever plant and container choice you make, the idea is for the plants to sit tight against the container. With pot-hugging designs, the entire container becomes the focal point, and people take notice because it's uncommon.

As you design and build your containers every year, remember that these are just starting recipes. With a little experience, you can build on these design techniques and adjust them to your taste. Good container garden design is a mixture of elements, and none are to be taken too seriously. Don't let the pressures of proper design ruin the fun.

▲ The plant material in this collection of monoculture containers is fairly common, but when several pots are grouped together in this way, the resulting design is very attractive.

◀ Pot-hugging plantings, such as this container of low-growing succulents, make a very striking display.

DESIGNING WITH EDIBLE PLANTS

Containerized fruits and vegetables are often grown in a very utilitarian manner, with very little thought put into the container's design and layout. Many gardeners tend to be more concerned with productivity than appearance when it comes to container vegetable gardening, but they can have both function and form in one pot.

Containers of fruit and vegetable plants deserve to be beautiful, too. Tomato plants don't have to be plunked in a big pot all by themselves. You can utilize all five design styles for growing vegetables, just as you do for ornamentals. In fact, by following the guidelines outlined above, you'll have an edible container garden that's as gorgeous as it is productive.

For example, the thriller, filler, and spiller concept also works for edible plants. Good thrillers can include large-statured veggies such as tomatoes, peppers, or eggplants. Or, the thriller could also be an obelisk in the center of the pot covered with pole beans or cucumbers— or even a fig tree or blueberry bush. Around these, plant bush beans, basil, lettuce, chard,

or root crops such as carrots and beets as the filler layer. Then, fill in the outer edge of the pot with spillers such as thyme, strawberries, sweet potatoes (*Ipomoea batatas*), or cascading cherry tomato varieties.

Later in this chapter, you'll find a table of excellent vegetable varieties for container culture.

Flat-backed style works for vegetable container gardeners, too. Select crops that fit each height

This fabric container filled with vegetables and edible flowers utilizes the thriller, filler, and spiller design concept.

niche and build your layers just as you would build them for ornamental plants.

Excellent edible plant choices for containers designed using the featured specimen style include columnar or dwarf fruit trees, large tomato plants, figs, papayas (*Carica papaya*), citrus trees (*Citrus* spp.), bananas, a trellis of hardy kiwi vines (*Actinidia arguta*) or pole beans. Then, surround this focal point with a low-growing crop, such as mixed herbs, a combination of lettuce and other greens, or a skirt of edible flowers like nasturtiums (*Tropaeolum* spp.), marigolds (*Tagetes* spp.), and pansies (*Viola tricolor* var. *hortensis*).

One important word of caution when it comes to designing containers of edibles: be careful not to overcrowd them. Veggies need lots of air circulation to reduce the risk of fungal diseases and plenty of room to grow and produce their best. Take the time to create beautiful combinations, but don't jam too many plants into any one container. Pay careful attention to the pot size guidelines offered in Chapter 1; they'll help you determine how many vegetable plants to include in any given container.

▲ Monoculture-style vegetable containers are filled with a single species of edible plant, and though they're certainly utilitarian, there's not much room to flex your creative muscles.

▼ This featured specimen style container of edible plants includes a citrus tree surrounded by a skirt of low-growing thyme.

CHOOSING PLANTS FOR YOUR CONTAINERS

There are few things more enjoyable than walking up and down the aisles of your favorite local nurseries, shopping for plants every spring. I purchase plants for my container garden from five or six different garden centers every year because each one carries different varieties. Although I'm often armed with a list of must-have varieties based on research I've done over winter, I also make a lot of impulse buys, which has lead to some pretty eclectic containers over the years—a habit you may or may not want to copy.

Understandably, some people plant the same things in their containers every year, to save themselves time and because it's easy and familiar. Others buy premade plant combinations and plant them into containers for an instant container garden. Those are great options, but don't be afraid to develop your creative side by mixing and matching new plants.

To give you a little guidance to aid your efforts, I've separated the plants you're likely to find at the garden center into eight distinct categories:

- Annuals for flowers and foliage
- Perennials
- Bulbs and tubers
- Tropical plants
- Small trees and shrubs
- Herbs
- Vegetables
- Backyard fruits

◀ There are dozens of succulent plants that make wonderful container plantings.

For each of these categories (except backyard fruits) you'll find a brief introduction followed by a chart of some of the best plants for that particular group. Each chart shares information on the best growing conditions for the plant, along with growth specs and other items worth noting, followed by a gallery of images, including more favorite varieties. Because the backyard fruit category is quite complex, this section will be presented in narrative form rather than in a chart.

There is one group of plants, however, that did not get its own category: the succulents. For recommendations on succulents, refer to the Cement Bin Succulent Planter project in Chapter 1.

You'll notice that the sections on backyard fruits and vegetables for containers are much longer than the others—that's because when it comes to growing edible plants in containers, variety selection matters a whole lot more than it does for ornamental plants. In the chart in the vegetable section, I also include a list of varieties bred specifically for container culture.

Annuals for Flowers and Foliage

Technically, an annual plant is one that completes its entire life cycle in a single year. It germinates, grows, flowers, sets seed, and then dies in a single growing season. Annuals are popular garden plants because most of them remain in bloom for months in an attempt to disperse as many seeds as possible before dying at season's end. But many of the plants we grow as annuals are actually frost-sensitive perennials. For example, fuchsias and coleus are not true annuals, but perennials that do not survive freezing temperatures and are therefore usually planted again each year, as though they were annuals. For the purposes of this book, the term *annual* refers both to true annuals and also to any perennials that are killed

The term *annual* technically refers to a plant that completes its entire life cycle in one year, however gardeners also use the term when referring to a tropical perennial, such as this upright fuchsia (*Fuchsia* 'Gartenmeister Bonstedt'), that's killed by frost at the end of the growing season.

Foliage-based annuals, such as this variegated copperleaf (*Acalypha wilkesiana* 'Beyond Paradise'), add a great amount of interest and texture to container plantings.

by frost. If you live in a gardening zone where winter temperatures seldom dip below freezing, know that some of these plants may continue to thrive in your container garden for many seasons. For those gardeners in northern climes, Chapter 5 offers tips on how to overwinter these frost-sensitive perennials indoors so you can keep them for many years, too.

Although flowers are a common reason for including annuals in your container plantings, foliage-based annuals are another important group to consider. These plants create varied interest through unique foliage coloration or leaf texture, and are beautiful even when not in bloom. In fact, many gardeners pinch or cut off flower buds as they develop on these plants in an attempt to further highlight their unique foliage. I try to include at least one or two foliage-based annuals in each of my ornamental container designs. Not only are they gorgeous and interesting plants, but foliage-based annuals may require less care than their flowering kin.

The following chart includes nineteen of my favorite annuals for flowers and foliage in container gardens (I could have listed hundreds!). The chart offers design usage ideas, growing requirements, and other general information for the species, and will be applicable to many different varieties beyond the ones listed.

Recommended Annuals

COMMON NAME	BOTANICAL NAME	USED FOR FOLIAGE OR FLOWERS?	DESIGN USE	HEIGHT	GROWING CONDITIONS	COMMENTS
Variegated Swedish ivy	*Plectranthus forsteri* 'Marginatus'	Foliage	Filler	12 in.	Full sun to part shade	Green and white variegated foliage plant; vigorous grower.
Silver falls	*Dichondra argentea* 'Silver Falls'	Foliage	Spiller	2 in.	Full sun to part shade	Long cascades of small, fuzzy, gray leaves; low-maintenance; drought tolerant.
Licorice plant	*Helichrysum petiolare*	Foliage	Spiller	6 in.	Full sun to part shade	Gray leaves except on chartreuse cultivars; fast-growing.
Heliotrope	*Heliotropium arborescens*	Flower	Filler	12 to 18 in.	Full sun	Flat-topped clusters of deep purple, vanilla-scented flowers; dark green foliage.
Lantana	*Lantana camara*	Flower	Filler and Spiller	1 to 4 ft.	Full sun	Attracts butterflies and hummingbirds; clusters of small, tubular flowers followed by dark purple berries.
Persian shield	*Strobilanthes dyerianus*	Foliage	Thriller and Filler	1 to 2 ft.	Full sun to part shade	Broad, purple leaves with dark veins and a silvery flush; keep as houseplant during the winter.
Million bells	*Calibrachoa cultivars*	Flower	Spiller	4 to 8 in.	Full sun	Covered in small flowers that look like mini petunias; blooms all summer; trails over edge of containers; lots of colors.
Nemesia	*Nemesia hybrids*	Flower	Spiller	6 to 12 in.	Full sun to part shade	Delicate-looking plants covered with small, spurred flowers; prefers cooler summers; many colors available.
Diamond frost euphorbia	*Euphorbia hypericifolia* 'Inneuphe' Diamond Frost	Flower	Spiller	12 to 18 in.	Full sun to part shade	Dark green foliage topped with tiny frothy white flowers; blooms all summer; drought tolerant.
Hanging begonias	*Begonia boliviensis*	Flower	Filler and Spiller	1 to 2 ft.	Full sun to part shade	Cascading plant with tapered leaves and elongated, four-petaled flowers; orange, red, yellow, or pink flowers are the most common.

Continued

COMMON NAME	BOTANICAL NAME	USED FOR FOLIAGE OR FLOWERS?	DESIGN USE	HEIGHT	GROWING CONDITIONS	COMMENTS
Beefsteak plant	*Perilla frutescens*	Foliage	Thriller and Filler	1 to 3 ft.	Full sun	Grown primarily for their deep burgundy foliage, but white flower spikes are fragrant; keep bushy by pinching plants.
Bacopa	*Sutera cordata*	Flower	Spiller	2 to 6 in.	Full sun to part shade	Small-leaved plants covered with tiny flowers; stems trailing and can grow up to 4 feet; great spiller for tall planters.
Creeping zinnia	*Zinnia angustifolia*	Flower	Spiller	8 to 12 in.	Full sun	Sun-loving, drought-tolerant plants covered in small, daisy-like flowers; low maintenance; blooms all summer long.
Lobelia	*Lobelia erinus*	Flower	Spiller	6 to 10 in.	Part shade	Covered in tiny pink, blue, or white flowers; performs best in spring and fall; heat-tolerant varieties are available.
Signet marigolds	*Tagetes tenuifolia*	Flower	Spiller and Filler	10 to 18 in.	Full sun	Covered in tiny red, yellow, or orange flowers; small, fern-like leaves; profuse bloomer; heat tolerant; edible flowers.
Zonal geranium	*Pelargonium* x *hortorum*	Flower	Filler	1 to 3 in.	Full sun to part shade	Hundreds of varieties with different colored blooms and unique foliage variegation; good, old-fashioned plant.
Bidens	*Bidens ferulifolia*	Flower	Spiller	10 to 15 in.	Full sun	Trailing plants covered in small, daisy-like flowers; profuse bloomer; heat tolerant; low maintenance.
Globe amaranth	*Gomphrena globosa*	Flower	Filler	1 to 2 ft.	Full sun	Red, purple, white, or pink globe-shaped flowers; excellent cut flower; great for drying; drought resistant.
Sunset lysimachia	*Lysimachia congestiflora*	Foliage and flower	Spiller	2 to 6 in.	Full sun to part shade	Variegated varieties have striking gold and green foliage topped with small clusters of yellow flowers; trailing habit.

Angelonia (*A. angustifolia*), fan flower (*Scaevola* hybrid), golden dewdrop (*Duranta erecta* 'Gold Mound')

Verbena (*Verbena* hybrid), golden pineapple sage (*Salvia elegans* 'Golden Delicious', and Dark Dancer™ clover (*Trifolium repens* 'Atropurpureum')

Nasturtiums (*Tropaeolum majus*)

▲ Wishbone flower (*Torenia*)

◀ Coleus varieties (*Solenostemon scutellarioides*)

Popcorn plant (*Cassia didymobotrya*)

HANGING BEGONIA BASKET

This sweet, three-tiered hanging basket planter uses a combination of foliage and flowering annuals to make a unique display. But instead of using an expensive wire hanging basket, the project repurposes an old set of hanging fruit or vegetable kitchen storage baskets. Styled in the same manner as expensive coconut fiber-lined baskets, this DIY version costs a lot less and looks just as beautiful.

Though you can grow any number of small-statured flowering and foliage annuals in this planter, I chose a shade-loving combination of begonias and a few spiller plants to tumble over the edges.

This planter includes the following plants:

- 2 golden creeping Jenny (*Lysimachia nummularia* 'Aurea')
- 1 English ivy (*Hedera helix*)
- 5 mixed-foliage Rex begonias (*Begonia* rex hybrids)
- 1 trailing begonia for the top tier (I used *Begonia* 'Summerwings Rose'®)

HOW TO MAKE A HANGING BEGONIA BASKET

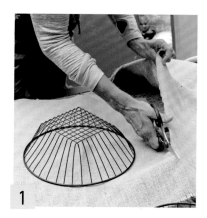

1

2

3

4

STEP 1 Begin by removing the chain hanger from the bottom two baskets to disconnect all three baskets from each other. Then, place each basket face-down on the piece of burlap. Use scissors to cut a circle of burlap that's a few inches larger than the rim of each basket.

STEP 2 Flip the baskets back over and line the inside of each of them with pieces of sheet moss covering all the metal, then press the circle of burlap down onto the moss. Use scissors to cut off the excess. It's okay if the burlap hangs over the edge a bit.

STEP 3 Replace the chain hanger by reconnecting it to each of the baskets. Hang the baskets from a ceiling hook, tree branch, or shepherd's hook, and make sure the chains are positioned so each basket is level. Fill each basket with the 50/50 potting soil blend until it's ¾ full. Begonias are shade-lovers, so this basket will do best under trees or in another shady area.

STEP 4 Arrange the plants in the baskets so the spillers are toward the outer edge. Each basket should have one spiller and two begonias. Once all the plants are in place, fill in around their roots with more potting

soil blend until each basket is filled to within 1 in. of its upper rim. Water each basket well. Rex begonias like to be watered regularly, but they do not like constantly wet soil. Since the soil volume is so small, the baskets should be watered fairly frequently, but Rex begonias are quite forgiving, even if they're left high and dry for a few days.

NOTE: At the end of the growing season, before the arrival of fall's first frost, this planter can be moved indoors and grown as a houseplant. Rex begonias are wonderful houseplants, though they do like higher humidity than that found in most homes. If you can, hang your begonia basket next to a bathroom window where the humidity from the shower will prove helpful. Indoors, Rex begonias like bright, but not direct, sunlight.

Perennials

By definition, perennial plants are those that survive for many growing seasons. Generally, the top of the plant dies back to the ground during the winter, but the root system survives, though many perennials do retain some ground-hugging foliage year-round.

Perennials are a surprisingly useful group in container gardening. Though their flowering season is typically shorter than most flowering annuals, they really add a unique design element to containers. Much like annuals, perennials are selected for their flower power, or for the texture, color, and form of their foliage. Perennials grown primarily for their foliage, such as ornamental grasses, hostas, coral bells, ferns, and spurges make both excellent focal points and accent plants in container designs, especially when mixed with complementary species.

Aside from adding unique physical attributes to the design, another perk of using perennials is that you can plant them elsewhere in your garden at the end of the season, or overwinter them in their containers and grow them for many seasons.

The following chart includes fifteen of my favorite perennial plants for container gardens, each with a unique attribute that lends itself well to container designs. Though there are many different named varieties of each of these perennials, as a whole, each species works well in containers. There is a great amount of variety among the different cultivars of these plants, so do a bit of experimentation to determine which ones work best with your personal design style.

Many perennials make excellent container plants. Those grown primarily for their foliage, such as this coral bell, hosta, and dwarf Japanese painted fern (*Athyrium* 'Silver Slippers'), add a lot of color, texture, and form to container designs.

Recommended Perennials

COMMON NAME	BOTANICAL NAME	USE	DESIGN USE	HEIGHT	GROWING CONDITIONS	COMMENTS
Dwarf bee balm	*Monarda didyma* 'Petite Delight'	Flower	Thriller and Filler	1 to 2 ft.	Full sun	Attracts hummingbirds and bees; blooms midsummer.
Coral bells	*Heuchera* cultivars	Foliage	Filler	6 to 12 in.	Full to part shade	Some varieties have unique and striking foliage colors; flowers are tiny on tall stems.
Black-eyed Susans	*Rudbeckia* spp.	Flowers	Thriller and Filler	2 to 3 ft.	Full sun	Attracts pollinators; long bloom time; birds enjoy the seeds.
Yarrow	*Achillea millefolium*	flowers	Thriller and Filler	2 to 3 ft.	Full sun	Flat-topped flower clusters; lacy foliage; long bloom time.
Aromatic aster	*Symphyotrichum oblongifolium*	Flowers	Filler	12 to 18 in.	Full sun	Late-season bloomer; many small flowers; great for pollinators.
Daylilies	*Hemerocallis* spp.	Flowers	Thriller and Filler	1 to 3 ft.	Full sun	Many different flower colors; strap-like foliage; look for repeat blooming.
Tick seed	*Coreopsis* spp.	Flowers	Filler	1 to 3 ft.	Full sun	Small, bright flowers; long bloom time; easy to care for.
Golden hakone grass	*Hakonechloa macra* 'Aureola'	Foliage	Spiller	10 to 12 in.	Part to full shade	Soft, flowing, shade-tolerant, grass-like plant; gorgeous yellow variegation.
Cranesbill	*Geranium* spp.	Flowers	Filler and Spiller	1 to 2 ft.	Full sun	Lots of round flowers; round leaves with a serrated edge; many different varieties.
Hosta	*Hosta* spp.	Foliage	Filler	6 in. to 3 ft.	Full shade	Many varieties have unusual variegation and/or coloration; come in many different sizes; deer favorite.
Creeping Jenny	*Lysimachia nummularia* 'Aurea'	Foliage	Spiller	2 to 6 in.	Full sun to part shade	Excellent low-growing, trailing plant for the edge of containers.
Garden phlox	*Phlox paniculata*	Flowers	Thriller	2 to 4 ft.	Full sun	Tall stems topped with large flower clusters; attracts butterflies and bees; look for resistance to powdery mildew.
Astilbe	*Astilbe* spp.	Flowers	Thriller and Filler	1 to 3 ft.	Part to full shade	Plume-like flowers; do not let plants dry out or the foliage will crisp.
Blanket flower	*Gaillardia* spp.	Flowers	Filler and Spiller	1 to 2 ft.	Full sun	Lots of bright, daisy-like flowers atop loosely mounded foliage.
Cushion spurge	*Euphorbia polychroma*	Foliage and flowers	Filler	12 to 18 in.	Full sun to part shade	Flowers are actually colored leaves called bracts; early-season interest; tight, mounded foliage.

Hosta (*Hosta* spp.)

Salvia (*Salvia sylvestris* 'Blue Hill')

Ornamental grass (*Miscanthus sinensis* 'Variegatus')

▲ Stonecrop (*Sedum spectabile* 'Autumn Joy')

▶ Coneflowers (*Echinacea* cultivars)

Bulbs and Tubers

Another group of plants well-adapted to container culture are plants that grow from bulbs. Bulbs are underground, fleshy storage organs. Though bulbs and tubers are botanically different, they are often lumped together as bulb plants, which is what I've done here.

Both hardy spring-blooming and summer-blooming bulbs, as well as tender tropical bulbs, can be included in containers, though careful consideration has to be given to seeing them safely through the winter. In northern climates, most potted flowering bulbs will not survive the winter if the pot's exterior is left exposed to the elements, even if the bulbs are winter hardy when they're planted in the ground. But if you insulate the pots according to the instructions given in Chapter 5 or move the pots into an unheated garage or root cellar that's cold but not freezing, hardy bulbs will do quite nicely. Tropical bulbs, on the other hand, have to be overwintered as houseplants or lifted from their pots and stored indoors in a dormant state. Typically, spring-blooming bulbs are planted in the autumn, while summer-blooming bulbs and tender tropical bulbs are planted in the spring.

Including pots of spring-blooming bulbs in your container garden is a great way to add early season color to your landscape because many of them are in bloom long before the weather is warm enough to plant annuals and warm-season vegetables. When these bulbs are finished blooming, they can be lifted from the containers and planted elsewhere in the garden.

In the following chart, you'll find fifteen great bulbs and tubers to add to your container garden.

Hardy, spring-flowering bulbs, such as these tulips (*Tulipa* spp.), do well in containers, provided the bulbs are not allowed to freeze out during the winter. Keep the container in a cold garage or insulate the pot from planting time until the spring.

Recommended Bulbs and Tubers

COMMON NAME	BOTANICAL NAME	WINTER HARDY?	USE	HEIGHT	GROWING CONDITIONS	COMMENTS
Upright elephant ear	*Alocasia* spp.	No	Foliage	2 to 5 ft.	Full sun to part shade	Bold and tropical; great thriller plant.
Tuberous begonias	*Begonia* x *tuberhybrida*	No	Flower	6 in. to 1 ft.	Shade	Flowers come in many different colors; overwinter dormant bulbs in a box of peat moss.
Oriental lily	*Lilium orientalis*	Yes	Flower	2 to 3 ft.	Full sun	Fragrant and striking.
Montbretia	*Crocosmia* spp.	Yes	Flower	2 to 3 ft.	Full sun to part shade	Butterflies and hummingbirds love it.
Freesia	*Freesia corymbosa*	No	Flower	1 to 2 ft.	Full sun	Sweet fragrance.
Tulips	*Tulipa* spp.	Yes	Flower	3 to 2 ft.	Full sun to part shade	Wide range of colors and sizes available.
Ranunculus	*Ranunculus asiaticus*	No	Flower	1 to 2 ft.	Full sun to part shade	Papery petals; great cut flower.
Peacock orchids	*Gladiolus acidanthera*	No	Flower	2 to 3 in.	Full sun	Blooms midsummer; lovely fragrance.
Wood sorrel	*Oxalis* spp.	No	Foliage	6 in. to 2 ft.	Part to full shade	Seek out varieties with colorful or variegated foliage.
Crinum	*Crinum bulbispermum*	No	Flower	1 to 5 ft.	Full sun to part shade	Bulbs like to be pot-bound; overwinter container in an unheated garage in the north.
Alliums	*Allium* spp.	Yes	Flower	6 in. to 3 ft.	Full sun to part shade	Deer-resistant; globe-shaped flowers atop straight stems.
Rain lily	*Habranthus robustus*	No	Flower	6 to 12 ft.	Full sun	Plant in spring for summer bloom.
Saffron crocus	*Crocus sativus*	Yes	Flower	3 in.	Full sun to part shade	Stamens are harvested and dried for use in cooking; not fully hardy in the far north.
Amaryllis	*Hippeastrum* spp.	No	Flower	1 to 2 ft.	Full sun to part shade	Grow in containers for winter blooms indoors; enjoy the foliage in the summer garden.
Gloriosa lily	*Gloriosa superba*	No	Flower	5 to 6 ft. vine	Full sun to part shade	Beautiful vine; red and yellow recurved petals; overwinter dormant tubers in the pot indoors in a cool area.

Sweet potato vine
(*Ipomoea batatas* cultivar)

Dahlia (*Dahlia* spp.)

Canna (*Canna* spp.)

Asiatic lily (*Lilium asiaticum*)

Calla lily (*Zantedeschia* spp.)

Caladium (*Caladium* x *hortulanum*)

▲ Daffodils (*Narcissus* spp.)

◀ Elephant ear (*Colocasia esculenta*)

There are many tropical plants that do beautifully in containers. One of the most popular is the tropical hibiscus (*Hibiscus rosa-sinensis*), which comes in dozens of different flower colors.

Tropical Plants

Tropical plants are species native to tropical regions. They are well-adapted to warm and humid environments, though with the right care, tropical plants can be grown almost everywhere. Tropical plants are not winter hardy except in very warm climates, and they often have large leaves to maximize sunlight exposure. Many houseplants are foliage tropicals that happen to be adaptable enough to thrive indoors.

In addition to large leaves, many tropical plants have brightly colored flowers with a heavy fragrance or exotic forms and shapes, all designed by nature to tempt and lure very specific pollinators. Tropical forests offer a wealth of plants with unique attributes perfectly suited to container gardens.

Because of their beauty and uncommonness, tropical plants are a bit pricier than most garden plants. They require optimal care, so greenhouses charge a premium price for these beauties, but you shouldn't let that stop you from growing them, if you're willing to put forth a little effort. They aren't winter hardy, but most tropical plants are easily overwintered either in a dormant state or as houseplants. I delve into exactly how to accomplish this in Chapter 5.

The following chart features ten of my favorite tropical plants that thrive in containers. Because each of these plants is big and bold and beautiful, tropicals are perfect for featured-specimen and monoculture-style container designs, though they also work well as the thriller in layered designs.

Recommended Tropical Plants

COMMON NAME	BOTANICAL NAME	USE	HEIGHT	GROWING CONDITIONS	COMMENTS
Tropical hibiscus	*Hibiscus rosa-sinensis*	Flowers	3 to 10 ft.	Full sun to part shade	Large, disc-shaped flowers come in many different colors; each flower lasts only one day; tree or shrub forms.
Gardenia	*Gardenia jasminoides*	Flowers	4 to 6 ft.	Part shade	Fragrant, pure white flowers on dark, glossy foliage; look for cultivars with double-petaled flowers.
Bird of paradise	*Strelitzia reginae*	Flowers and foliage	3 to 4 ft.	Full sun to part shade	Broad, gray-green, stiff, upright leaves; orange and purple flowers resemble plumage on a bird's head; excellent cut flower.
Angel's trumpet	*Brugmansia* spp.	Flowers	4 to 8 ft.	Full sun	Huge, pendulous, trumpet-shaped flowers hang from the tree-like plants; highly fragrant flowers can be white, yellow, peach, or pink.
Frangipani	*Plumeria* spp.	Flowers	10 to 15 ft.	Full sun to part shade	Fragrant flowers pollinated by moths; keep plants on the dry side; flowers can be white, yellow, pink, or peach colored.
Red Abyssian banana	*Ensete ventricosum* 'Maurelii'	Foliage	8 to 10 ft.	Full sun to part shade	Broad, deep red, tropical leaves.
Variegated ginger	*Alpinia zerumbet* 'Variegata'	Flowers and foliage	4 to 5 ft.	Full sun to part shade	Yellow and green striped upright leaves; fragrant white flowers.
Variegated Japanese aralia	*Fatsia japonica* 'Variegata'	Foliage	4 to 5 ft.	Full to partial shade	Glossy, lobed, dark green leaves with creamy yellow variegation.
Stromanthe	*Stromanthe sanguinea* 'Triostar'	Foliage	2 to 3 ft.	Full shade	Visually striking, variegated green and white leaves with bright pink undersides; impressive plant makes a great thriller in containers.
Variegated rubber tree	*Ficus elastica* 'Tineke'	Foliage	Up to 20 ft.	Full sun to part shade	Prune to maintain a shorter height; leaves are variegated white and pale green with striking pink and burgundy splotches; needs bright light if overwintering indoors.

New Zealand flax
(*Phormium tenax*)

Iochroma (*Iochroma*
'Royal Queen'™)

Ti plant (*Cordyline*
fruticosa cultivar)

Mandevilla (*Mandevilla* hybrids)

Bougainvillea (*Bougainvillea* spp.)

Variegated croton (*Codiaeum*
variegatum)

Small Trees and Shrubs

Consider including small trees and shrubs in your plans if you want to add shade and structure to your container plantings. A containerized tree or shrub on a small balcony, patio, or deck adds height and visually expands the space while providing shade and cover.

The best trees and shrubs for container culture are those with a smaller stature. Unless you have an extremely large container, skip trying to grow trees that grow much bigger than 15 or 20 feet in height. And remember that when winter arrives, most containerized trees and shrubs need a little root insulation, especially if you live where winter temperatures drop below freezing on a regular basis. I'll cover this type of root insulation in Chapter 5, too, but another option is to remove the tree or shrub from its pot and plant it in the ground at the end of the growing season to ensure it survives the winter.

Because trees and shrubs are such large design elements, they are best used in a featured specimen design style.

The following chart features ten favorite selections that thrive in containers. Some bloom, while others are appreciated primarily for their foliage, but all add height and structure to your container garden.

▶ Small-statured or slow-growing evergreen trees and shrubs make great container plants. Just be sure to use a large enough container to accommodate the root mass.

Recommended Small Trees and Shrubs

COMMON NAME	BOTANICAL NAME	USE	HEIGHT	GROWING CONDITIONS	TREE OR SHRUB?	COMMENTS
Kousa dogwood	Cornus kousa	Flowers	15 to 20 ft.	Full sun to part shade	Tree	White flowers followed by red fruits.
Japanese maple	Acer palmatum	Foliage	10 to 20 ft.	Full sun to part shade	Tree	Seek out varieties with cut-leaf foliage or unique coloration for added interest.
Stewartia	Stewartia pseudocamellia	Flowers and fall foliage	12 to 35 ft.	Full sun	Tree	White, camellia-like flowers; striking fall foliage; peeling bark.
Japanese snowbell	Styrax japonicus	Flowers	20 to 30 ft.	Full sun to part shade	Tree	White pendulous, bell-shaped flowers; great structure.
Red twig dogwood	Cornus sericea	Foliage and showy stems	6 to 9 ft.	Full sun	Shrub	Red stems in winter; clusters of small white flowers followed by white berries.
Blue mist shrub	Caryopteris x clandonensis	Flowers	2 to 3 ft.	Full sun	Shrub	Clusters of medium blue flowers in midsummer; great for pollinators.
Red-veined enkianthus	Enkianthus campanulatus	Flowers and foliage	6 to 10 ft.	Full sun to part shade	Shrub	Tiny, bell-shaped flowers in early summer; nice fall color.
Boxwood	Buxus spp.	Foliage	2 to 8 ft.	Full sun	Shrub	Broad-leaved evergreen; deer resistant.
Virginia sweetspire	Itea virginica	Flowers and fall foliage	3 to 6 ft.	Full sun to part shade	Shrub	Long panicles of creamy white flowers; bright red fall foliage.
Daphne	Daphne spp.	Flowers	2 to 5 ft.	Part shade	Shrub	Very sweet fragrance; clusters of small flowers.

Virginia magnolia (*Magnolia virginiana*)

Fringe tree (*Chionanthus virginicus*)

Dwarf Hinoki cypress topiary (*Chamaecyparis obtusa* 'Nana Gracilis')

Deciduous azalea/Exbury azalea (*Rhododendron* hybrids)

Hydrangea species (*Hydrangea macrophylla* 'Paraplu')

Popcorn viburnum (*Viburnum plicatum f. pilcatum* 'Popcorn')

Herbs

Herbs are plants grown for their flavor, fragrance, or medicinal properties. Some herbs are frost-sensitive annuals, while others are perennials that return year after year. There are even a few herbs that are shrub-like in nature. And some even grow into small trees, if they're grown in the right climate or the plants are overwintered indoors.

Culinary herbs are ideal candidates for container gardens. Most are quite content to grow in a pot either by themselves or in a mixed design. Depending on their structure and growth habit, herbs can serve as thrillers, fillers, or spillers in any given container. The portion of the plant used in the kitchen can be the foliage, flowers, stems, or seeds.

Almost any herb is suitable for container gardening, but there are some bred specifically to thrive in container conditions. The following chart features fifteen favorite culinary herbs ideal for container gardening. Most require full sun conditions to perform their best. Many herbs perform double duty in a container garden—they're useful in the kitchen, but they also attract pollinators and other beneficial insects when they're in flower.

Regularly harvest your herbs to encourage more growth and to keep them from going to flower (flowering sometimes alters the flavor). Use a sharp pair of scissors or pruners to remove tender new herb shoots or leaves for drying. If you harvest whole shoots, tie them into small bundles and hang them up to dry in a cool, dry room for several weeks. If you harvest individual leaves, they can be dried in a food dehydrator for 1 to 3 hours. Or, if you're harvesting chamomile, harvest the small white and yellow flowers by plucking them off with your fingers in a rake-like

This container is filled with a mixture of culinary herbs, including a bay tree (*Laurus nobilis*), thyme, parsley (*Petroselinum crispum*), and variegated sage.

fashion, then dry them by spreading them out on a cloth and turning them over once a day for 10 to 20 days. Dried herbs are best stored in air-tight plastic or glass containers and kept away from direct sunlight.

Recommended Herbs

COMMON NAME	BOTANICAL NAME	PLANT TYPE	EDIBLE PORTION	HEIGHT	COMMENTS
Italian oregano	*Origanum vulgare* var. *hirtum*	Perennial	Leaves	1 to 2 ft.	Small pink flowers are attractive to bees and other beneficial insects.
Cilantro coriander	*Coriandrum sativum*	Annual	Leaves for cilantro; seeds for coriander	10 to 18 in.	Cool-season herb best grown in the spring and fall; white flower clusters; look for slow-bolting varieties for heat tolerance.
Chives	*Allium schoenoprasum*	Perennial	Leaves and flowers	8 to 10 in.	Slender, hollow, grass-like leaves have mild onion flavor; round clusters of small, pink, edible flowers occur in spring.
Sweet marjoram	*Origanum majorana*	Tender perennial	Leaves	4 to 6 in.	Unique flavor; small whitish-pink flowers; trailing plant with sparse form.
Sweet basil	*Ocimum basilicum*	Annual	Leaves	18 in. to 2 ft.	Classic, summery flavor; try dwarf, small-leaved varieties such as 'Spicy Globe' and 'Fino Verde' for containers.
Parsley	*Petroselinum crispum*	Biennial grown as an annual	Leaves	6 to 12 in.	Biennial that produces leaves the first season and umbels of white flowers the second; flat- and curly-leaved types both do well in containers.
Lemongrass	*Cymbopogon citratus*	Tropical	Base of leaf stalks	2 to 4 ft.	Large grass with distinct citrus flavor; to harvest, snap off a leaf cluster at the base of the plant and peel off outer leaves to reveal the white interior flesh.
Dill	*Anethum graveolens*	Annual	Leaves and seeds	2 to 3 ft.	Host plant for swallowtail butterflies; yellow umbrella-shaped flower clusters; delicate, ferny foliage.
Sage	*Salvia officinalis*	Perennial	Leaves	8 to 12 in.	Broad, gray-green leaves with strong flavor; blue to purple flowers in mid- to late-summer; variegated forms available.
Rosemary	*Rosemarinus officinalis*	Tender perennial	Leaves	1 to 3 ft.	Needle-like leaves on woody stems; can grow into a shrub where winters don't freeze; perfumed flavor; flowers pink or purple and borne tight against the stem.
Bay laurel	*Laurus nobilis*	Tender perennial	Leaves	Up to 20 ft.	Can grow into a large tree where winters don't freeze; broad, glossy leaves are harvested and dried.
Lemon verbena	*Aloysia triphylla*	Tender perennial	Leaves	2 to 4 ft.	Snappy lemon-flavored leaves are long and tapered; can grow into a woody shrub if overwintered properly; tiny, white flowers.
Mints	*Mentha* spp.	Perennial	Leaves	1 to 2 ft.	Highly invasive, perfect for containers; many types—*M.* x *piperita* is peppermint; *M. spicata* is spearmint; also try apple, chocolate, and pineapple mints for more subtle flavors.
Thyme	*Thymus vulgaris*	Perennial	Leaves	2 to 6 in.	Low-growing plant with tiny leaves and small pink, purple, or white flowers; flowers are attractive to pollinators.
Fennel	*Foeniculum vulgare*	Perennial	Leaves and seeds	4 to 6 ft.	Large plant with licorice-flavored foliage; yellow umbrella-shaped flower clusters in summer; seeds are dried for cooking; prolific self-sower.

Vegetables

If you've wondered if it's possible to grow your favorite veggie in a container, the answer is yes—as long as you have the right plant partnered with the correctly sized container. Large-statured veggies need very large containers for optimal production. And if you're growing long, tapered root crops, the containers also need to be deep enough to handle the full length of the mature roots.

Vegetables need good air circulation to fend off fungal diseases and maximize growth, which makes choosing the right varieties extremely important. If you try to sandwich giant veggie plants into pots that are too small, you're likely to find yourself disappointed at the end of the season. Thankfully, there are a few ways around this problem.

First, if you want to grow vine crops but you don't have enough room, know that breeders have developed smaller, bush-type varieties of almost all of your favorites. These vegetables are perfect choices for container gardens because they've been bred to have good production from compact plants. Among these smaller varieties you'll find bush cucumbers, watermelons, pumpkins, cantaloupes, winter squash, and summer squash. I've included my favorite bush vine crop varieties in the chart at the end of this section.

Peas and beans also have specific varieties bred to have more compact growth, but tall, vining pea varieties and pole beans also do great in containers, provided you give them a sturdy trellis. In Chapter 3, you'll find lots of ideas for creating unique trellises and staking systems for containers.

Partnering the right vegetable plant with the right size container is essential.

Dwarf pea varieties, such as 'Peas-in-a-Pot' and 'Half Pint' do great in container gardens. But so do standard pea varieties, as long as you have a sturdy trellis for them to climb.

In addition to bush-type vine crops, miniature or patio-type vegetable varieties are also ideal for container gardening. There are many varieties of tomatoes, eggplants, peppers, okra, and even sweet corn bred just for containers, and more and more are being developed each year. Because they're more compact, a smaller soil volume is required for optimum growth, but they still produce a great harvest.

There are dwarf and miniature varieties of many other vegetables as well. Some were bred to look cute on a plate, while others were created specifically with container gardeners in mind. These dwarf crops are not the same as "baby" vegetables, which are simply full-sized veggies that have been harvested early. Instead, these are tiny marvels even when fully mature. From orb-shaped carrots, mini heads of lettuce, and pint-size cabbages to petite broccoli plants, dwarf kale, and beets no bigger than a ping-pong ball, these mini veggies are real stand-outs in a container. There are even semi-dwarf varieties of Brussels sprouts!

Of course not all container veggies need to be dwarf or compact varieties. There are plenty of crops that perform beautifully in a pot just as they are. You can grow just about any variety of radish, cauliflower, turnip, kohlrabi, chard, lettuce, spinach, onions, and tomatillo in containers, too.

In addition to considering which varieties to plant, it's also important to think about timing. Some vegetables are warm-season crops that don't tolerate frost, while others prefer the cool temperatures of spring and fall. Warm-season

Miniature or patio-type vegetable varieties, such as this 'Amethyst' eggplant, are ideal for container gardening.

Cool-season crops, such as this 'French Breakfast' radish, love the cool temperatures of spring and fall.

crops are best planted after the danger of frost has passed, but cool-season crops prefer to be planted very early or very late in the growing season. Chapter 5 digs deeper into the differences between these two groups of plants and teaches you how to maximize production by using a technique called succession planting.

A final consideration when it comes to growing vegetables in containers is their preferred method of planting. Because some crops take longer to mature, it's best to give them a head start by sowing seeds indoors under grow lights or purchasing transplants from a local nursery. Typically, warm-season fruiting crops such as tomatoes, peppers, eggplants, and okra are best grown from transplants that are already 6 to 8 weeks old. Northern gardeners with shorter growing seasons may also want to start cucumbers, pumpkins, melons, and other vine crops in the same way. Vegetables that grow quickly are easily started by sowing seeds directly into a container.

Recommended Vegetables

COMMON NAME	BOTANICAL NAME	COOL OR WARM SEASON	START AS SEEDS OR TRANSPLANTS	FAVORITE VARIETIES FOR CONTAINERS	COMMENTS
Artichoke	*Cynara cardunculus var. scolymus*	Warm	Transplants	'Green Globe', 'Emerald', and 'Imperial Star'	Difficult to grow in cold climates where plants need to be overwintered indoors; in warm climates, artichokes are perennial and may produce a crop for several years.
Bush beans	*Phaseolus vulgaris*	Warm	Seeds	'Provider', 'Gold Rush', 'Yellow Wax', 'Gold Mine', 'Jade', 'Mascotte', 'Blue Lake'	Any bush bean grows well in a container; also try 'Fordhook Bush Limas' if you want to grow lima beans, too.
Beets	*Beta vulgaris*	Both	Seeds or transplants	Baby varieties include 'Baby Ball', 'Little Ball', and 'Babybeat'	Though all beets are suitable for containers, baby-types stay small even when mature; for variety try 'Golden' beets and candy-striped 'Chioggia' beets.
Broccoli	*Brassica oleracea var. italica*	Cool	Transplants	Miniature varieties include 'Small Miracle' and 'Green Magic'	Full-sized varieties need larger pots than mini varieties, but still do well; look for varieties with good side shoot production for a longer harvest.
Brussels sprouts	*Brassica oleracea var. gemmifera*	Cool	Transplants	Short-statured varieties: 'Catskill', 'Half-Dwarf French', 'Long Island Semi-Dwarf'	If you plan to grow a full-sized variety of Brussels sprouts in a container, choose a large, heavy pot, as the plants can become quite top heavy.
Cabbage	*Brassica oleracea var. capitata*	Cool	Transplants	'Golden Acre', 'Gonzales', 'Caraflex', 'Earliana', 'Integro', 'Golden Cross', and 'Tiara'	Harvest when heads are tight and fully formed by cutting them from the plant with a sharp knife; if left on the plant too long, the head will split.
Carrots	*Daucus carota* subspp. *sativus*	Cool and warm season	Seeds	Round and short varieties: 'Yaya', 'Romeo', 'Caracas', 'Oxheart', 'Parisienne', 'Thumbelina', 'Little Finger', and 'Short n' Sweet'	Thin seedlings after they develop first true leaves; any carrot variety can be grown in containers, just make sure the pot is deep enough to handle the full-grown roots.
Corn	*Zea mays*	Warm season	Seeds	Only dwarf corn does well in containers; try 'Yukon Chief', 'On Deck', 'Blue Jade Dwarf', and 'Golden Midget'	Full-sized corn does poorly in containers, but newer dwarf selections require just a few plants per pot for good ear production; grow only one variety of corn at a time.

COMMON NAME	BOTANICAL NAME	COOL OR WARM SEASON	START AS SEEDS OR TRANSPLANTS	FAVORITE VARIETIES FOR CONTAINERS	COMMENTS
Cucumbers	Cucumis sativus	Warm season	Seeds or transplants	Bush-types: 'Salad Bush', 'Bush Champion', 'Spacemaster', 'Picklebush', 'Patio Snacker', 'Miniature White'	Standard cucumbers need a sturdy trellis to climb or a lot of room for them to spread; make sure plants receive ample water when fruit is developing.
Eggplant	Solanum melongena	Warm	Transplants	Small-statured varieties: 'Fairy Tale', 'Morden Midget', 'Patio Baby', 'Bride', 'Hansel', 'Gretel', 'Little Fingers', 'Amethyst', 'Emerald Isle', 'Pinstripe', and 'Pot Black'	A great variety of patio-type eggplants available for container gardeners, including purple, white, pink, and striped eggplants, as well as elongated, Japanese types.
Kale	Brassica oleracea var. sabellica	Cool	Seeds	Small varieties: 'Dwarf Green Curled', 'Dwarf Blue Curled Vates', 'Dwarf Blue Curled Scotch', and 'Improved Dwarf Siberian'	Any type of kale grows well in containers; the flavor is best after the plants have experienced a few frosts.
Lettuce	Lactuca sativa	Cool	Seeds or transplants	Miniature lettuce varieties include 'Little Gem', 'Tom Thumb', 'Bambi', and 'Red Cash'	All varieties are suited to containers; plants will bolt (go to flower) when summer's heat arrives, so plant them early in the spring or late in the fall for an autumn harvest.
Okra	Abelmoschus esculentus	Warm	Seeds or transplants	Dwarf okras such as 'Baby Bubby', 'Vidrines Midget Cowhorn', and 'Green Fingers' are best for containers	Requires a long growing season so northern gardeners should plant transplants; southern gardeners can sow seeds directly into containers.
Peas	Pisum sativum	Cool	Seeds	Small-statured: 'Karina', 'Laxton's Progress', 'Peas-in-a-Pot', 'Tom Thumb', and 'Half Pint'; or snap pea varieties: 'Sugar Daddy' or 'Little SnapPea Crunch'; and snowpeas: 'Snowbird'	Full-sized peas need a sturdy trellis or teepee to support the plants, as some varieties can grow 6 ft. tall.

Continued

COMMON NAME	BOTANICAL NAME	COOL OR WARM SEASON	START AS SEEDS OR TRANSPLANTS	FAVORITE VARIETIES FOR CONTAINERS	COMMENTS
Peppers	*Capsicum annuum*	Warm	Transplants	'Sweet Bellina', 'Basket of Fire', 'Baby Belle', 'Mohawk Patio', 'Cheyenne Patio', 'Tequila Sunrise', 'Miniature Yellow Bell', 'Oda', 'Bangles Blend', 'Tangerine Dream', and 'Yum Yum Gold'	Both hot and sweet peppers do great, but compact varieties require a smaller container and don't need to be staked or caged; make sure plants receive plenty of water when fruiting.
Popcorn	*Zea mays* var. *everta*	Warm	Seeds	Miniature varieties include 'Tom Thumb', 'Dakota Black', 'Mini Blue', and 'Mini Pink'	For best pollination, grow as many plants as you can, but grow only one type of corn at a time so the varieties don't cross pollinate and produce starchy kernels.
Pumpkins	*Cucurbita* spp.	Warm	Seeds or transplants	Bush-type pumpkins: 'Neon', 'Kandy Korn Plus', 'Orange Cutie', 'Amazonka', and 'Windsor'	Full-sized pumpkins require a very large container and a sturdy trellis to support the vines or plenty of room for them to ramble.
Radish	*Raphanus sativus*	Cool	Seeds	Favorites include 'French Breakfast', 'Easter Egg', 'Cherry Belle', 'Amethyst', and 'Starburst'	Radish are very fast-growing, making them a great crop to grow with kids; wide, shallow bowl-type containers are best.
Squash, summer	*Cucurbita pepo*	Warm	Seeds or transplants	Compact, bush varieties: 'Dunja', 'G-Star', 'Burpee's Best', 'Saffron', 'Patio Star', 'Bush Baby', 'Buckingham', 'Patio Green Bush', and 'Patio Silver Bush'	Summer squash grown from seed do better than transplants, but northern gardeners can get a jump start by putting transplants into their pots instead of seeds.
Squash, winter	*Cucurbita* spp.	Warm	Seeds or transplants	Compact, bush varieties: 'Sugarbush', 'Bush Delicata', 'Butterbush', 'Tivoli', 'Reno', 'Honey Bear', 'Table King Bush', 'Bush Buttercup', 'Table Gold Acorn', and 'Table Queen Bush'	Full-sized winter squash vines can grow up to 20 ft. long, making these bush types the perfect choice for container gardeners with limited space.

COMMON NAME	BOTANICAL NAME	COOL OR WARM SEASON	START AS SEEDS OR TRANSPLANTS	FAVORITE VARIETIES FOR CONTAINERS	COMMENTS
Swiss chard	*Beta vulgaris*, Cicla group	Both	Seeds	Any variety does beautifully; favorites include 'Golden', 'Bright Lights', 'Peppermint Stick', 'Electric Neon Blend', and 'Lyon'	Chard planted in the very early spring will produce edible greens well into the fall; the colored stems of some varieties look beautiful when mixed with other veggies and flowers.
Tomatoes, full-sized fruits	*Lycopersicon esculentum*; *Solanum lycopersicum*	Warm	Transplants	Determinate, patio-type tomatoes: 'Mountain Princess', 'Iron Lady', 'Glacier', 'Bush Big Boy', 'Bush Steak', 'Patio Paste', 'Fresh Salsa', 'Bush Goliath', 'Totem', and 'Patio Princess'	Provide each plant with a stake, cage, or trellis; choose deep, large containers for tomatoes and water regularly to fend off blossom end rot.
Tomatoes, cherry-sized fruits	*Lycopersicon esculentum*; *Solanum lycopersicum*	Warm	Transplants	Dwarf cherry tomato varieties: 'Sweetheart of the Patio', 'Red Robin', 'Tumbling Tom', 'Minibel', 'Tiny Tim', 'Small Fry', 'MicroTom', 'Sweet 'n Neat Cherry Red', 'Sweet 'n Neat Yellow', 'Gold Nugget', 'Sweet Zen', and 'Merlot'	Small-fruited, dwarf tomatoes are perfect for salads or fresh snacking; plants are highly productive, but they stay small; tumbling varieties do well in hanging baskets too.
Tomatillo	*Physalis philadelphica*	Warm	Transplants	Any tomatillo will do well in containers; favorites include 'Miltomate', 'Mexican', and 'Purple'	Tomatillos are covered with a papery husk; they're ready to harvest when the husk folds back and fruits begin to drop from the plant.
Watermelon	*Citrullus lanatus*	Warm	Seeds or transplants	Bush-type watermelons: 'Bush Sugar Baby' and 'Sugar Pot' are best for containers	Northern gardeners will want to start from transplants; full-sized varieties require large containers; bush-types offer the best chance of success.

Tomato 'Red Profusion' (*Solanum lycopersicum* 'Red Profusion')

Okra 'Green Fingers' (*Abelmoschus esculentus* 'Green Fingers')

▲ Tomato 'Red Robin' (*Solanum lycopersicum* 'Red Robin')

▶ Kale (*Brassica oleracea* var. *sabellica*)

Broccoli 'Small Miracle' (*Brassica oleracea* var. *italica* 'Small Miracle')

Cucumbers in grow bag (*Cucumis sativus*)

▲ Lettuce blend (*Lactuca sativa*, mixed cultivars)

◀ Hot pepper (*Capsicum annuum*) and yellow Swiss chard (*Beta vulgaris* subsp. *vulgaris* 'Golden')

Backyard Fruits

Choosing the right fruit varieties is extremely important because not every backyard fruit variety can handle the stress of container culture. Toward the end of this section, you'll find step-by-step plans for a containerized berry garden featuring a combination of blueberries and strawberries, but there are lots of other options for backyard container-grown fruits and berries.

Essentially, backyard fruit is grown on five different types of plants: trees, shrubs, brambles, vines, and herbaceous plants. Let's look at each of them in turn.

Fruit Trees

Fruit trees make a great addition to the container garden, but not all fruits are a good fit. Most fruit trees (except for citrus) require a specific number of chill hours below 45°F to properly grow and bud. If you live in a warmer climate, be prepared to do some research to find the specific varieties that require a lower number of chill hours. For example, some apples require as little as 100 chill hours while others need well over 500. Up north, look for varieties with a higher number of required chill hours to keep the trees from breaking dormancy too soon.

There are two different types of fruit trees that work well in containers: dwarf and columnar.

Dwarf Fruit Trees

First and foremost, look for dwarf or mini-dwarf selections. If you'd like to grow apples, pears, peaches, and other fruit trees in containers, only dwarf or mini-dwarf varieties will do. Dwarf fruit trees are created by grafting the fruiting buds of a desired variety onto a dwarfing rootstock (or root system) of another variety.

Apples (*Malus pumila*). Any apple that's grafted onto a dwarfing rootstock is a good candidate for container culture as long as you have a large enough container, but apples grafted onto special rootstocks such as EMLA 27 and G65 are known as

Apple trees need a cross-pollination partner to produce fruit. That means you'll need to grow two different trees, each of a separate variety. Or, grow trees with multiple varieties grafted onto the same tree.

mini-dwarf apples, and they reach only 4 to 6 ft. in height but are highly productive. They're perfect for small yards and container gardens.

Since apple trees are not self-fertile (meaning the pollen from one particular variety is not able to fertilize the flowers of the same variety), you'll need at least two different varieties to ensure ample pollination. The varieties must be compatible pollination partners, and they must be in bloom at the same time. Nurseries specializing in fruit trees often provide lists of good pollinizer partners.

If you can only grow a single apple tree due to space restrictions, consider growing a combination tree. These trees are created by grafting multiple apple varieties onto the same tree. The different varieties serve to pollinate each other, so only one tree is needed. Each branch bears one of the varieties.

Pears (*Pyrus communis*). Pears aren't the best choice for container gardens, as even dwarf varieties can grow quite large, but if you're able to find a variety that's grafted onto a specialty dwarfing rootstock, specifically one named Pyrodwarf, you'll have better luck. Trees grafted onto these specialty rootstocks stay under 15 ft. at full maturity with one annual pruning. Pears bear some fruit without a cross-pollination partner but do far better with a pollinator variety nearby, which means you'll need two or more trees, each of a different variety.

Apple trees (*Malus pumila*) do quite well in large containers, but only if they're dwarf varieties.

There are several exceptional genetic dwarf varieties of peaches and nectarines that do great in containers. This one is growing in a pot with basil and flowers.

Peaches and nectarines (*Prunus persica*).

These stone fruits are among my favorite fruits for container gardens. Though regular grafted dwarf trees do well enough in containers, varieties that are true genetic dwarfs do even better. They top out at just 5 ft. in height, but they produce full-sized fruits. Peaches and nectarines are self-fertile, so you don't need a pollination partner, but most do require a good number of chill hours, making them a good choice for gardeners with colder winters. A few excellent genetic dwarf varieties include 'El Dorado', 'Pix Zee', 'Honey Babe', and 'Empress' peach, and 'Necta Zee' and 'Nectar Babe' nectarine. Because peaches and nectarines are so closely related, the two can even be grafted onto the same tree.

Plums (*Prunus* spp). Plums are another good choice for container gardens, if you select varieties grown on dwarfing rootstocks. Combination plum trees are also fairly easy to find—some even come combined with other stone fruits, such as peaches and apricots. Look for plums grafted on a dwarfing rootstock and be prepared to prune them yearly for the best height control.

Sweet cherry (*Prunus avium*). Cherry varieties grown on dwarfing rootstocks, such as Gisela 5 and 3, mean you don't have to climb a huge ladder to harvest cherries as long as you prune them properly. These trees top out between 10 and 12 ft. tall with a single annual pruning. Cherries grafted on New Root 1 Zaiger rootstock grow only 6 to 8 ft. tall. As you choose which varieties to grow, keep in mind that most (but not all) sweet cherries will need another variety for cross-pollination, while most tart cherries (*P. cerasus*) are self-fertile and don't require another variety

Dwarf sweet cherries grafted on New Root 1 Zaiger rootstock reach only 6 to 8 ft. tall, but you'll need to protect the fruits from marauding birds with netting.

to about 10°F. Pomegranates are self-fertile and can be readily pruned to maintain a small stature. 'Red Silk' and 'Parfianka' are excellent dwarf varieties that grow great in containers.

Columnar Fruit Trees

If you want to grow even more compact containerized fruit trees, consider columnar trees. These straight, vertical trees have extremely short fruiting branches that stay close to the main trunk. Currently, apples are the most common columnar fruit trees, with mature specimens reaching about 8 to 10 ft. tall. Standard columnar apple varieties include 'North Pole'™, 'Golden Sentinel'™, and 'Scarlet Sentinel'™, as well as a line branded under the name Urban Apples® from a breeder in the Czech Republic that includes varieties such as 'Tasty Red'™, 'Blushing Delight'™, 'Golden Treat'™, and 'Tangy Green'™.

for pollination. Combination cherry trees offer multiple varieties grafted onto one tree. Almost all cherry trees require a high number of chill hours, making them another good fit for northern gardeners. 'Syliva' is an excellent dwarf cherry to keep on your radar, as it's great for containers and is a self-fertile sweet cherry.

Pomegranate (*Punica granatum*). This wonderful plant is grown as a small tree or a bush. It produces delicious fruit and lovely foliage but grows best in the southern United States and California, as pomegranates are only hardy down

Dwarf pomegranates like this one do best in southern climates and other regions where temperatures don't drop below 10°F.

Fruiting Shrubs

Fruits that grow on shrubs are also good choices for container gardens. Though there are certainly fruiting shrubs capable of growing quite large, as long as you keep a keen eye out for varieties with a shorter growth habit, these backyard fruits are exceptional additions to edible container gardens.

Blueberries (*Vaccinium* spp.)

With their shallow, fibrous root systems, blueberries are ideally suited to container growing, but some varieties do better than others.

Blueberries perform their best in soil that's slightly acidic, so for container gardeners, that means incorporating an acid-specific granular organic fertilizer into the potting soil before planting. Follow the directions on the label to determine how much fertilizer to add (more on container fertilization in Chapter 3).

Blueberries are extremely hardy (some varieties survive down to -35°F) and thrive in acidic soils with a pH range of 4.0 to 5.0 and full to partial sun. There are many different types of blueberries, including high-bush, low-bush,

Miniature blueberries, such as the one on the right side of this wheelbarrow planter, grow only 18 in. high but provide lots of berries.

half-high, rabbit-eye, and lots of assorted hybrids. Container gardeners would do best to grow either half-high varieties, which reach 3 to 4 ft. at maturity, or miniature varieties.

Most blueberries require two or more varieties for maximum pollination and berry production, but there are a number of self-pollinating, miniature blueberries that are the perfect fit for container gardens. 'Top Hat', 'Jelly Bean'™, and 'Blueberry Glaze'™ top out at just 18 to 24 in. in height and are excellent for containers in most gardening zones.

If you live in the south, your best choices are the rabbit-eye varieties, as they produce well in areas with warm winters. The 3-ft.-tall 'Sunshine Blue' is a great choice for southern container gardeners; it's self-fertile but does better when a cross-pollination partner is present. 'Northsky' is a favorite for up north—a mid-season ripener that's extremely hardy and reaches only 18 in. high, though it does require another variety for cross-pollination.

Gooseberries (*Ribes hirtellum*)

These unique fruits are a delightful addition to the container garden. Though many tart-flavored varieties exist, choose one of the many available sweet gooseberry selections instead, including 'Jeanne', 'Black Velvet', 'Poorman', and 'Amish Red'. They grow anywhere but in very hot southern regions and survive down to -40°F during the winter. Gooseberry shrubs reach 2 to 4 ft. in height and produce a substantial number of berries. Though many gooseberry plants are spined, thornless varieties are a better choice.

Currants (*Ribes* spp.)

This pretty little berry bush matures to a height of only 3 to 5 ft. Currants are fully hardy to -40° F and are resistant to most diseases and pests. Most currants are self-fertile, though they all produce better yields when partnered with a different variety. Not all varieties of currants are good for fresh eating, as the flavor can be quite tart, but they're great for jams, jellies, sauces, and syrups.

Currants come in many beautiful colors, including red, black, white, and pink, with most being good producers across most of North America, except where winters drop below -40° F or in the extreme south where summers are very hot. In some states, however, the planting of certain currant and gooseberry varieties (particularly black, red, and white currants) is restricted due to the plant's ability to serve as a vector for white pine blister rust. Please pay attention to any restrictions in your state.

Figs (*Ficus carica*)

These delectable fruits are an excellent choice for container gardening. Even in the north, where they must be carefully overwintered, container culture is perfect for figs because the plants are easily moved indoors for the winter.

Figs can be grown as a tree or a shrub, depending on how the plant is pruned. There are dozens of fig cultivars, some of which have very specific climactic preferences. Talk to other gardeners who grow figs in your area, or stick with varieties that are more widely adapted, including 'Excel', 'Hardy Chicago', 'Petite Negri', 'Brown Turkey', 'Black Mission', and 'Norland'.

Honeyberries
(*Lonicera caerulea* var. *edulis*)

Though this fruiting shrub isn't widely grown in North America, its popularity is on the rise. Also known as blue honeysuckle, this lovely shrub is a close relative of ornamental flowering honeysuckle and produces white, tubular flowers in very early spring that are followed by oblong, blue fruits in late spring. Honeyberries are the first fruits to ripen in my garden every year, with a flavor reminiscent of a mixture of cherries and grapes. My plants are 6 years old, and they began to bear fruit in their 3rd year. Once mature, honeyberry bushes continue to bear fruit for 50 years. To improve pollination rates, be sure to plant two or more varieties. Full-grown honeyberry shrubs reach about 4 ft. in height; they're extremely hardy and can be grown everywhere except in very hot southern regions.

Bramble Fruits

Brambles are plants that grow in a thorny thicket of long stems. Though there are some uncommon bramble fruits (including thimbleberry, dewberry, nagoon berry, and salmonberry), there are two brambles that are far more familiar to gardeners: raspberries and blackberries. While in the past these plants have not been good candidates for container gardening due to their rambunctious growth habits, times have changed. There are now dwarf raspberry and blackberry varieties that thrive in containers.

These fig trees are growing in 32-gallon trashcans in the rooftop garden of Dinette Restaurant in Pittsburgh, Pennsylvania.

Red raspberry 'Shortcake'™ plants surround a dwarf apple tree in this 45-gallon fabric pot.

Raspberries (*Rubus idaeus*)

'Shortcake'™ raspberries from Bushel and Berry® are not only super cute, they're also thornless and very productive. Reaching only 3 ft. in height, 'Shortcake'™ plants produce full-sized red raspberries on short, stocky plants. They're hardy in the same regions as regular red raspberries and have performed great in my own garden for several years.

Blackberries (*Rubus* spp. and hybrids)

Most blackberry varieties are vigorous growers, with long, arching stems that outgrow a container quickly. But 'Baby Cakes'™ is a thornless dwarf blackberry that reaches just 4 ft. in height. The plants even produce two crops per season in most regions. The berries are large, dark, and sweet.

Fruiting Vines

Though there are some very unusual fruiting vines, including Akebias and passionfruits, the two most popular fruiting vines for container gardening are grapes and hardy kiwis. Both are surprisingly easy to grow in pots if you choose the best varieties and care for them properly. I also grow a hops vine (*Humulus lupulus*); however, hops are very aggressive growers and climbers, so restricting their roots in a container keeps them from getting out of hand.

Grapes (*Vitis vinifera, Vitus labrusca*)

Because most grape varieties can grow quite large, growing them in containers can be a challenge, unless you have a good trellis or fence to support them. Grape vines can also be pruned into a weeping tree form for container culture, but it requires a lot of regular pruning maintenance. A better bet is to plant dwarf grape varieties, such as those in the 'Pixie'® series. These little cuties reach only 2 ft. in height but bear 4- to 6-in.-long bunches of delicious grapes all season long.

Hardy Kiwis (*Actinidia arguta*)

For home container gardening, the best kiwis are not the brown, fuzzy grocery store variety (A. *chinensis*), but the hardy kiwi (A. *arguta*), which is native to northern China and Russia and can survive temperatures as low as -25°F. Hardy kiwi fruits do not have to be peeled. The skin is beautiful and smooth, and the fruits can go straight into your mouth. Female vines produce a lot of fruit starting at about 8 years of age. Because individual kiwi plants are either male or female, you'll need one male plant for every eight or nine female vines (the vines are already "sexed" and labeled when you purchase them). The vines grow very tall and very quickly, so plan to have a good climbing structure for them.

Herbaceous Fruiting Plants

There is only one real entry in this category of fruits suitable for container gardening, but it is an important one.

Strawberries (*Fragaria ananassa*)

Probably the easiest of all the small fruits, strawberries are ideal container garden plants. Though there are many wild strawberry species, cultivated types fit into two different categories: June-bearing and ever-bearing. June-bearing varieties produce berries that all ripen within a period of a few weeks in early summer, while ever-bearing types spread a more moderate harvest from June through late September.

Hardy kiwis are small, smooth, green, and delicious.

Strawberries are classic small fruits for container gardens. These pink-flowering strawberries are growing in a type of container known as a strawberry jar.

Alpine strawberries are sweeter and smaller than their large-fruited cousins.

Both types of strawberries are great plants for containers; they work well in hanging baskets, vertical planters, and pots of every shape and size. Because their growth needs are similar to many vegetables, strawberries also do well when grown in a mixed container of veggies. Two more compact strawberry varieties ideal for containers are 'Loran' and the pink-flowered 'Tristan.'

Alpine strawberries (*Fragaria vesca*)

These little guys are a slice of heaven unlike anything else you can grow in your garden— sweeter, and more fragrant and flavorful than their large-fruited cousins. Though the fruits of alpine strawberries are less than 1 in. long, their flavor is unsurpassed. Tasting like a combination of berries and pineapple with a floral twist, alpine strawberries are surprisingly easy to grow. These

perennial, woodland berries have been bred and selected from wild strains over many generations.

Unlike cultivated strawberries, most alpine types do not send out runners. Instead, the size of the mother plants increases, and you can divide the crowns in spring to get more plants. This means that alpine strawberries are extremely well-behaved and do quite well in containers. Plants should be divided every 3 or 4 years.

Even when planted from seed, alpine strawberries quickly produce fruits, often the same season the seeds are sown. Their tiny, sweet fruits are produced continually all summer long, providing you with a handful of berries every day from just a dozen plants. In addition to the popular red-fruited alpine strawberry varieties, such as 'Alexandria' and 'Mignonette', there are also several yellow-fruited types, including 'Pineapple Crush' and 'Yellow Wonder.'

BEGINNER'S BERRY GARDEN

MATERIALS NEEDED

6- or 28-gallon galvanized metal utility tub

Enough 50/50 potting soil and compost blend to fill the tub

1 cup granular fertilizer, formulated specifically for acid-loving plants

Blueberry plant

10 to 15 strawberry plants

TOOLS NEEDED

Scratch awl

Hammer

Eye protection

You don't need a lot of room to grow berries. This container planting combines two of the most popular small fruits—blueberries and strawberries, into one container. Though the two have slightly different soil requirements (blueberries like more acidic soil), they both do quite well in a peat-based potting soil and compost blend with a bit of acid-specific fertilizer mixed in. A little extra care is required to see this container through the winter if you live where temperatures regularly dip below freezing.

Blueberries have wide, shallow, fibrous root systems, so you don't need a particularly deep container to grow them. This makes galvanized utility tubs the perfect blueberry-growing vessels.

HOW TO MAKE A BEGINNER'S BERRY GARDEN

STEP 1   Flip the metal tub over and use the hammer to pound the tip of the scratch awl through the bottom of the tub in six to eight places to create drainage holes. Fill the tub with the potting soil blend to within an inch of the tub's upper rim. Mix the cup of acid-specific granular fertilizer into the growing mix, being sure to incorporate it throughout.

STEP 2   Plant a single blueberry bush in the center of the tub. Pay careful attention to the type of blueberry you select, because not all of them are suited to container culture. For the best results, look for a variety of blueberry that's been bred to grow well in containers. Larger varieties will quickly out-grow the space. Self-pollinating miniature blueberry varieties, such as 'Top Hat', 'Jelly Bean'™, and 'Blueberry Glaze'™ that top out at 18 to 24 in. are a perfect fit for northern regions. In southern climates, use a rabbit-eye variety of blueberry instead (just plan on planting two berry tubs because rabbit-eyes are not self-fertile and need a pollination partner).

STEP 3   Plant ten to fifteen strawberry plants around the base of the blueberry bush, spacing them 3 to 6 in. apart. If possible, choose an ever-bearing variety that will produce a constant harvest of fruit from early summer through autumn. Also be on the lookout for varieties with natural disease resistance. Water the plants well and continue to care for them throughout the growing season. Some folks recommend you pinch off all the strawberry flowers during the first growing season to strengthen the plant roots, but with container-grown strawberries, it's okay to allow the plants to produce berries their first season.

NOTE: When winter arrives, it's important to give your berry tub a little added protection by surrounding the metal tub with a ring of chicken wire or cattle fencing that's about 2 to 3 feet wider than the tub and the same height. Stuff some straw, hay, or autumn leaves between the tub and the fence to insulate the roots. Do not cover the top of the tub or plants, or you might inadvertently promote fungal diseases. Remove the fencing and insulating materials the following season, 4 to 6 weeks before the last expected frost. When you remove the fencing, it's a good time to make an additional yearly fertilization of ½ cup of granular, acid-specific fertilizer.

Encourage pollinators, including European honeybees and North American native bee species such as this bumblebee, by including lots of flowering plants near your fruiting trees, shrubs, and brambles.

About Fruit Pollination

If you've done everything right and the plants flower prolifically but don't bear fruit, poor pollination is probably to blame. To solve the problem, first make sure you have the correct pollination partner for your plant. Remember, many fruits are not self-fertile and without another variety with which to swap pollen, fruit production will be minimal or nonexistent. Next, most fruits require insects to move pollen from flower to flower, and some plants rely heavily on certain pollinators. Blueberries, for example, are best pollinated by bumblebees. To ensure the presence of ample pollinators, also include plenty of flowering plants in your container garden. Surround potted fruit trees, shrubs, vines, brambles, and herbaceous fruits with lots of annuals, perennials, herbs, and other pollinator-attracting flowers. The more pollinators you have around, the more fruit you'll be able to grow.

PLANTING YOUR CONTAINERS

Once the plants for your containers have been carefully selected and your pots have been filled with soil, it's time to get planting, following a simple rule of thumb: arrange first, plant second.

Keep the plants in their nursery pots and arrange them on top of the soil before doing any actual planting—this allows the plants to be moved around and reorganized. Confirm the mature height of all the varieties by reading the pot tag or checking online before settling on where to place each plant. As you shuffle the plants around, keep a particular design style in mind, then, when satisfied with their placement, start the planting process.

When slipping a plant out of its nursery pot, carefully put one hand over the top of the pot and weave your fingers around either side of the stem. Use the other hand to flip the pot over and gently knock the mass of soil and roots out of the container and into your waiting hand. Once the plant is out of its nursery pot, inspect the roots prior to planting. If they are circling around inside of the container, loosen them prior to planting. Skipping this step means the roots will continue to circle around in a ball instead of growing out into the soil and filling their new, larger home.

To loosen pot-bound roots, use your fingers, a soil knife, or a trowel to gently rip apart the outer surface of the root mass. Don't be afraid of tearing the fine root hairs and even a few of the bulkier roots. Doing so only encourages a more branched root structure that will more quickly spread out into the potting soil. If the roots are extremely pot-bound, you may need a pair of pruning shears or even a small folding saw to loosen them.

Plant each plant to the same depth it was inside its nursery pot. You may need to add more soil to your container as you plant, or perhaps take some of the soil out to make room for all of the plants.

If you're planting seeds directly into containers, study the seed packet prior to planting to determine seed spacing, planting depth, and timing.

Once everything has been planted, water the container thoroughly. If you find the potting mix settles too far and exposes the tops of root balls or drops way below the upper rim of the pot, add a bit more potting mix to the top, but be careful not to pile it around plant stems or you could risk girdling the plants.

Before planting your containers, arrange and rearrange the nursery pots on the soil surface until you're satisfied with the layout. Only then should you begin planting your arrangement.

DESIGN GALLERY

This black urn is host to only three plants. But, the combination creates a striking effect. The urn is designed in a flat-backed style because it's only meant to be viewed from one side.

Recipe:

1 Coleus 'Fishnet Stockings'

2 purple false shamrocks (*Oxalis triangularis* subsp. *papilionacea* 'Triangularis')

1 small fuchsia stem to hang over the edge (*Fuchsia* spp.)

Design tip: Keep the coleus just off center toward the back of the pot, then plant the false shamrocks in front of it. The fuchsia should dangle down on the opposite side of the coleus to bring balance to the design.

This lovely window box has a light, frothy appearance. Choosing plants with smaller flowers and slender stems keeps the design from becoming too visually heavy.

Recipe:

2 Euphorbia 'Diamond Frost'® (*Euphorbia* hybrid)

2 dark purple African daisy (*Osteospermum* 'Asti Purple'™)

1 lavender African daisy (*Osteospermum* 'Asti Purple Bicolor'™)

1 coleus (*Solenostemon scutellarioides* 'Dark Star')

2 licorice plants (*Helichrysum petiolare*)

1 Bluebird nemesia (*Nemesia fruticans* 'Hubbird')

2 Supertunias® (*Petunia* hybrid 'Vista Silverberry')

Design tip: When designing window boxes or other hanging planters, keep the light colors toward the front and the darker colors toward the back. It helps balance the design and stop it from looking too bulky.

For gardeners who complain about having too much shade, this one's for you! This striking combination of plants is very bold, but it thrives in even the densest shade. There are only three plants in this container, but it's lush and full of interesting textures and leaf forms.

Recipe:

1 ZZ plant (*Zamioculcas zamiifolia*)

3 Dragon Wing™ begonias (*Begonia* x *hybrida* 'Dragon Wing Pink')

2 swirl-leaf Rex begonias (*Begonia* 'Escargot')

Design tip: This combination of plants looks great when partnered with a dark container. Choose black, slate blue, or dark gray to really make the plants "pop."

Another lush and lovely trifecta of plants for the shade! This combination relies primarily on its unique foliage (though the parakeet flower is really cool when it blooms). Each of these plants can be grown indoors all winter long at the end of the growing season, provided they have enough light. The spiller in the container is one of my all-time favorite ornamental plants for container gardening—a climbing begonia vine (not a begonia at all, but a relative of the grape). Choose a tall container for this combination to really show off the vine.

Recipe:

1 climbing begonia vine (*Cissus discolor/Cissus javana*)

1 variegated Ti plant (*Cordyline fruticosa* 'Kiwi')

1 parakeet flower (*Heliconia psittacorum* x *spathocircinata*)

Design tip: The climbing begonia vine in this design can both tumble down over the front of the container and grow up a lattice, trellis, or fence placed behind the pot. The vining tendrils will ramble up the parakeet flower plant too, so you'll have to trim them from time to time to keep them from taking over.

◄ This simple design is for shade gardeners who like to grow perennials in their containers so they can add them to the garden at the end of the growing season. The mixture of foliage textures in this planting creates a soft and interesting appearance. The upright structure and lacy nature of the fern provide a vertical element to offset the rounded leaves of the coral bell. The soft grass-like plant tumbling over the pot's edge adds yet another textural element.

Recipe:

1 Coral bell (any variety of Heuchera will do, but try to choose one with attractive coloration)

1 red-stemmed lady fern (*Athyrium angustum forma rubellum* 'Lady in Red' or another upright fern)

1 soft, grass-like plant: Try prairie blue-eye grass (*Sisyrinchium campestre*), a low-growing sedge such as Bowles' golden sedge (*Carex elata* 'Aurea') or broad-leaf sedge (*Carex siderosticha* 'Variegata')

Design tip: The flowers of some coral bell varieties are more ornamental than others. If you're not impressed with the flower spikes, don't hesitate to cut them off at the base of the plant. The primary focus of this container is foliage texture and color, so removing the flowers won't hurt the design.

▶ This hot-colored container design is ideal for bright, sunny spots. To really make this color combo shine, chose a brightly colored container.

Recipe:

2 yellow creeping stonecrop (*Sedum rupestre* 'Angelina')

3 purple salvias (*Salvia splendens*)

3 apricot Profusion zinnias (*Zinnia* hybrid 'Profusion Apricot')

3 Bonfire® begonias (*Begonia boliviensis* 'Bonfire')

1 orange FlameThrower™ coleus (*Solenostemon scutellarioides* 'FlameThrower Habanero')

Design tip: Though this container is designed in a flat-backed style, the same collection could also be arranged in thriller-filler-spiller fashion.

This cute pot is an excellent example of a thriller-filler-spiller design. The purple stems of the thriller plant, plectranthus, are highlighted by the purple leaves of the shamrock plant, and the balance and simplicity of the design are quite nice.

Recipe:

1 purple plectranthus (*Plectranthus* 'Mona Lavender')

2 Purple Charmed® Wine shamrocks (*Oxalis* hybrid 'Charmed Wine')

1 creeping wire vine (*Muehlenbeckia axillaris*)

1 pink cuphea (*Cuphea ramosissima* 'Cuphoric Pink')

Design tip: To keep the plants in any container design in proper proportion with the container itself, be prepared to do some trimming and pinching throughout the season.

I love the soft, rustic blue of this container partnered with the pink, tropical-looking caladiums and the striking variegation of the begonia. The top-tier plant has interesting speckled foliage, too, helping give this container design an extra punch.

Recipe:

1 Japanese spotted laurel (*Aucuba japonica* 'Gold Dust')

3 caladiums (*Caladium* cultivars)

3 Rex begonias (*Begonia rex* cultivars)

Design tip: This design would also look nice with an added spiller plant. If you'd like to include a few plants to cascade over the edge of the container, consider using silver falls, creeping Jenny (*Lysimachia nummularia*), or white or pale pink bacopa (*Sutera cordata*).

This combination of plants was put together specifically to attract butterflies. The soft colors of the plants in this container are a bit different from the bright color combos typically seen in butterfly gardens. The monarch's sole larval food source, milkweed, serves as the central thriller plant. It's surrounded by another butterfly host plant, *Artemisia*, which is a larval host for American lady butterfly caterpillars. These are layered with two other plants selected for their nectar quality as well as for their beauty.

Recipe:

1 swamp milkweed (*Asclepias incarnata*)

3 pink pentas (*Pentas lanceolata*)

3 ornamental oreganos (*Origanum rotundifolium* 'Kent Beauty')

3 artemisia (*Artemisia stelleriana* 'Silver Brocade')

Design tip: Using butterfly larval host plants in your container garden is an excellent idea. Other good caterpillar plants to include in your container garden are dill, violets, lupine, borage, and fennel.

chapter 3

Caring for Your Containers

One of the most important things to remember about gardening in any form is that plants are surprisingly forgiving. A rhododendron pruned into a meatball shape will eventually outgrow its odd form, a small tree with hacked branches will look fine once it's properly trimmed, and a perennial that was aggressively cut back by an overzealous gardener will quickly outgrow even the worst "haircut." There are very few mistakes you can make in a garden that can't be corrected.

In this chapter, I'm going to share many plant care tips and maintenance techniques, but be aware that not a single one of them is carved in stone. Yes, completing every task outlined in this chapter definitely results in a gorgeous, healthy, and productive container garden, but skipping a few of them from time to time is not going to spell certain disaster. Care for your containers to the best of your ability, make mistakes and learn from them. When things go wrong, remember: you can always try again next year.

But although you can skip some of the following maintenance tasks from time to time, there is one job you absolutely cannot forget when it comes to container gardening. And, because this one core duty is so critical, it's the first thing we'll talk about.

◀ Little containers like this clay pot hold a small volume of potting mix and need to be watered more frequently.

WATERING

The vast majority of failed container-grown plants are the result of the gardener either failing to water or watering improperly. There's no doubt about it: if you want a beautiful container garden, you have to make sure the plants receive regular and consistent moisture.

How Often?

The irrigation needs of a particular container are directly related to the volume of potting soil contained in it. Smaller containers need to be watered more frequently—so frequently, in fact,

To reduce watering needs, select larger containers whenever possible and make smart plant choices.

Large, glazed ceramic pots, like this one, hold a lot of soil and therefore need to be watered less frequently than smaller, porous containers.

Succulents and cacti are some of the best choices for filling terra-cotta containers because they have low-water requirements and prefer to stay on the dry side.

Stylish, light-weight plastic containers are a great choice for gardeners who want a bigger container without the weight of traditional clay or ceramic pots.

that if a small clay pot is in the full summer sun, you may have to water it two or three times a day. The large volume of potting soil found in bigger containers can store more moisture, so in general, the larger the pot, the less frequently you'll need to water it.

Since irrigation needs are also dependent on the size and type of plants, there are other factors to consider. No matter what size container they're growing in, bigger plants need more water (unless, of course, you're growing a cactus or another plant with low-water requirements). Mature plants also tend to need more water than immature ones. That means a container generally needs more and more water as the season progresses and the plants grow. Porous containers, like unglazed clay or moss-lined planters, dry out more frequently,

as well. If you want to limit how often you have to water, opt for glazed ceramic, plastic, metal, or fiberglass containers over terracotta.

Rainfall also plays a role. Invest in a rain gage and stick it right into one of your containers at or just above the soil level. It will collect and measure the amount of rainfall that finds its way there. Keep in mind, however, that rain may slide and bounce off foliage, diverting it away from where it's needed. You may find your rain gage empty, even after a heavy rain, simply because the leaves scatter the droplets before they reach the soil. The only way to know for sure is to head outside and check the moisture level of your pots in person.

There are many ways to check the moisture level of a container. You can purchase a fancy moisture sensor meter or soil water monitor to insert into the soil, you can feel the weight of the pot, or you can wait for the plant to wilt. But the most reliable way to assess soil moisture levels also happens to be the easiest: stick a finger into the pot up to your knuckle. If the soil is dry, water it. If it's not, don't. And if you've done a good job selecting a pot with adequate drainage, you'll never be in danger of overwatering, because excess water simply drains out the hole in the bottom of the pot. Which brings us to the next consideration . . .

How Much?

Another common mistake is using the "splash-and-dash" method of irrigation: sprinkling a little water on top of each plant every morning, maybe splashing a bit onto the soil as you go. The foliage gets peppered with water, but the roots remain parched. The plants suffer, and the gardener can't understand why their containers are underperforming when they're "watering them every day."

This kind of "splash-and-dash" irrigation, where a small amount of water is added every day, is not good for in-ground gardens or lawns either. Plants need deep, thorough irrigation that penetrates down through the soil to reach the entire root system. Shallow irrigation promotes shallow root systems that cannot access ample nutrition or withstand any amount of drought, while deep irrigation promotes deep, self-sufficient root systems. In containers, this means you need to apply irrigation water directly to the root zone, and you need to drench the soil repeatedly until at least a quarter of the water applied runs out the drainage hole in the bottom of the pot.

The argument that frequent light watering prevents overwatering is a fallacy. Overwatering

Overwatering occurs when the soil is constantly wet and the plant roots can't breathe. Never allow water to sit in a saucer beneath a plant for longer than a few hours.

is most often the result of applying water too frequently. Roots need access to air, and when the soil is constantly wet, the roots can't breathe and the plant wilts and eventually dies. Unfortunately, the symptoms of overwatering look a lot like the symptoms of underwatering.

The trick to proper container irrigation is balance. Aim to supply your plants with plenty of water, but do it on an as-needed basis. Allow the growing mix to dry out a bit between waterings, but not enough to induce any plant stress.

If you're worried about forgetting to check the moisture levels of your containers, set a reminder on your smart phone. Or, if you don't have time to regularly check for irrigation needs, consider growing your container garden in self-watering planters, like the commercial brands discussed in Chapter 1 or by making the DIY self-watering planter featured in the next project sidebar.

SELF-WATERING PATIO CONTAINER

MATERIALS NEEDED

2 plastic storage bins of the same type and size

1 old cotton hand towel

Enough 50/50 potting soil and compost blend to fill one of the bins

Old bricks or blocks

Plants

TOOLS NEEDED

Utility knife

Work gloves

Scissors

Purchasing manufactured self-watering containers is expensive, especially if you want more than one or two. The following step-by-step plan lets you make five or six self-watering containers for the cost of a single manufactured one. Use large, 50-gallon storage bins like the ones in the photographs, to grow tomatoes, zucchini, and other big veggies, or choose smaller bins for smaller plants or smaller spaces. Simply follow the steps to turn a pair of plastic storage bins of any size into an inexpensive, self-watering planter.

HOW TO MAKE A SELF-WATERING PATIO CONTAINER

1

2

3

STEP 1   Use a utility knife to cut a 2-in. square hole in the middle of the bottom of one of the storage bins, near the center. Cut the cotton hand towel lengthwise, to make four strips of the same approximate width.

STEP 2   Position the second bin wherever you'd like your planter to be located, then stack columns of bricks or blocks 4 to 8 in. high in the bottom to create a water reservoir. For larger bins, make three columns of bricks; smaller bins will only need two columns. Do not place a column in the exact center of the bin, as it could restrict the movement of water. Use the utility knife to cut a 2-in. square hole into the back of this bin. The top of the hole should be the exact same height as the top of your brick columns. This hole will be where you fill the water reservoir, but it will also serve as an overflow outlet.

STEP 3   Fill the reservoir with water up to the bottom of the fill/overflow hole. Place the first bin into the second, nestling it securely inside and making sure the bottom of the inside bin is resting on top of the brick columns.

Continued

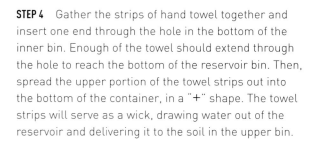

STEP 4   Gather the strips of hand towel together and insert one end through the hole in the bottom of the inner bin. Enough of the towel should extend through the hole to reach the bottom of the reservoir bin. Then, spread the upper portion of the towel strips out into the bottom of the container, in a "+" shape. The towel strips will serve as a wick, drawing water out of the reservoir and delivering it to the soil in the upper bin.

STEP 5   Fill the inner bin with a 50/50 mixture of high-quality potting soil and compost. Don't overfill with the soil blend; leave 1 in. of headspace at the top to collect any rainfall. Now you can plant. This 50-gallon self-watering planter will house two patio-type bush tomatoes, two basil plants, a cucumber vine, a miniature watermelon vine, and a hot pepper plant. If you use smaller bins, you'll have to whittle down your plant list. Water the plants after planting. This will be the only time you'll need to water from the top.

STEP 6   Insert stakes and cages, if necessary. For this example, we used two colored tomato cages to support the tomato plants as they grow, but you could also incorporate any of the trellising ideas discussed later in this chapter.

STEP 7   Though you won't have to add water to the reservoir every day, you will have to check it from time to time. Fill the reservoir by inserting a hose into the hole in the back of the planter and letting it run until water starts coming back out of the hole. The amount of water needed depends on how empty the reservoir was when you started.

The Water Delivery System

There's no single best way to deliver water to your container garden—it's only important that the water is focused on the plants' root zone rather than on the foliage. Plenty of gorgeous container gardens are watered by hand, with watering cans, buckets, or pitchers full of water. Others are hand-watered with a gentle spray from a water wand nozzle attached to the end of a hose. But if you really want to cut down on the amount of time you spend watering, consider setting up an automatic irrigation system to water your containers.

This is a particularly useful method if you grow a large number of containerized fruits and vegetables, or if you're growing for commercial purposes. Automatic irrigation systems deliver water to containers drop by drop, which is very efficient because the water is delivered straight into the pot with very little lost to evaporation or misapplication. This type of system is usually installed by distributing irrigation tubing along rows of containers, and then running a section of small, flexible tube out from the main tubing and into each of the pots. Irrigation kits are sold at nurseries, farm supply stores, specialty greenhouse and irrigation supply companies, or you can build your own automatic irrigation system by following the step-by-step instructions found in the next project sidebar.

Once installed, irrigation systems can be hooked up to a programmed timer, or the system can be turned on or off with a simple twist of whatever spigot it's connected to.

▲ Commercial container growers often use automatic drip irrigation to water many pots at the same time. The next project shows you how to make a similar system to use at home.

◄ This bucket-in-bucket system at the rooftop garden of Dinette Restaurant in Pittsburgh, Pennsylvania, utilizes an automatic irrigation system to make watering easier. Water is added to the bottom bucket via a drip system and then wicked up into the top grow bucket as needed.

DIY CONTAINER IRRIGATION SYSTEM

MATERIALS NEEDED

½-in. black poly
  irrigation tubing

¼-in. black micro poly
  tubing

½-in. poly tube end cap
  or shut-off valve

6 dripper stakes with
  baskets, or 6 mini
  in-line drippers

6 double barbed
  connectors, ¼ in.

1 drip irrigation faucet
  connection kit for
  ½-in. tubing

1 programmable hose
  timer (optional)

TOOLS NEEDED

Scissors

Tape measure

Irrigation tube hole
  puncher, ¼ in.

This DIY system irrigates up to six pots, but you can adjust the design for your needs, adding more tubing and dripper stakes to water up to ten pots at a time or even using T couplings to add additional branches. Commercial drip irrigation kits contain all the components you'll need to make a similar system, but it's cheaper to buy the materials and construct the system yourself.

HOW TO MAKE A DIY CONTAINER IRRIGATION SYSTEM

STEP 1   Put all the pots you want served by your irrigation system in their places. Measure the amount of ½-in. black poly irrigation tubing you'll need to go from the nearest pot to the furthest pot on the line. Lay the tubing out and cut it to size with a sharp scissors.

STEP 2   Cap the end of the tubing that's farthest away from the hose spigot with either a poly tube end cap or a shut-off valve (shown in photo). If you use a shut-off valve, make sure it's in the closed position. Attach the faucet connection kit to the end of the tube closest to the hose spigot. (After construction of the system, you'll need to run a length of garden hose from the spigot out to the faucet connection kit.)

STEP 3   Now it's time to add lengths of micro tubing line to go into each container. Use the hole puncher to punch a small hole through the ½-in. black poly irrigation tubing you've laid out. Punch one hole for each drip line that will extend from the main line.

Continued

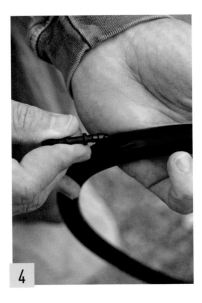

STEP 4   Once each hole has been punched, put one end of a ¼-in. double-barbed connector into each of the holes. Measure and cut a piece of ¼-in. black micro poly tubing to reach from each barbed connector to the container, allowing a little slack in each line. Slide one end of the micro poly tubing down over the exposed end of the double-barbed connector.

STEP 5   Attach a dripper stake with basket or a mini in-line dripper to the other end of each micro poly tubing by pushing the tubing down over the nipple. Insert the dripper stake with basket into the container's soil; or, if you're using mini in-line drippers instead, lay the end of the in-line dripper on top of the soil.

STEP 6   Test your system by connecting it to a hose and turning the faucet on. Depending on the type of dripper stakes you used, you may be able to control the flow of water coming out of them by twisting the top of the basket. Check the system carefully for leaks and repair any you happen to find.

STEP 7   If you'd like, connect a programmable timer to the spigot to control when and how much water is supplied. How long it will take to fully irrigate your pots depends on your water pressure and how many containers are being watered on the same line. Run a test from time to time to determine how long the timer needs to run before the containers are fully watered.

STEP 8   To see your new irrigation system safely through the winter, disconnect it from the spigot before freezing temperatures arrive. Drain the system completely, then lift it out of the garden and overwinter it in a garage or shed. Or, if you want to leave it in place, use an air compressor to blow air through all the lines to make sure there's no moisture remaining in them.

TIP: To use this DIY system in conjunction with a rain barrel, hook it up to a small, submersible pond pump (a 250- or 400-gallons-per-hour pump should work just fine). Submerge the pump into the rain barrel and plug it in. The pump will draw water out of the barrel and send it down the irrigation tubing to water the pots. If you need to move the water uphill, you'll need a more powerful pump.

FERTILIZING

Garden centers and nurseries are beautiful places, but they can also be very confusing. Endless shelves and end caps overflowing with fertilizer choices are enough to make your head spin.

By definition, a plant fertilizer is either a synthetic chemical or a natural material added to the soil or growing media to increase its fertility and aid in plant growth. Your mother may have drenched her potted plants with a water-soluble chemical fertilizer every week, but there's been a major shift in thinking over the past decade. We've moved away from the idea of "feeding the plants" and toward the idea of "feeding the soil."

When you use naturally derived fertilizers, your plants are provided with a much more balanced nutrient source—one that provides mineral nutrition for growing plants by feeding the soil's living organisms. These microscopic organisms (most of which are fungi and bacteria) process these fertilizers, breaking them down into the nutrients plants use to grow. In addition, many of these microbes live in a mutually beneficial relationship with the roots of plants, providing the plants with certain mineral nutrients in exchange for small amounts of carbohydrates. When we feed the soil, our plants reap the benefits.

Gorgeous container plants are the result of encouraging healthy, biologically active soil through the addition of compost to the planting mix and feeding with natural fertilizers.

You may think all this doesn't matter for container gardens, since the root system is contained in a small area, but if you use a 50/50 blend of compost and potting soil to fill your containers, quite the opposite is true. The compost in your containers is alive with beneficial soil organisms. Plus, compost contains myriad macro- and micronutrients essential for plant growth. Science has shown us that encouraging healthy, biologically active soil is the best way to promote optimum plant growth, even when plants are growing in containers.

Nevertheless, there are times when our container-grown plants need more nutrition, such as when the nutrients contained in the compost are depleted or unavailable. For those times, there are a number of easy-to-use natural fertilizers that do an excellent job of feeding the soil. These fertilizers are derived from assorted combinations of naturally-sourced materials, and they can readily be added to containers throughout the growing season. An added benefit of using these natural fertilizers is that many of them contain trace nutrients, vitamins, amino acids, and plant hormones that aren't usually noted on the label and are rarely found in chemical fertilizers. These compounds act as natural growth enhancers and play a vital role in the health and vigor of plants.

Reading the Label

When shopping for fertilizers, spend some time reading the labels. Natural fertilizers have four main ingredient sources.

1. **Plant materials.** These are fertilizer ingredients derived from plants. A few examples include corn gluten meal, alfalfa meal, kelp meal, and cottonseed meal.

2. **Manure materials.** You may also see pelletized poultry manure, dehydrated cow manure, cricket manure, bat guano, and worm castings or worm "tea" on the label of a natural fertilizer.

3. **Animal byproducts.** Fertilizer components found in this category are often derived from the byproducts of our food industry. They include things like fish emulsion, bone meal, feather meal, blood meal, and crab meal.

Dehydrated cow and poultry manure can be found in bags at your local garden center, but it's also a common ingredient in many natural granular fertilizer blends.

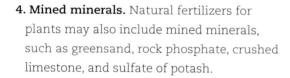

4-2-2

NET WEIGHT 20 LBS (9.07 kg)

Garden Manure

4-2-2

GUARANTEED ANALYSIS

Total Nitrogen (N) 4%
  2% Water Soluble Nitrogen
  2% Water Insoluble Nitrogen
Available Phosphate (P_2O_5)........................2%
Soluble Potash (K_2O) 2%

Derived from: Poultry Manure   F1381

The Espoma Co. • 6 Espoma Rd. • Millville, NJ 08332

ion regarding the contents and levels of metals in this product is available on the internet at www.regulatory-inf

Carefully read the labels of any fertilizers you use in your container garden. Pay special attention to both the N-P-K ratio of the product and the ingredient list to determine if it's the right fertilizer for your needs.

Commercially available granular fertilizer blends are a great way to add nutrition to your container garden.

4. Mined minerals. Natural fertilizers for plants may also include mined minerals, such as greensand, rock phosphate, crushed limestone, and sulfate of potash.

Using fertilizers containing a combination of these ingredients is a terrific way to feed your soil when nutrients become depleted and adding more compost isn't an option.

Before choosing any type of fertilizer for your container garden, however, it's important for you to understand the numbers you see on the label. In addition to listing their ingredients, natural fertilizers also state their N-P-K ratio somewhere on the bag. This ratio exhibits the percentage by weight of three macro-nutrients—nitrogen, phosphorous, and potassium. For example, a bag of 10-5-10 holds 10% N, 5% P, and 10% K. The remaining 75% of the bag's weight is filler products. For natural-based fertilizers, the numbers in the N-P-K ratio are often smaller (2-3-2 or 1-1-6, for example). This is due to the fact that the label percentages are based on levels of

immediately available nutrients, and many of the nutrients in natural fertilizers are not available immediately upon application; it takes some time for the soil microbes to process these nutrients and release them for plant use. Although this may seem like a disadvantage, natural fertilizers release their nutrients gradually, serving as a slow-release fertilizer.

It's also important to understand how plants use these different macronutrients.

Nitrogen is a component of the chlorophyll molecule, and it promotes optimum shoot and leaf growth. Adding a fertilizer high in nitrogen (such as 6-2-1 or 10-5-5) to a fruiting or flowering plant, such a tomato or a petunia, will result in excessive green growth, often at the expense of flower and fruit production. But adding it to a green, leafy vegetable plant, such as spinach or lettuce, makes much more sense.

Phosphorus, on the other hand, is used for cell division and to generate new plant tissue. It promotes good root growth and is used in fruit and flower production. Phosphorous is particularly important for root crops, such as beets, carrots, and onions, as well as for encouraging flower and fruit production. That's why fertilizers that contain bone meal and rock phosphate are often recommended for use on root crops: both are rich in phosphorous.

Potassium helps trigger certain plant enzymes and regulates a plant's carbon dioxide uptake by controlling the pores on a leaf's surface, called stomata, through which gasses pass. Potassium levels influence a plant's heartiness and vigor.

Making a Choice

To make your decision easier, you have two basic choices when it comes to natural fertilizers for your container garden. Let's talk about each of them in turn.

Complete Granular Fertilizer Blends

There are dozens of different brands of complete granular fertilizer blends. Most combine assorted plant, manure, animal, and mineral-based ingredients, and depending on the brand, they may have an N-P-K ratio of 4-5-4 or 3-3-3 or something similar. What makes them "complete" is that they contain a combination of ingredients that provides some amount of all three macronutrients, in addition to many trace nutrients, vitamins, and other things. All of these products have different formulations and compositions, so be sure to choose appropriately according to what plants you're growing. Some complete granular fertilizer blends are even tailored for specific crops, such as tomatoes or flowers or bulbs, and are labeled as such.

Different plants have different nutritional needs. These radish roots and other root crops, for example, require the right level of phosphorous to form properly.

Vegetables such as Swiss chard, lettuce, spinach, and other leafy greens utilize nitrogen to produce optimum leaf growth.

Fertilizer spikes are another easy way to add fertilizer to your container garden. These are formulated especially for tomatoes, peppers, and other fruiting crops and are pushed down into the soil around the base of the plant.

Natural liquid fertilizers are absorbed into plants through both their roots and their foliage. Mixing liquid fertilizers in a watering can is the simplest way to apply them.

For the best results, add granular fertilizer to your containers according to the label instructions. Many gardeners find they get the best results by fertilizing their containers with granular fertilizers two or three times throughout the growing season.

With granular products, it's possible to have too much of a good thing. Even natural fertilizers can be easily overapplied, leading to nutrient deficiencies, pH imbalance, and/or fertilizer "burn" (yes, even some natural fertilizers are capable of this). To avoid these issues, don't apply too much, too often. Again, be careful to follow all label instructions.

Liquid Fertilizers

Liquid fertilizer products are absorbed into plants via both their roots and their foliage. In general, nutrients provided to plants via a liquid solution are more readily and rapidly available for plant use. Like all fertilizers, water soluble ones provide plants with some of the necessary nutrients for increasing yields and improving growth and vigor, but not all liquid fertilizers are created equal.

While chemical-based, water soluble fertilizers certainly supply plants with the macronutrients specified on the label, these products are made from salts that can harm beneficial soil organisms. Instead of chemical salt-based fertilizers, look for organic or natural-based liquids, which will reduce the risk of fertilizer burn and offer a more balanced "diet" for your plants. In addition to the three macronutrients, most natural liquid fertilizers also contain dozens of trace nutrients, vitamins, amino acids, and plant hormones, each of which plays a vital role in the health and vigor of a plant.There are many different types of liquid fertilizers available on the shelf of your local garden center, or, in some cases you can even make your own. Here are some of the most popular types of natural liquid fertilizers.

Liquid kelp or seaweed is created by processing sea kelp at cool temperatures. It's rich in many trace minerals and amino acids and is a source of several plant hormones known to aid in shoot and root growth, improve soil structure, and increase hardiness and fruit development. Research has shown that liquid kelp is adept at increasing yields and drought resistance. It's one of the least expensive yet most highly beneficial liquid fertilizers. Liquid kelp can also be applied in combination with any of the other products listed below, with very little chance of fertilizer burn.

Fish emulsion is made when whole fish is cooked and filtered. Before the finished fertilizer emulsion is created, the oils and proteins are removed for use in other products, leaving the resulting fertilizer bereft of many of the amino acids, vitamins, and hormones most beneficial to plant growth. Still, fish emulsion is a good natural alternative to chemical water-soluble fertilizers, albeit a smelly one. Because the aroma of fish emulsion is so strong, it's wise to use it only in the mornings, so the odor has time to dissipate before nightfall. Otherwise, every raccoon and cat in the neighborhood will happily dig up your containers in search of dead fish.

Fish hydroslate (or liquid fish) is another, less odorous form of fish-based fertilizer. Instead of cooking the fish, they're digested with enzymes at cooler temperatures to make hydroslate products. Then, the partially dissolved fish are ground up and liquefied, resulting in a nutrient-rich fertilizer containing many trace minerals. The fish used in hydroslate products come from either commercial fishing by-catch, or are the byproducts of the fish-farming industry. The enzymes used in the creation process also help break down the fishy odor and some manufacturers even add mint and other essential oils to help mask the smell, but it's still a good idea to use fish hydroslates in the morning.

Compost tea is getting a lot of attention these days for its ability to nurture beneficial soil life, suppress certain diseases, and stimulate optimum plant growth. But the compost tea of old, created simply by steeping some compost in water for a few days, isn't what it's cracked up to be. The anaerobic conditions of bucket steeping can lead to some pretty funky concoctions.

Today's compost tea is aerated. Air is pumped through the water as a blend of quality compost and a microbial food

Liquid kelp or seaweed is an excellent fertilizer for container-grown plants.

Fish emulsions and fish hydroslate products are nutrient-rich, but they often have a bad odor.

source (often unsulphured molasses) brews to perfection. The tea is finished and ready to use a few days later. High-quality compost tea is teeming with beneficial microbes, adept at boosting soil and plant health and fighting off foliar diseases. Making compost tea is an involved process, but it's not a difficult one. You'll find plenty of information and how-to instructions on various websites devoted to the topic.

Companies that brew compost tea for purchase are popping up in cities across the country, but because the tea needs to be used a few hours after the brewing process is complete, this may prove to be a difficult business model.

Worm tea is a variation of compost tea. It is created in the same way, using a homemade or commercial brewing system. But instead of using regular compost, this tea is made from worm castings. The resulting liquid is nearly odorless, rich in a diversity of beneficial microbial life, and perfect for watering containers and houseplants. Worm tea is especially good if you have your own worm bin and have a regular source of castings.

The above products are useful on their own, but they're also quite valuable when combined with other ingredients. Natural liquid fertilizer combination products blend the products described above with ingredients such as liquid bone meal, blood meal, feather meal, and rock phosphate to create a well-rounded fertilizer and growth stimulant.

When using any natural liquid fertilizer, follow label instructions for mixing rates and application instructions. Generally, most liquid fertilizers are applied either by mixing the product in a watering can and watering by hand, or by using a hose-end fertilizer distribution system to automatically deliver the fertilizer with the irrigation water.

Liquid fertilizers are best absorbed when the plants growing in your containers are not under stress. Do not fertilize your plants when they're wilting or suffering from heat stress. Water them first, a few hours before fertilizing them, to maximize their absorption of nutrients.

Though overdoing natural liquid fertilizers is seldom possible in terms of plant health, overdoing it can be hard on the budget. Don't use more than you need. Most liquid fertilizers should be applied every 2 to 4 weeks throughout the growing season.

Hose-end sprayers are a great way to deliver liquid fertilizers with irrigation water. Some brands, such as this one, come with the hose-end sprayer attached to a siphon bottle, but reusable hose-end sprayers are also available at most garden centers and hardware stores.

Deadheading is the term used when removing an old, spent flower head from a blooming plant.

DEADHEADING AND PINCHING

Two other tasks to be performed from time to time are deadheading and pinching. While you can take these two jobs off your to-do list if you're growing vegetables, they're important chores for keeping flowers and herbs in tip-top shape.

Deadheading

Deadheading is a term we gardeners use when removing the old, spent flower heads from a blooming plant. The practice encourages the production of new blooms by preventing the plant from setting seed (and using lots of energy to do so). Removing spent flowers often cues the plant to produce another set of blooms.

Deadheading is an ongoing chore, beginning as soon as the first peony petals fall and continuing until the last annual has been touched by frost, but midsummer is the prime deadheading season. Perennials such as peonies (*Paeonia* spp.), lilies (*Lilium* spp.), Oriental poppies (*Papaver orientale*), delphiniums (*Delphinium* spp.), and bearded

iris (*Iris germanica*), typically bloom only once per season, so deadheading these plants won't encourage more blooms. Instead, it tidies them up and encourages further growth on the rest of the plant. In other words, these plants are deadheaded mostly for aesthetic reasons.

There are, however, many other plants that flower repeatedly throughout the growing season, and as long as they're regularly deadheaded, the plant will continue to generate more blooms. Deadheading freshens up the plant's overall appearance and often generates fresh, new foliage as well. When the spent bloom is removed, side-buds are formed and go on to develop subsequent flushes of flowers. Most flowering annuals fit in this category, along with some perennials, including Shasta daisies (*Leucanthemum* x *superbum*), perennial sage (*Salvia* spp.), bee balm (*Monarda* spp.), yarrow (*Achillea* spp.), butterfly bushes (*Buddleia* spp.), garden phlox (*Phlox paniculata*), coneflowers (*Echinacea* spp.), Coreopsis (*Coreopsis* spp.), and some black-eyed Susans

(*Rudbeckia* spp.). Deadheading flowering plants several times throughout the growing season is a great way to ensure constant color in your container garden.

Tips for Deadheading

- For plants whose flowers occur on stalks that have leaves along them, follow the tip of the faded bloom all the way back to where you see the first few leaves emerging from the stem. Snip or snap off the flower stalk just above these leaves. Do not leave a lengthy stump behind, as it could succumb to botrytis or another fungal disease as it naturally rots away. Plants in this category include butterfly bush, Monarda, cosmos, snapdragons, black-eyed Susans, zinnias, annual geraniums (*Pelargonium* x *hortorum*), salvias, Shasta daisies, sedums, dahlias (*Dahlia* spp.), and many, many others.
- For plants with large flowering stalks that do not have foliage along them, like daylilies (*Hemerocallis spp.*), hosta, or bearded iris, cut the entire flowering stem all the way back down to the crown of the plant, where the foliage emerges from the ground.
- For plants with mounded foliage and many small flowers, it's often easier to shear back the entire plant rather than removing the spent flowers one by one. Plants like coreopsis, bidens, sweet alyssum, French marigolds, ageratum, nepeta, dianthus (*Dianthus* spp.), and lavender (*Lavandula* spp.) should be sheared once or twice throughout the growing season to encourage more blooms.
- Some flowering plants don't need to be deadheaded at all. There is a hearty handful of plants that pump out new blooms and always look fresh, even without deadheading.

These easy-care plants might need to be pinched back from time to time (see the next section), but they'll be in constant bloom almost all season long. Plants on this list include impatiens, lobelia, nemesia, torenia, oxalis, wax begonias, dragon- and angelwing begonias, calibrachoa, diascia (*Diascia* spp.), and some petunias, among others.

There is, however, one occasion when you don't want to deadhead. If you'd like a particular plant to purposefully set seed, then don't remove its spent flowers. It's easy to collect and save your own seed from lots of different flowering annuals, perennials, and herbs. You can save a lot of money by using collected and saved seeds to start the following year's container garden. Cosmos, zinnias, amaranth, calendula, dill, and sunflowers are easy plants to start with. Simply wait for a few of the seed heads to fully dry, then cut them from the plant and allow them to finish drying in a cool, dry room for a few weeks. Then crack the seed heads apart, pull out the seeds, and store them in sealed glass jars or plastic containers until next spring.

Some gardeners also stop deadheading as late-summer approaches to allow some of their plants to set seed for birds such as goldfinches, cardinals, chickadees, and other seed-eaters.

Deadheading is an especially important task if your container garden is serving double-duty as pollinator habitat. Pollinating insects, such as butterflies and bees, need a constant source of nectar, and if you want these beneficial bugs to stick around, having a container garden that's in continual bloom is a must. The following two projects are great ways to start supporting these two groups of important insects with a specialized container garden created just for them.

BUTTERFLY GARDEN TUBS

MATERIALS NEEDED

2 or more plastic
  bucket tubs with rope
  handles, 17 to 20
  gallons each

Enough 50/50 potting
  soil and compost blend
  to fill the tubs

6 to 8 butterfly plants
  for each tub, selected
  from the lists on
  page 145

TOOLS NEEDED

Utility knife

Soil scoop

Work gloves

Gardening to attract and support wildlife is a great way to be an eco-conscious gardener. Incorporating the right kind of plants into your landscape influences which types of insects call your garden home. This project uses a combination of bright, colorful blooms to entice some of the world's most-beloved insects—butterflies.

Since most species of butterflies need different plants at different stages of their life, it's important to combine flowers that supply nectar to adult butterflies with the specific plants their caterpillars use as food. Most gardeners already know monarch caterpillars can only feed on milkweed plants, but there are many other species of butterflies that require a particular host plant to feed their young. For this project, begin by selecting a mixture of plants that serve as either a nectar plant, a host plant, or both.

Popular Nectar Sources for Adult Butterflies:

- Coneflower (*Echinacea* spp.)
- Bee balm (*Monarda* spp.)
- Goldenrod (*Solidago* spp.)
- Asters (*Symphyotrichum* spp.) `
- Joe Pye weed (*Eutrochium purpureum*)
- Milkweed (*Asclepias* spp.)
- Buttonbush (*Cephalanthus occidentalis*)
- Pentas (*Pentas lanceolata*)
- Zinnia (*Zinnia elegans*)
- Million bells (*Calibrachoa* spp.)
- Salvia (*Salvia* spp.)
- Cosmos (*Cosmos bipinnatus* and *C. sulphureus*)
- Mexican sunflower (*Tithonia rotundifolia*)
- Sunflower (*Helianthus annuus*)
- Ironweed (*Vernonia* spp.)
- Black-eyed Susan (*Rudbeckia* spp.)
- Verbena (*Verbena* spp.)
- Heliotrope (*Heliotropium arborescens*)
- Phlox (*Phlox* spp.)
- Blanket flower (*Gaillardia* spp.)
- Lantana (*Lantana camara*)
- Liatris (*Liatris spicata*)
- Coreopsis (*Coreopsis* spp.)
- Yarrow (*Achillea* spp.)

Caterpillar Host Plants and Butterflies These Plants Benefit:

- Milkweed: Monarchs
- Violets (*Viola* spp): Several species of fritillary butterflies
- Passionflower (*Passiflora* spp.): Gulf fritillary
- White turtlehead (*Chelone glabra*), hairy beardtongue (*Penstemon hirsutus*), and speedwell (*Veronica* spp.): Baltimore checkerspot
- Yarrow, borage, and sunflowers: Painted lady
- Hops (*Humulus lupulus*): Eastern comma and the red admiral
- Dill, fennel, and golden Alexanders (*Zizia* spp.): Eastern black swallowtail
- Asters: Pearly crescent
- Pussytoes (*Antennaria* spp.), hollyhock (*Alcea rosea*), and lupine (*Lupinus* spp.): American lady
- Blueberries and viburnums (*Viburnum* spp.): Spring azure

NOTE: As you build Butterfly Garden Tubs of your own, include as many of these plants as possible. Use a combination of the annuals, perennials, and shrubs listed above for season-long color and a varied food source for the butterflies.

Continued

HOW TO MAKE BUTTERFLY GARDEN TUBS

STEP 1 Flip the plastic bucket tubs upside down and use a utility knife to cut a triangular hole in the bottom of each bucket for drainage. Make sure the hole is about 1 in. across. Fill each bucket three-quarters of the way to the top with the 50/50 potting soil and compost blend.

STEP 2 Carefully pull the plants from their containers and situate them in the plastic buckets, moving them around until you're happy with their placement. If your butterfly garden tubs are located against a wall or fence, put the tallest plants toward the back of the containers and the shortest plants in the very front. If the tubs can be viewed from all sides, put the tallest plants in the center, surround them with mid-sized plants, and then put the shorter plants around the outer edge. Once happy with the arrangement, loosen any pot-bound roots and fill in around each plant with potting soil and compost blend. Do not overfill the buckets; there should be 1 in. of headspace between the soil and the top edge of the bucket's rim. Water the plants well.

STEP 3 Maintain your Butterfly Garden Tubs by regularly deadheading the flowers. Carefully inspect host plants for caterpillars on a frequent basis and don't disturb any you happen to find. Avoid using pesticides or fungicides of any sort on your Butterfly Garden Tubs as they could negatively affect both the adult butterflies and the caterpillars.

POLLINATOR CAN

There are over 4,000 species of native bees in North America, and while supporting European honeybees is important, helping our native bees is even more so. Bees are responsible for pollinating more than $20 billion dollars of food crops each year, and many species are suffering from population declines due to pesticide exposure, diseases, and habitat loss. Even urban gardeners with small patio gardens or containers can provide important habitat for these insects.

If every homeowner and apartment dweller built a Pollinator Can like this one, what a huge difference we'd make!

Excellent Host Plants for Bees:
- Goldenrod
- Liatris
- Phacelia (*Phacelia tanacetifolia*)
- Culver's root (*Veronicastrum virginicum*)
- Asters
- Bee balm
- Meadowsweet (*Spirea alba*)
- Boneset (*Eupatorium perfoliatum*)
- Penstemon (*Penstemon* spp.)
- Coneflower
- Black-eyed Susans
- Sunflowers
- Agastache
- Globe thistle (*Echinops* spp.)
- Coreopsis
- Milkweed
- Mountain mint (*Pycnanthemum* spp.)
- Dill
- Oregano
- Nepeta (*Nepeta* spp.)
- Salvia

MATERIALS NEEDED

Large, 31-gallon galvanized trashcan

Empty 5-gallon bucket

Enough 50/50 potting soil and compost blend to fill the can

8 to 12 pollinator-friendly plants, selected from the list to the left

1 piece of untreated 2x4 lumber, 4 to 5 ft. long

30 to 50 natural bamboo garden stakes, 2 to 3 ft. long

3 pieces of 2x6 lumber, 18 in. long. Cedar, redwood, or another untreated wood is best

Wood glue

1 brick

A small roll of aluminum hobby wire

A piece of burlap, approximately 1 ft. x 3 ft.

A roll of natural jute twine

TOOLS NEEDED

Scratch awl

Hammer

Scissors

Pruning shears

Wire cutter

Cordless drill with 5/16-in. and 7/16-in. twist bits

Continued

HOW TO MAKE A POLLINATOR CAN

STEP 1   Flip the trashcan upside down and hammer the awl through the bottom of the can in eight to ten places to create drainage holes. Turn the can back over and locate it where it will receive eastern or southeastern exposure on its front.

STEP 2   Place an upturned, empty 5-gallon bucket in the bottom of the trashcan. This will fill up some of the space and reduce the amount of potting soil/compost blend you'll need.

STEP 3   Stick one end of the 2x4 down into the can, propping it vertically between the 5-gallon bucket and the wall of the trashcan. Fill the can three-quarters of the way to the top with the potting soil blend, straightening the 2x4, if necessary.

STEP 4   Carefully slide the plants out of their pots and arrange them in the can, keeping the taller plants closest to the 2x4 and the shorter plants along the outer edge of the can. Once happy with the placement of plants, loosen any pot-bound roots and fill the spaces in between the plants with more potting mix until the container is filled to within an inch of the top. Leave a small, empty space somewhere close to the front edge of the can. Lay the brick in this space.

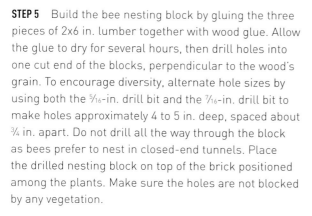

STEP 5   Build the bee nesting block by gluing the three pieces of 2x6 in. lumber together with wood glue. Allow the glue to dry for several hours, then drill holes into one cut end of the blocks, perpendicular to the wood's grain. To encourage diversity, alternate hole sizes by using both the ⁵⁄₁₆-in. drill bit and the ⁷⁄₁₆-in. drill bit to make holes approximately 4 to 5 in. deep, spaced about ¾ in. apart. Do not drill all the way through the block as bees prefer to nest in closed-end tunnels. Place the drilled nesting block on top of the brick positioned among the plants. Make sure the holes are not blocked by any vegetation.

STEP 6   Next, lay the piece of burlap on the ground and place the bundle of bamboo stakes in the center of it. Use a pair of sharp pruners to cut the stakes to approximately 2 ft. in length. Use the wire cutters to cut two 18-in.-long pieces of aluminum hobby wire. Wrap the wire around the bamboo stakes, one close to each end, to fasten them into a secure bundle. Roll the burlap around the center of the bundle and use a piece of natural jute twine to secure it in place.

STEP 7   Fasten the burlap-wrapped bundle of bamboo stakes to the top of the 2x4, using more jute twine. Make sure the stakes are parallel to the ground and fairly level. If any of the cut ends of the bamboo pieces are blocked with dried bamboo pulp, use the awl to clear out the debris and give the bees better access.

8

STEP 8   Care for your new Pollinator Can by watering the plants regularly. When winter arrives, do not cut the plants back or otherwise disturb them. Some species of native bees may take shelter in the plant debris for the winter. Instead, do your cleanup when spring arrives and the weather is consistently warm. By then the bees will have emerged from their overwintering sites. You can also replace any plants that didn't make it through the winter at that time.

NOTE: You'll know the bees are using your nesting sites when the ends of the openings are sealed over with mud or plant debris. To prevent pathogens and predators from taking over your nesting sites, replace the wood nesting block and bamboo stakes every 2 years in the early summer, after the young bees have emerged and before new eggs are laid.

Pinching

Pinching is another important practice for container gardens, especially when it comes to maintaining many different flowering annuals and herbs. Pinching involves removing a portion of the plant's shoot system in order to promote branched, bushy growth. Pinching serves to either encourage more flowers, or in some cases, to prevent the plant from flowering altogether.

Most, but not all, annual plants benefit from being pinched back several times a year, starting in the late spring. Licorice plant, impatiens (*Impatiens walleriana*), salvias, torenia, petunias, geraniums, plectranthus, ageratum (*Ageratum houstonianum*), cosmos, verbena, snapdragons (*Antirrhinum* spp.), and many other annuals should be pinched back on a regular basis to generate new growth and future flowers. But, there are a handful of plants that are pinched for the opposite reason: to *prevent* the formation of flowers. Plants in this category include basil, whose flavor alters when the plant comes into flower; coleus, which is grown primarily for its colorful foliage; and chrysanthemums (*Dendranthema* spp.), which are pinched several times before the arrival of the July 4 holiday to delay flowering until the autumn.

Many gardeners are hesitant to pinch back flowering plants, but it really is the best way to freshen-up container plantings and keep plants from getting too leggy. Here are a few tips for pinching back plants the right way.

A properly pinched plant doesn't look like it's been pinched at all. The sweet potato vine and geranium in this container were pinched back several times throughout the growing season, resulting in the bushy, highly branched plants you see now.

Hardy chrysanthemum is one common plant that's pinched to delay its flowering period.

STAKING, CAGING, AND TRELLISING

Whether it's to keep heavy blossoms off the ground, to prevent fruits and veggies from hitting the dirt, to keep foliage from splaying, or simply to maintain a sense of order, supporting certain container-grown plants with stakes, cages, or trellises preserves their form and beauty. And, in the case of vining vegetables, staking and trellising can also increase yields and reduce pest issues. Not all plants need to be supported, but for those that do, it is essential.

- Pinching does not equal shearing. When you shear a plant, you remove every single growing point, leading to a plant that's covered with leafless, blunt stumps. Pinching, on the other hand, is the selective removal of just a few plant stems.

- Use a sharp pair of scissors or pruners for tougher stems. Though the term *pinching* comes from the fact that, traditionally, gardeners have used their thumb and forefinger to pinch off a plant's stem, it's much better to use a scissors or pruning shears on thicker stems, to avoid tearing them. Torn stems welcome fungal and bacterial infections and are unsightly.

- Remove about ⅓ of the total growth. To pinch a plant, follow the stem tip down from the tip until you reach a set of side-buds. Snip the stem off just above these side-buds. By removing the stem tip, you'll encourage those side shoots to develop into two flowering stems where you used to have only one.

- A little at a time is best. Pinch off a few stems every week or two. This keeps the plant full and lush.

Make sure your staking or trellising system is big enough to support the mature plant. This Malabar spinach plant is quickly outgrowing its tiny trellis.

Staking the plants in your container garden while they're still young keeps fruits and veggies from hitting the ground. It also supports blossoms so you can enjoy them longer.

When to Stake or Trellis Plants

When it comes to supporting plants with a stake, cage, or trellising system, completing the job at the start of the growing season is critical. Better to stake early and allow the foliage to mask the materials holding the plant up than to tie them up after they've already become unruly. If you wait too long to provide a support system to a plant that needs it, you'll begin with a wrestling match and end up with a plant that looks like it's been strapped up in a corset.

Install supports for containerized plants at planting time, if possible. The stakes, cages, and trellises will look naked for a few weeks, but soon the plants will be off and running and quickly begin to rely on their support system.

For the most part, flowering plants grown in containers seldom need to be staked, caged, or trellised, unless they are a vining plant, like a black-eyed Susan vine, a hyacinth bean, or a morning glory—or if they produce heavy blooms on wimpy stems. Some dahlias grown in containers may require a hardwood stake to keep the flowers upright, but most flowering and foliage plants grow quite well in containers without the need for support. But for a lot of container-grown veggies, staking and trellising are essential chores.

When it comes to supporting potted veggies, always choose a system that's stronger than you think you'll need. Some plants are vigorous growers, and they can take down a wimpy stake or cage before summer even arrives. But remember, strong and sturdy doesn't have to mean unattractive. There are tons of beautiful options, both in commercially available systems and DIY projects just about anyone can make. The following project is a great example of a container trellis that's both good looking and hard working.

SQUASH ARCH

MATERIALS NEEDED

2 large, 31-gallon galvanized trashcans

2 empty 5-gallon buckets

Enough 50/50 potting soil and compost blend to fill both cans

2 pieces of pre-cut ½-in. rebar, 10 ft. long

7 pieces of pre-cut ½-in. rebar, 2 ft. long

Roll of aluminum hobby wire

A packet of winter squash seeds

8 to 10 mixed flowering annuals, such as nasturtiums, salvia, marigolds, etc.

Jute twine

TOOLS NEEDED

Scratch awl

Hammer

Tape measure

Marker

Wire cutter

Level

This creative system uses two large containers to support a curved rebar arch extending between them. Though I'm growing tromboncino squash on this arch, the system can also be used to grow pole beans, gourds, cucumbers, melons, or any other vining crop.

This example uses two pieces of 10-ft.-long rebar to make the arch, but if you'd like a taller arch, opt for longer pieces of rebar and increase the number of 2-ft.-long pieces used as cross braces. Use your creativity and make X-shaped cross braces, if you'd like. Paint the rebar for a splash of color, or hang little ornaments from the arch to add a touch of whimsy. The possibilities are infinite.

Building this squash arch is a two-person job, and you'll need a big tree to use as a form to bend the rebar. But both the containers and the arch last for years, making it well worth your time and effort.

HOW TO MAKE A SQUASH ARCH

STEP 1 Flip the cans upside down and hammer the scratch awl through the bottom of each can in several places to make multiple drainage holes. Flip the cans right-side-up, and place them 4 to 5 ft. apart.

STEP 2 Put an upended, empty 5-gallon bucket into each empty trashcan. This helps fill some of the empty space and reduce the amount of potting mix you'll need. Fill both galvanized trashcans with the 50/50 potting soil and compost blend until there's only 1 in. of headspace remaining below the top of the can.

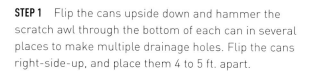

STEP 3 Using a large tree (at least 2 ft. in diameter) as a bending form, bend each long piece of rebar exactly in the middle to form an arch. For this step, it is essential to have two people, one holding each end of the rebar. Begin by holding the rebar straight with the center

against the tree, then slowly walk around the tree to bend the rebar until the legs of the arch are nearly parallel. Repeat with the second long piece of rebar, making sure that both arches are exactly the same.

Continued

4

5

STEP 4   Insert the ends of the two rebar arches into
the trashcans, keeping the bars about 18 in. apart.
For added interest, you can keep the arches close
together at the bottom and lean the tops outward.
Now cut 14 pieces of aluminum hobby wire, each
16 in. to 18 in. long.

STEP 5   Attach the rebar cross braces to the arches
by using wire wrapped in a figure-8 around the
intersections. Use a level and tape measure to ensure
that the crossbars are level and spaced evenly along the
arches. This, too, is a step that will be easier with the
assistance of a helper.

STEP 6   Fill each can with 8 to 10 flowering annuals,
then sow 3 to 5 squash seeds at the base of the rebar
arch. As the squash plants grow, train the young vines
to climb the arch by tying them with jute twine and
guiding them in the right direction until their tendrils
are mature enough to provide support.

6

BIKE-RIM SWEET POTATO TRELLIS

Many gardeners avoid planting sweet potatoes simply because they don't have enough room for the vines to ramble all over their garden. But it's easy to grow a great crop of sweet potatoes by planting them in a container and training the vines to grow up a trellis.

Sweet potatoes require a fairly long growing season, and they love hot summer weather, so if you live in the north, look for varieties that have been bred to produce a good crop in a shorter period of time. 'Beauregard' and 'Georgia Jet' are two good choices for growers north of the Mason-Dixon Line.

Sweet potato vines are easily trained to grow up this bike-rim trellis; as they grow, simply weave the vines through the spokes. You can even make patterns and designs by weaving the vines around the spokes in a spiral fashion.

Continued

HOW TO MAKE A BIKE-RIM SWEET POTATO TRELLIS

STEP 1 Position the two bicycle rims on the ground, one above the other, and measure the total height. Add this to the height of the container; this combined measurement will be the length of the conduit stake you need to cut.

STEP 2 Cut the conduit pipe to the desired length with a copper tube cutter or a hacksaw.

STEP 3 Fill the container most of the way with the 50/50 potting soil and compost blend, then insert the piece of EMT conduit into the center. Fill the rest of the container with the soil mix until it's within an inch of the pot's rim.

5

6

7

STEP 4   Use aluminum hobby wire to secure the bike rims to the conduit stake, one above the other. If your bike rims are two different sizes, use the larger one on the bottom. Wrap the wire securely to hold the rims in place on the conduit stake, and to one another.

If you want to add a splash of color, paint the rims and conduit pole before continuing.

STEP 5   Plant 3 to 6 sweet potato plants or slips in the container, depending on the size of the pot. Water them well.

STEP 6   As the vines grow, weave them between the spokes. To keep the container from toppling over, do not place the container in an area with high winds, and make sure the plants receive at least 6 to 8 hours of full sun per day.

STEP 7   The sweet potatoes are ready to harvest as soon as the leaves begin to yellow, but the longer you leave them in the ground, the better. Just remember to dig them up immediately if the vines get blackened by a frost. Store the dug tubers in a warm room (80° to 90°F) for 8 to 10 days to cure them and sweeten the flavor. After the curing period passes, move the tubers to a cool location, such as a basement or root cellar, where temperatures are between 50° and 60°F.

Support Options

When selecting the appropriate stake, cage, or trellis system for container-grown plants, vegetables in particular, there are several things to keep in mind:

• Veggies that produce heavy fruits, such as beefsteak tomatoes, full-sized eggplants, and bell peppers, will no doubt need to rely on a 1x1 hardwood stake, a metal tomato cage, a teepee, or some other staking system for support. Their stems don't grip the staking system as vine crops do, so you must fasten the plant to them.

There's no need to build a trellis when one's already in place. Use existing fences, arbors, and even window bars as support structures for climbing container plants. These hyacinth beans (*Lablab purpureus*) and morning glories (*Ipomoea purpurea*) are quite happy to cling to whatever they can.

Upcycled trellises are perfect for container gardens. Here, the skeleton of an old patio umbrella is soon to be covered with pea vines.

- Twining crops such as pole and runner beans and malabar spinach (*Basella alba*), have twining stems that coil around their support system. These plants look great growing up just about anything they can wrap themselves around, including hardwood stakes, tree branches, sunflower stalks, bamboo poles, teepee legs, and the like.

- Vining crops with tendrils growing off their main stems will grow up and over just about anything. Cucumbers, winter squash, gourds, pumpkins, peas, and melons produce small tendrils at their leaf nodes, and will easily grow up anything from chicken wire and chain link fencing, to nylon garden netting and hardware cloth. To keep them under control, you'll need a very sturdy trellis.

Repurposed household items also make great garden trellises. Keep your eyes peeled for things like closet organizers, wire shelving units, and store displays, all of which are easily transformed into vertical supports for container plants.

A simple arch of cattle fencing makes an excellent support for flowering vines and climbing veggies. Extend the arch between two containers to make a unique arbor over a walkway or gate.

Wooden trellises and cages are excellent choices for supporting plants in your container garden. With a little finesse, you, too, can build custom wooden trellises like this one to fit a particular size and shape of container.

Wooden ladders make great trellises. Place them over containers filled with vine crops, like these pole beans, and you'll soon discover it makes harvesting a snap.

While white PVC pipes aren't necessarily pretty, they sure do make versatile, inexpensive, and sturdy trellises. This gardener built super-sturdy cages out of PVC pipe and surrounded his containerized tomato plants with them.

◀ If there's nothing in your container for a plant to climb, try placing the container in front of a wall with a trellis attached to it. This mandevilla plant is quite happy to cover the wall behind it with flowers.

As with all things gardening, there are a hundred different ways to complete a project, and staking your plants is no exception. There's no right or wrong way to do it, as long as the end result maintains the plants' natural form and habit without making it look restricted or soldierly. This page shows some great ideas for staking, caging, and trellising your container garden.

In addition to using commercially made plant stakes, cages, and trellises, it's also fun to use natural materials to build support structures for plants. It's easy to build a teepee made from tree branches and vines and place it over a container to support the pea crop growing there. Here's a project that uses a recycled container and natural materials to grow a hearty harvest of pole beans.

BEAN TRELLIS BIN

MATERIALS NEEDED

1 large, 30- to 40-gallon plastic storage bin

Enough 50/50 potting soil and compost blend to fill the bin

2 branches, 1 to 2 in. diameter and 4 to 5 in. longer than the length of the bin

8 branches, 1 to 2 in. in diameter and 4 to 6 ft. tall.

Aluminum hobby wire

1 packet of pole bean seeds

8 to 10 flowering annuals, if desired

TOOLS NEEDED

Utility knife

Wire cutter

Pruning saw

Pole beans are one of the most productive garden crops you can grow, but because the plants grow so large, they require a lot of support. Their twining vines wrap around whatever they touch, and unless you give them some type of trellis to climb, they'll quickly get out of hand.

This simple trellis, made from a recycled storage bin and some branches is perfect. It gives the vines plenty of room to grow while taking up very little real estate. Use it to grow pole beans on an apartment patio, a deck, or a balcony. For something a little different, try growing yellow or purple pole beans, pole limas, runner beans, Chinese yard-long beans, or winged beans on it, too.

HOW TO MAKE A BEAN TRELLIS BIN

STEP 1   Flip the plastic storage bin over and use the utility knife to cut a 1-in.-square drainage hole in the bottom of the bin. Use the wire cutters to cut eight pieces of aluminum hobby wire, each about 30 in. long. Put them aside, but keep them within arm's reach.

STEP 2   Lay the two shorter branches across the top of the container, spacing them about 2 in. apart. Insert one of the taller branches in between the shorter branches, just inside one of the container's side edges. Wrap a piece of aluminum hobby wire around the vertical branch and both horizontal branches in a figure-8 fashion to secure them together. Repeat with another vertical branch on the edge of the opposite side of the container.

STEP 3   Place two more branches in between the horizontal support branches, about 3 in. in from the first vertical branches. Use aluminum hobby wire to secure these to the horizontal branches.

Continued

STEP 4 Fill the container about halfway with the 50/50 potting soil and compost blend. This helps support the remaining branches as they're installed. Continue to insert more vertical branches, spacing them evenly and then securing them to the horizontal branches with hobby wire wrapped in a figure-8 pattern. Once all the branches are installed and secured, fill the rest of the bin with the potting soil blend until there's only about an inch of headspace remaining.

STEP 5 Plant a row of your favorite variety of pole beans on either side of the branch trellis. Space bean seeds 2 in. apart. If you'd like to add some color, plant a handful of flowering annuals around the outer edge of the bin. Water everything in well and place your Bean Trellis Bin where it receives at least 6 to 8 hours of sun per day. As the beans grow, train them to grow up the branches by gently guiding them in the right direction.

Natural bamboo stakes fashioned into teepees and inserted into fabric pots work like a charm when it comes to growing a good crop of pole beans. Connect the teepees with a bamboo cross bar at the top for added protection against high winds and heavy plants.

As you can see, maintaining a container garden is, in many ways, far easier than taking care of a traditional garden in the ground. Though we have to water and fertilize a bit more often than other gardeners, container growers get to skip such tasks as weeding, mulching, and tilling. Instead, we get to focus on enjoying the garden's beauty and yields.

chapter 4

Troubleshooting

There will be times when things don't go as planned in your container garden. Plants might not perform as well as you'd hoped, combinations might look more gaudy than expected, or vegetable plants might not produce a single edible morsel. Don't worry; it happens to everyone. Keep growing and focus on the things that *did* work.

The goal of this chapter is to walk you through some of the troublesome issues you may face in your container garden, and provide you with all the tools you'll need to quickly overcome them.

First, I'll introduce you to several of the common pest insects you might encounter, with physical descriptions and photographs of each pest, along with multiple easy-to-employ control tactics for dealing with them. But I've also included photos and descriptions of some of the *good* bugs you're likely to find. These beneficial insects play a huge role in the health of your plants and should be encouraged. Next, I'll cover twelve of the more common plant pathogens and ways to combat them, along with several physiological disorders that are easily remedied by tweaking the way you care for your containers.

◀ Beautiful containers like this one are the result of much trial and error. Sometimes things don't go as planned, but don't let that stop you from trying to grow the best container garden you can.

Keep in mind that for new gardeners, one of the easiest ways to limit potential problems is to start small. Don't plant forty containers your first year, and don't spend a ton of money on fancy containers. Instead, focus on growing a handful of plants in recycled containers. The beginner's project that follows is a great way to dip your toes into the world of container gardening without feeling overwhelmed.

With any luck, you'll discover far more pollinators, such as this green metallic sweat bee, and other beneficial insects in your container garden than you do pests.

MILK-CRATE GARDENING

This is another excellent way to experiment with container growing, without having to invest a lot of time and money. What's extra fun about this technique is that you have lots of design options for displaying your milk crate garden:

- Stack the planted crates in layers, checkerboard-style, to make a wall of containers. Plant low, vining plants, such as cucumbers, melons, and winter squash, in the lower levels, then use crates with taller plants, like peppers, eggplants, and basil, as the top tier.

- For this project, I placed the plants in the open top of the milk crate, but you could also cut holes in the burlap sides and plant herbs and seeds of vining veggies right through the holes in the sides of the crate, allowing you to stack the crates directly on top of each other and save tons of space.

- Milk crates also make excellent hanging planters. Attach chains with S-hooks to the top edge of the crate and hang it from plant hangers or ceiling hooks.

- Prior to planting, secure the milk crates to a deck railing using L-brackets or bolts for another great way to save space.

The possibilities are endless with milk-crate gardening!

MATERIALS NEEDED

Plastic milk crates

Roll of burlap fabric

Enough 50/50 potting soil and compost blend to fill all the milk crates

Plants

TOOLS NEEDED

Scissors

HOW TO MAKE A MILK-CRATE GARDEN

STEP 1 Cut a piece of natural or synthetic burlap twice the size of the inside of the milk crate. For added interest, use patterned or printed burlap from a fabric store. Tuck the burlap down into the bottom of the crate and into the four corners, then pull the ends of the fabric out over the top edge of the crate. Don't line up the corners of the fabric with the corners of the crate; it looks far more interesting if they're off-set.

STEP 2 Fill the burlap with the potting soil/compost blend to within 1 in. of the top of the milk crates. As you water these containers, any excess water will drain right through the porous burlap, so there's no need to cut drainage holes. Choose a single specimen plant for each crate. Since each crate only holds a few gallons of soil, do not overstuff them. If you'd like, you can add one or two filler flowers or herbs to each crate, but don't overdo it or the plants won't perform their best.

STEP 3 Arrange your milk crates however you'd like.

NOTE: Because of the porous nature of the burlap, your milk crate garden might need to be watered a little more often than plants grown in non-porous plastic, metal, or glazed ceramic containers.

PEST PROBLEMS

Don't assume every insect is a bad, leaf-munching enemy. In fact, less than 1% of the world's identified insect species are classified as pests, while the vast majority are either benign or beneficial. There are tens of thousands of species of pollinators and pest-eating beneficial insects found in a healthy garden, and they should be encouraged and left unharmed.

Because we don't want to harm good insects while managing the bad, all the control techniques and products discussed in this section are highly effective and nature-safe when used according to label instructions. They're derived from naturally occurring compounds that target the pest while causing little if any collateral damage when used correctly. But before you apply anything to your plants, be sure to use any physical controls as your first line of defense. If it does become necessary to turn to a product for control, always follow the label instructions exactly when applying it, even if it's natural or organic. Protect yourself, and pay attention to application directions for optimum results and to best preserve beneficial insect species. Though this is not an insect-focused book, it's impossible to talk about container gardens and not talk about insect pests. Some bugs eat plants, and these herbivorous insects are just doing what nature intended. The truth is, you'll have to tolerate some amount of pest insects in your container garden. After all, without a few pests here and there, you won't have a good population of beneficial insects hanging around to manage larger pest outbreaks down the line. A less-than-perfect head of cabbage, a bit of pock-marked foliage, and the occasional slug-nibbled petunia are small prices to pay for an overall healthy container garden. It's only when pest insect numbers grow overwhelmingly large and the damage they cause becomes too extensive that we need to find a way to safely reduce their numbers to a tolerable level.

Proper identification is by far the most important facet of pest control. Take your time identifying any insect you find in your container garden. Use all the resources available to you, and don't jump to conclusions about the insect without careful investigation.

◄ Beneficial insects, such as this ladybug larva, are great at helping you control pests. Learn to identify them so you don't mistakenly eradicate them.

▲ Physical controls, such as hand-picking and covering plants with a layer of floating row cover, are always your first line of defense against pests.

▶ It's good to have some pest insects in your garden, because without them, you won't have beneficial insects hanging around to bring balance. Here, a spined soldier bug nymph is feasting on a young tent caterpillar on a container-grown blueberry.

Common Container-Garden Pests

Below you'll find identification information and ecologically safe management techniques for twenty of the pests you're most likely to encounter in your container garden.

Aphids (many species)

North American geographical range: All

Identification: Aphids are tiny, pear-shaped, soft-bodied insects up to ⅛ in. long. They can be green, yellow, brown, red, gray, or black. Some species have winged forms, others do not. At the hind end of each aphid are two small, tube-like structures called cornicles.

Plants affected: Highly susceptible plants include nasturtiums, roses, milkweed, mums, tomatoes, lettuce, peppers, geraniums, and members of the cabbage family. But since there are numerous species of aphids, there are many other potential host plants.

Aphids are prolific, sap-sucking pests often found in large numbers on leaf undersides and shoot tips. Here, they're lined up along a flowering stem.

Feeding habits and damage: Aphids feed by using a piercing-sucking mouthpart to penetrate plant tissue and suck out sap. They feed in groups on new plant growth or on leaf undersides, and cause stem tips, new leaves, and buds to be curled and distorted.

Physical controls: Removing aphids with a sharp stream of water from the hose knocks them off plants onto the ground where they quickly perish. Hand-crushing is also effective, but predatory beneficial insects usually bring aphid populations under control naturally.

Product controls: Horticultural oil, insecticidal soap, and neem-based insecticides.

Lacewing larva are one of many beneficial insect species that help gardeners control aphids.

Cabbageworm (*Artogeia rapae*)

North American geographical range: All

Identification: Cabbageworm caterpillars are light green with a faint yellow stripe down the back. They measure about 1 in. long. Adult butterflies have a 1-to-2 in. wingspan and are white to yellowish-white with up to four black spots on the wings.

Plants affected: All members of the cabbage family, including broccoli, cabbage, cauliflower, Brussels sprouts, kale, kohlrabi, radish, and turnip.

Cabbageworm caterpillars feed on all members of the cabbage family and can quickly skeletonize leaves.

Covering susceptible plants with floating row cover prevents adult cabbageworm butterflies like this one from laying eggs on the foliage.

Feeding habits and damage: Caterpillars chew ragged holes in leaves. They may also leave round holes through flower clusters of broccoli and cauliflower. Young cabbageworms are difficult to spot. Carefully examine leaf undersides and midribs for their presence.

Physical controls: Cover their favorite plants with floating row cover to keep the female butterflies from laying eggs on the plants. None of the susceptible vegetables needs to be pollinated before harvest, so row covers can stay in place until harvest. Handpick and crush any caterpillars you find. Many insectivorous birds find cabbageworms to be a real treat.

Product controls: *Bacillus thuringiensis* (*B. t.*), spinosad, botanical oils, citrus oils.

Colorado Potato Beetle (*Leptinotarsa decemlineata*)

North American geographical range: All areas of the United States., except the Pacific Northwest and the extreme South. Also Southern Canada.

Identification: ⅓ in. long adult beetles have a rounded, hard shell. The wing covers are black and tan striped, with the head having several irregular black spots. Full grown larvae are ½ in. long, fat, and reddish-pink, with rows of black dots on their sides.

Plants affected: All members of the tomato family, including potatoes, tomatoes, eggplants, peppers, and tobacco.

Feeding habits and damage: Colorado potato beetle larvae and adults quickly skeletonize foliage. They're most often found on the top-most leaves of the plant. You may also find pellets of their black excrement.

Physical controls: Cover potato plants with floating row cover, and leave it in place until harvest. On tomatoes and other crops, handpick the adults and larvae every few days. Clean up garden debris and rotate crops to keep the adult beetles from overwintering.

Product controls: *Bacillus thuringiensis* (B. t.) var. San Diego or B. t. var. *tenebrionsis*, spinosad-, and neem-based insecticides.

Colorado potato beetle larvae have a distinctive, rounded shape. They're fond of all members of the tomato family, but are most common on potatoes.

Cucumber beetle
(striped species: *Acalymma vittata*; spotted species: *Diabrotica undecimpunctata howardi*)

North American geographical range: All

Identification: Both common species, striped and spotted, measure ¼ in. long at maturity. Adult striped beetles are bright yellow with three broad black stripes. Spotted cucumber beetles are greenish-yellow with eleven (eastern species) or twelve (western species) black spots on the wing covers. Larvae live underground and feed on plant roots.

Plants affected: All members of the curcurbit family, including cucumbers, melons, pumpkins, and squash. Other plants occasionally damaged include: beans, corn, beets, potatoes, tomatoes, asparagus, flowers, and soft fruits.

In addition to feeding on host plant foliage, the spotted cucumber beetle also feeds on the nectar of various flowering plants.

The striped cucumber beetle is a major pest of cucumbers and other vine crops. Damage appears as small, ragged holes in plant leaves and flowers.

Feeding habits and damage: Feeding damage creates small, ragged holes in plant leaves and flowers. The biggest issue with cucumber beetles, however, is their ability to transmit deadly bacterial wilt to plants.

Physical controls: Plant only bacterial wilt-resistant cucumber varieties. Cover susceptible plants with floating row cover when they're young, but remove it when the plants come into flower. Place yellow sticky cards above plant tops to trap the adult beetles. Mulch newly planted seedlings with a loose material, like straw or hay, as soon as they're planted, creating a barrier for females who need to access the soil to lay eggs.

Product controls: Neem, spinosad, and pyrethrins.

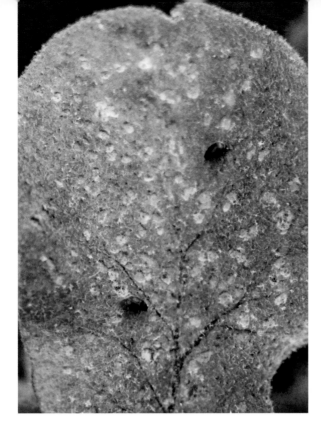

Flea beetles are small, hopping insects that feed on many different crops, including radishes, eggplants, and tomatoes.

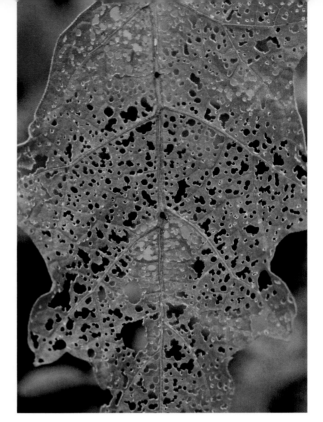

Flea beetles are most damaging to young, tender seedlings. Protect plants such as the eggplant pictured here, with kaolin clay-based sprays.

Flea Beetle (many species)

North American geographical range: All

Identification: Extremely small, these members of the beetle family measure only about 1/10 in. long and hop like a flea. Most species are shiny and black, though some are iridescent or striped. They move very quickly and are often seen hopping around damaged plants.

Plants affected: Many different plants are susceptible to flea beetle damage, but some of their favorites include cole crops, corn, eggplant, pepper, potatoes, radishes, tomatoes, and turnips.

Feeding habits and damage: The damage flea beetles cause is very distinctive. Small, round holes make the plant look as if it's been riddled with tiny buckshot. The larvae live underground and can do minor damage to plant roots and potato tubers.

Physical controls: Place yellow sticky cards just above the plant tops to attract and trap adult beetles. While floating row cover is not an effective way to keep flea beetles off plants in an in-ground vegetable garden (it often ends up trapping *in* the beetles as they emerge from their underground pupation), it *is* an effective way to keep the beetles off containerized plants, especially if they were planted in a fresh batch of potting mix at the start of the season.

Product controls: Citrus oil, garlic oil, kaolin clay-based sprays, hot pepper wax, neem, and spinosad.

Four-Lined Plant Bug
(*Poecilocapsus lineatus*)

North American geographical range: East of the Rockies and into southern Canada

Identification: Four-lined plant bugs are extremely fast moving. They have greenish-yellow wing covers with four black lines down them. Adults measure ¼ in. long at maturity, but they start out as tiny, red and black nymphs in the early spring.

Plants affected: These insects are most attracted to plants with highly fragrant foliage. Basil, lavender, mint, oregano, and sage are among their favorites, though you'll also find them feeding on ornamentals like azaleas, Russian sage, peonies, mums, Shasta daisies, and viburnums, among many others.

Four-lined plant bugs feed on host plants for only a few weeks every year. Their distinctive greenish-yellow coloration and four black stripes make them easy to identify, if you manage to catch these fast-moving bugs in action.

As four-lined plant bugs suck out plant juices, they leave distinctive pockmarks behind. Thankfully, the damage is mostly aesthetic and can be pruned out easily.

Feeding habits and damage: Four-lined plant bug damage is unmistakable. Small, sunken, round pockmarks occur in groups on new plant foliage. The damage is caused by the insect's piercing and sucking mouthpart. Eventually, the pockmarks turn brown and the damaged tissue may fall out, leaving small holes in the leaves. The damage they cause is purely aesthetic and can easily be pruned out.

Physical controls: These insects only have one generation per year, in early summer, and they complete their life cycle in 4 to 6 weeks. Prune out affected plant material in mid- to late summer, after feeding damage ceases. Cover susceptible plants with floating row cover until midsummer when the bugs are no longer active.

Product controls: Product controls are seldom necessary as their damage is only aesthetic.

Fungus Gnats (*Bradysia* species and *Lycoriella* species)

North American geographical range: All; considered an indoor nuisance pest

Identification: Mature gnats are tiny black flies that measure a mere ⅛ in. and live for about 2 weeks. During this time, females lay eggs in soil fissures. The resulting translucent, minute larvae feed largely on the assorted fungi growing in potting soil, though they can also feed on fine roots and plant debris. In a few weeks, they pupate into adults within the soil and the cycle continues with several generations occurring together at any given time. When a cloud of tiny, black flies rises from the pot of a houseplant, it's a clear sign of trouble. That cloud may consist of hundreds of adult fungus gnats and, while individually they are barely noticeable, in large numbers they are hard to miss.

Plants affected: Any indoor plant is susceptible

Feeding habits and damage: Because fungus gnat larvae feed primarily on fungi growing in the potting soil, these insects typically don't cause a significant amount of damage to infested plants. However, in extreme cases where the larvae also feed on plant roots, the plant may wilt and show signs of stunted growth.

Physical controls: Constantly damp soils promote fungal growth, which serves as an excellent food source for the larvae. Simply cut down on watering to solve most fungus gnat issues. Water infested houseplants deeply (but not frequently) and only when the soil is dry. Be sure the pot itself has good drainage and the saucer underneath

doesn't hold standing water. If this doesn't clear up the problem, repot the plant with new, sterile potting soil. You can also trap adult fungus gnats on yellow or blue sticky cards placed vertically an inch or two above the soil surface. Another option is to remove the top half-inch of potting soil completely and replace it with a small gravel-like substance, such as Gnat Nix or chicken grit.

Product controls: Two biological control products are highly effective: beneficial nematodes (*Steinernema feltiae*) and Bti (*Bacillus thuringiensis* var. *israelensis*) can be applied to the soil as a drench or spray. The first is a microscopic nematode that burrows into the soil and consumes the gnat larvae. The second is a biological insecticide made from a strain of bacteria that kills the gnat larvae. One popular brand is named Gnatrol®.

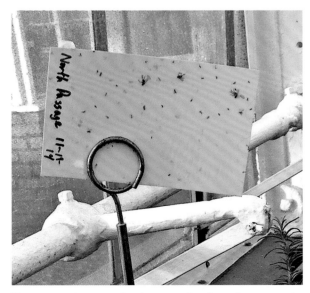

Fungus gnats are a classic example of a nuisance pest. Thankfully, they aren't harmful to plants unless present in large numbers, and they're easy to trap on yellow sticky cards.

Adult Japanese beetles skeletonize leaves and damage flower buds of over 300 different garden plants.

Japanese Beetle (*Popillia japonica*)

North American geographical range: Populations are heaviest east of the Mississippi River and north into the lower part of Canada, but they're found throughout most of the United States, except in the extreme Southeast.

Identification: Metallic green with copper wing covers, adult beetles are ½ in. long and ¼ in. wide. They stick up their two back legs when threatened and drop off plants when disturbed. The ground-dwelling larvae are C-shaped, plump, grayish-white grubs with light brown heads.

Plants affected: Adults feed on over 300 different landscape plants. Favorites include grapes, raspberries, blueberries, roses, rhubarb, zinnias, and many others. Grubs feed underground, on the roots of turf grass and many ornamental plants.

Feeding habits and damage: Adults skeletonize leaves and damage flower buds. They emerge in midsummer and feed heaviest at temps between 85° and 95°F. Grub damage appears as irregular brown patches in the lawn that peel back in a carpet-like fashion.

Physical controls: Withhold water from the lawn in summer when females are laying eggs and allow your lawn to go dormant. The eggs need moisture to survive, so doing so reduces next year's population. Knock adult beetles into a jar of soapy water. Handpicking the adults early and often limits the release of the congregating pheromone the beetles release to lure in more beetles for mating. Avoid using Japanese beetle traps unless they're placed far from your container garden. Several studies have shown these traps attract more beetles than they actually trap.

Product controls: Beneficial nematodes (*Heterorhabditis* species or *Steinernema carporcapsae*) are incredibly effective against the grubs when applied to the lawn every spring. Useful product controls to battle adult Japanese beetles include neem and spinosad.

Leaf hoppers, such as this candy-striped leafhopper, feed by sucking out leaf juices with their piercing-sucking mouth part. There are about 2,500 species of leafhoppers in North America, but most are not problematic to gardeners.

Leafhoppers (many species)

North American geographical range: All

Identification: Adults are wedge-shaped, slender insects, measuring as much as ¼ in. long. They can be green, yellow, brown, or brightly colored. Leafhoppers move sideways, like a crab, or jump when disturbed. Nymphs look like adults, only smaller and without wings. Leafhopper adults and nymphs are often found on leaf undersides side by side. The old, molted skins of leafhoppers are sometimes present on leaf undersides as well, along with the dark specks of their excrement.

Plants affected: Leafhoppers feed on hundreds of different plants; many are host-specific. Choice hosts include roses, potatoes, grapes, beans, lettuce, beets, and many others.

Feeding habits and damage: Feeding damage appears as mottled stippling or pale spots on infested leaves caused by the insect's sap-sucking behavior. Severely damaged leaves may curl up and fall from the plant. Some species of leafhoppers transmit various plant diseases, leading to problems that extend beyond their feeding damage.

Physical controls: Leafhoppers are fast-moving, making them somewhat difficult to control. Adults overwinter in crop debris and unmowed areas. Remove debris soon after the last garden harvest to reduce overwintering sites. Use floating row covers early in the season to prevent leafhoppers from damaging plants.

Product controls: Insecticidal soap and horticultural oil help reduce populations, but covering the leaf undersides when spraying is a must. Pyrethrins are also somewhat effective.

Leaf Miner (many species)

North American geographical range: All

Identification: Leaf miner damage is fairly easy to spot in your garden, though you seldom see the insects themselves. Leaf miners are the larvae of several different species of flies. Adult flies are about ¼ in. long and are often black with yellow markings. The larvae are tiny, green or brown maggots that feed inside plant leaves.

Plants affected: Different species of leaf miners feed on different species of plants. A few likely victims include spinach, Swiss chard, beets, hollies, columbine, nasturtiums, peas, blueberries, and boxwood.

Feeding habits and damage: These tunneling insects feed between layers of leaf tissue, "mining" out the material in between. They leave behind clear evidence of their presence in the form of squiggly trails and splotches on the leaves. In most cases, their damage is not severe enough to warrant using any control products. It's largely aesthetic damage, particularly on ornamental plants.

Leaf miners are tiny insect larvae that tunnel between layers of leaf tissue, leaving squiggly lines and splotches behind. Swiss chard is a common host plant.

Physical controls: A layer of floating row cover over spinach, beet, and chard plants is enough to prevent the adult leaf miners from laying eggs on the plants' leaves. If you do see their distinctive squiggly feeding pattern on a leaf, simply cut off and destroy that individual leaf. Wait to plant beets and chard until after the lilacs bloom; the species of leaf miner they host is no longer active at that time. There are also several species of parasitic wasps that help control leaf miners by laying eggs inside of them while they're still inside the leaf. You can encourage these beneficial insects by including plants like dill, fennel, and cilantro in your container garden. These three plants provide nectar to the tiny, non-stinging parasitic wasps.

Product controls: Since leaf miner maggots are nestled between layers of plant tissue, it's difficult to manage them with spray products, but neem and spinosad are the most effective. Early season sprays of hot pepper wax deter the females from laying eggs on any plants where it's been applied.

While some leaf miner species feed on spinach, chard, beets, and other vegetable crops, others use ornamental plants, including this columbine, as hosts.

Mealybugs (several species)

North American geographical range: All

Identification: Adult female mealy bugs are ⅛ in. long, oval-shaped, and usually covered with a soft white or gray fuzz. Both adult females and smaller larval mealybugs use their piercing-sucking mouthparts to suck sap from plants. They often feed in clusters and produce clumps of wax or fuzz. Males do not feed and only live long enough to breed. These insects secrete a sticky excrement known as honeydew. It leaves a shiny, tacky residue on the infested plant itself and on anything beneath it.

Plants affected: Many plants are potential hosts, but common ones include citrus, grapes, fruit trees, orchids, hibiscus, dracena, ficus, and many others.

Feeding habits and damage: Heavily infested plants may have reduced and distorted growth. A few mealybugs will not cause much damage, but large numbers could cause defoliation. These insects are more common outdoors in warm, humid parts of North America, but are common pests of houseplants and greenhouses.

Physical controls: Mealybugs are easily removed from plants by wiping stems and leaf surfaces with cotton balls or squares soaked in isopropyl rubbing alcohol. A sharp stream of water also knocks insects off plants. Do not overfeed houseplants, as mealybugs thrive on heavily fertilized plants.

Product controls: Insecticidal soap, horticultural oil, citrus oil, pyrethrins, neem.

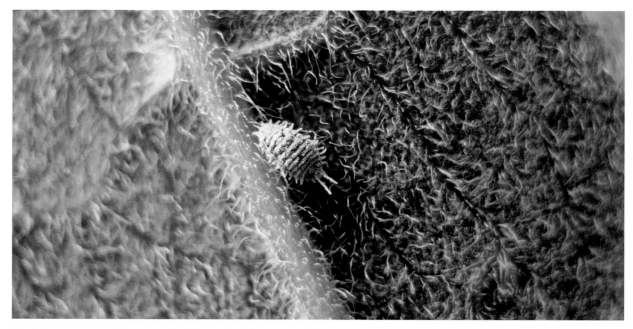

Mealybugs are usually covered with a soft white or gray fuzz. They often feed in groups and leave a sticky residue on leaves and other nearby surfaces.

Mexican Bean Beetle
(*Epilachna varivestis*)

North American geographical range: East of the Rockies in the United States into Southern Canada. Also present in certain regions of the Western United States.

Identification: Adult beetles look like a large ladybug. They have copper-colored wing pads with sixteen black spots on them. Larvae are ⅓ in. long, light yellow, and covered in soft, bristly spines.

Plants affected: All beans are potential hosts, including: black-eyed peas, cow peas, green beans, pole beans, runner beans, snap beans, lima beans, and soybeans.

Adult Mexican bean beetles look like ladybugs on steroids. But unlike ladybugs, these guys aren't good for the garden. They feed on all types of bean plants, including pole, runner, lima, snap, and others.

Feeding habits and damage: Both adult and larval Mexican bean beetles skeletonize leaves, leaving only the veins intact, and occasionally feed on flowers and developing beans. Larvae are most often found on the undersides of the leaves.

Physical controls: Handpick and crush both the larvae and adults when you find them. Though the larvae have spines, they're soft and pliable. A tiny, non-stinging beneficial, predatory wasp (*Pediobius foveolatus*) from India is regularly released in several Eastern states to control Mexican bean beetle numbers. You can purchase the larval wasps for release in your own garden when Mexican bean beetle larvae are present.

Product controls: Citrus oil, hot pepper wax, and spinosad.

The spiky yellow larva of the Mexican bean beetle can quickly skeletonize bean leaves, but it's easily crushed between your fingers.

Scales (many species)

North American geographical range: All

Identification: There are both soft and hard scales. Both feed with piercing-sucking mouthparts and may have a hard, armor-like shell. Many species look like raised bumps on twigs, leaves, and leaf petioles, though some species look like small, white flecks. Some species may also be covered in a downy fuzz, and most excrete sticky honeydew, which is evident as a shiny, sticky layer on infested plants.

Plants affected: Most species of scale feed on a specific species or group of species, of plants. Common hosts include: magnolia, pachysandra, fruit trees, dogwood, lilac, birch, euonymus, holly, citrus, boxwood, and many others.

Azalea scale looks like white tufts of cotton along the length of the branches of azalea plants. Physically removing the scale insects on this plant is a good control method, as is a well-timed application of horticultural oil.

Feeding habits and damage: Heavy scale infestations may cause stunted growth and yellow foliage. Stems and branches may be weakened as well. Often wasps and ants are found on plants with a scale infestation, as both of these insects feed on the sticky honeydew excreted by certain species of scale.

Physical controls: Large species of scale can be crushed by running your fingers down the length of an infested branch and crushing the insects as you go. Scale reproduces more quickly on over-fertilized plants, so don't overfeed. Some scales can be eliminated by wiping them with a cotton ball or square soaked in isopropyl rubbing alcohol.

Product controls: Because of the hard, armor-like shell on many species of scale, control can be difficult. Some species are in a soft, crawler life stage for a few weeks each year, when it is the best time to try to control them. But, each species of scale enters its crawler stage at a different time, so a bit of research is required. Effective products include insecticidal soap, horticultural oil, and neem.

Scales can be hard or soft, and they may have a hard, armor-like shell like this one. But regardless of their appearance, all scales feed by sucking out plant juices.

Slugs/Snails (several species)

North American geographical range: All

Identification: Slugs and snails are land mollusks and can be gray, black, orange, brown, tan, or yellow. Snails have exterior shells; slugs do not. Both excrete a slimy coating to protect themselves and on which they glide. Their telltale slime trails are often the first clue to their presence. Both slugs and snails feed largely at night, but they also come out on overcast or rainy days.

Plants affected: Nearly all young seedlings are susceptible, as well as numerous flowering plants and vegetables, including lettuce, tomatoes, strawberries, hosta, and many others.

Most troublesome slug species are not native to North America; they're European introductions. Their mouths are lined with tiny teeth that quickly shred plant material and consume it.

Firefly larvae are major predators of young slugs and slug eggs. If you have a lawn, you can encourage them by not filling in low-lying, damp areas or using lawn pesticides.

Feeding habits and damage: Both slugs and snails have a mouth lined with tiny teeth that shred plant material in a cheese-grater-like fashion. They leave irregular holes in leaves, along the margin, or in the center. Often this culprit isn't present during the day, so inspect plants at night.

Physical controls: Many different creatures dine on slugs, so encourage birds, snakes, salamanders, frogs, toads, turtles, and ground beetles. Water only in the morning to discourage nighttime feeding on wet foliage. Copper strips placed around susceptible plants deliver a mild shock to slugs (the slime reacts to contact with copper). Handpick any you find and toss them into a cup of soapy water. Saucers of beer work to trap slugs, too, but they should be emptied daily.

Product controls: Do not use baits containing metaldehyde or methiocarb. These products are highly toxic to pets and other wildlife. Instead, sprinkle iron phosphate-based baits around plants.

Squash Bugs (*Anasa tristis*)

North American geographical range: All

Identification: Adult squash bugs are ⅝ in. long and dark brown or grayish in color. Their bodies are flattened and oval-shaped. Young nymphs are wingless and gray, with spindly legs and dark markings. They're often found feeding in groups. All stages of squash bugs emit an unpleasant odor when crushed. Eggs are bronze-colored and laid in groups on leaf undersides.

Plants affected: All cucurbit crops, including cucumbers, melons, pumpkins, squash, and zucchini.

Feeding habits and damage: Squash bugs use their needle-like mouthpart to pierce the plant and suck out the sap. They leave behind small specks that soon turn yellow and may lead to leaf death. Severe infestations cause the vines to wilt and turn crispy. Large populations of squash bugs are often found gathered around fruit stems and on the ground around infested plants.

Squash bugs are one of the most problematic pests for gardeners. Both adults and nymphs emit a foul odor when they're crushed or otherwise disturbed.

Physical controls: Start by planting resistant varieties. Use trellises to keep susceptible plants off the ground, and cover young plants with floating row cover until they come into flower. Regularly handpick the adults and nymphs and crush any egg clusters you find.

Product controls: Neem and pyrethrins are effective when used against nymphs.

▲ Squash bug eggs are oval and bronze-colored. They're often found in groups underneath the leaves of host plants. Use your fingernail to crush any you find.

◀ Squash bug nymphs are sway-backed, wingless, and gray. They're often found clustered together on susceptible plants.

Squash Vine Borer
(*Melittia satyriniformis*)

North American geographical range: Everywhere east of the Rocky Mountains in the United States and up into southeastern Canada.

Identification: Adults are red and black, clear-winged moths that are active during the daytime. They measuring 1½ in. long and look more like a large hornet than a moth. The larvae are the vine borers. These chubby white caterpillars have brown heads and can grow up to an inch long before pupating into an adult. Eggs are flat and brown, and are most often laid at the base of the plant, just above or below soil level.

Plants affected: All members of the cucumber family are potential host plants, including winter and summer squash, pumpkins, gourds, melons, and occasionally, cucumbers.

Feeding habits and damage: Borer damage exhibits as rapid wilting of plants. Often frass (the excrement of the borer) is noted at the base of the plant; sometimes a hole is present as well.

Adult squash vine borers are red and black, day-flying moths. Females lay eggs at the base of squash and melon plants.

Adults emerge from their underground pupation in the spring. Eggs are laid soon after, and the larvae spend just over a month eating the inner tissue of the plant stem. There are typically two generations per year.

Physical controls: Cover susceptible crops with a floating row cover immediately after planting and leave it in place until the plants come into flower to allow for pollination. If you notice the borer damage before the plant is killed, slice open the affected stems with a sharp razor blade and dig out and destroy the borer inside. Cover the cut area with soil. You can also wrap a 1 x 6 in. strip of aluminum foil around the base of the plant as soon as it develops its first true leaves. Nestle the bottom edge of the strip just below the soil surface. This covers the most vulnerable part of the plant and keeps female vine borer moths from laying eggs there.

Product controls: Because the borer is housed inside of the plant itself, product controls are difficult. But you can inject *Bacillus thuringiensis* (B.t.) into the base of the stem, directly into any borer holes, and it will kill any insects inside. You can also spray insecticidal soap around the base of the vine on a weekly basis to smother any eggs laid there.

Squash vine borer adults are deterred from egg-laying behavior by covering the base of the plant with a strip of aluminum foil when the plant is young.

Spider Mites (several species)

North American geographical range: All

Identification: You'll need a microscope to see these tiny relatives of spiders and ticks. Spider mites have eight legs and are a mere 1/20 in. long. They live in large colonies, collectively spinning fine webbing for shelter. Most gardeners notice the webbing before they spot the mites themselves. For a positive ID, shake the plant over a piece of white paper and look for tiny specks moving around on it.

Plants affected: The most common species of spider mite, the two-spotted spider mite, feeds on over 180 different plant species. Host plants include azalea, dwarf Alberta spruce, grapes, melons, phlox, and strawberries, among many others.

Spider mites are extremely tiny, but the tell-tale webbing they leave behind is hard to miss. They cause leaf stippling and distorted growth.

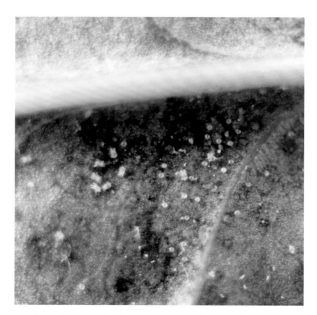

Spider mite populations are naturally kept in check by many species of beneficials, including larger predatory mites, ladybugs, and minute pirate bugs.

Feeding habits and damage: Spider mite damage appears as mottled, yellow foliage. Leaf undersides and stems are often covered in fine webbing. Mites can be carried from plant to plant on the wind, so they move around the landscape quite easily.

Physical controls: Beneficial predatory insects, like big-eyed bugs, damsel bugs, ladybugs, predatory mites, and minute pirate bugs, make a huge dent in spider mite populations. Encourage them by adding lots of flowering herbs and other tiny flowers to your container garden.

Product controls: Some chemical pesticides stimulate mite reproduction. Because these products also kill the beneficial insects that naturally keep mite numbers in check, refrain from spraying whenever possible. If absolutely necessary, effective product controls include horticultural oil and insecticidal soap.

Tobacco Budworms/Geranium Budworms (*Heliothis virescens*)

North American geographical range: Eastern and southeastern United States., up into Southern Canada. They may also be present in certain western states.

Identification: Adult tobacco/geranium budworms are nocturnal moths. They're light brown with three dark brown bands across the wings. Adults cause no harm to plants, but their larvae devour flower buds and plant foliage. Caterpillars measure up to an inch in length, and can be yellow, green, brown, and even pink or maroon, depending on their life stage and food source.

Plants affected: Tobacco/geranium budworms commonly feed on the flower buds of nicotiana (flowering tobacco), zinnias, petunias, geraniums, ageratum, chrysanthemums, marigolds, snapdragons, verbena, portulaca, and others.

They may also feed on certain vegetable crops, including tomatoes, collards, and okra.

Feeding habits and damage: Tobacco/geranium budworms don't typically survive cold winters, but their range is expanding northward as the climate changes. Damage is first noted as holes in flower petals or flower buds that fail to open or go missing. Budworms can quickly chomp all the flower buds off a plant or leave the flowers ragged and torn. If no flower buds are available, they'll also eat foliage. Northern gardeners typically see budworms late in the season, while southern gardeners may see them year-round.

Physical controls: Budworm caterpillars are most active at dusk. Head out to the garden and handpick any you find.

Product controls: *Bacillus thuringiensis* (B.t.) products work great. Spinosad is another option.

Geranium or tobacco budworms can be yellow, green, brown, or even pink or maroon, depending on their food source and age. Despite how cute this little caterpillar is, it will readily devour flower buds and plant foliage.

Tomato and Tobacco Hornworms (*Manduca quinquemaculata* and *Manduca sexta*)

North American geographical range: All

Identification: Hornworms are the large, green larvae of nocturnal moths commonly called sphinx or hawk moths. Mature caterpillars can grow up to 5 in. long. They pupate underground.

Plants affected: Members of the nightshade family, including tomato, tobacco, potatoes, peppers, and eggplants.

Feeding habits and damage: Gardeners often find the dark pellets of excrement left behind by hornworms before they spot the caterpillars themselves. Damage in the form of missing leaves is first noted on the tops of plants where the caterpillars feed at night. They shelter under or on interior leaves during the day, often making them difficult to find.

Tobacco and tomato hornworms measure up to 5 in. long before dropping off their host plant and burrowing into the ground to pupate.

This tobacco hornworm has been parasitized by the cotesia wasp. The white, rice-like cocoons hanging off its back contain the wasp pupae.

Physical controls: Hornworms frequently fall prey to non-stinging parasitic wasps that use them as hosts for their developing young. The tiny cotesia wasp inserts eggs under the caterpillar's skin that eventually hatch into larval wasps. The larval wasps consume the inside of the hornworm's body and soon emerge through the hornworm's skin to spin external cocoons. If you spot a hornworm with white, rice-like sacks hanging from its back, don't disturb it: it's already stopped feeding and will soon die. Hornworms are also easily handpicked from plants.

Product controls: *Bacillus thuringiensis* (B.t.) and spinosad work but are seldom necessary. Handpicking is far more effective when you're growing just a few plants.

Whiteflies (*Trialeurodes vaporariorum* and several other species)

North American geographical range: All. Greenhouse and indoor pests year-round in the north. Outdoor pests during the summer in the north. Active year-round in southern regions.

Identification: Adult whiteflies are tiny, white, moth-like flies that measure only ¹⁄₂₀ to ¹⁄₁₀ in. Infested plants emit a cloud of flying insects when disturbed. They exude a sweet excrement called honeydew that leaves a sticky, shiny film on leaves and other nearby surfaces. Whitefly larvae are extremely tiny and do not have wings.

Plants affected: Almost any plant can host whiteflies, but common hosts include tomatoes, geraniums, sweet potatoes, citrus trees, bedding plants, poinsettias, and flowering tobacco.

Feeding habits and damage: Adult and immature whiteflies both feed by sucking plant juices from leaf undersides. Outdoor populations seldom do significant damage, except in the south. In greenhouses, where populations can grow to significant levels, whiteflies can be very problematic. Whitefly feeding weakens plants, yellows leaves, and causes wilt and leaf drop.

Physical controls: Whiteflies are easily trapped on yellow sticky cards placed just above plant tops.

Product controls: Insecticidal soap, horticultural oil, neem, citrus oil, hot pepper wax.

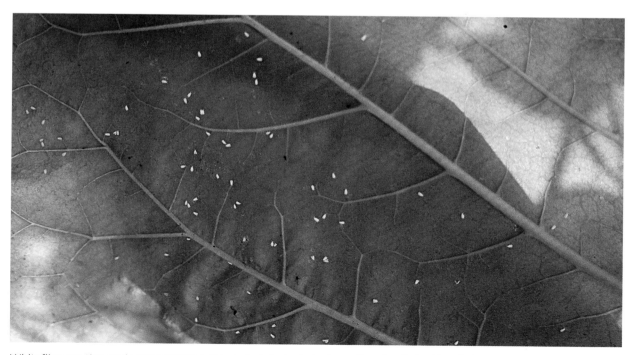

Whiteflies are tiny and very annoying. Severely infested plants emit a cloud of white, flying insects when disturbed.

COMMON BENEFICIAL INSECTS

The vast majority of the insects you'll encounter in your container garden are not harmful to your plants. Many serve to pollinate crops or break down organic matter, while others help you by consuming pest insects. Below you'll find seven common pest-munching, predatory, and parasitic insects you're sure to discover prowling around your plants in search of their next meal. All are found in a broad range of garden habitats across North America.

Hover or Syrphid Flies

Many species of hover flies look much like small wasps or bees, with a black and yellow striped abdomen, but they do not sting and aren't harmful to humans. The ¼ to ½ in. long adults can hover as they drink nectar from flowers, and they are important pollinators. It's the larvae that control pests. Hover fly larvae are small, brown or green maggots that hatch from eggs laid on plants infested with pests. Each larva can eat up to 500 pests before maturation. Adults cannot reproduce without pollen as a food source and since they don't have specialized mouthparts (nor do many other beneficial insects), plants with very shallow flowers are attractive to them. Plants like alyssum, aster, coreopsis, cosmos, daisies, fennel, mint, sunflowers, wild mustard, and dill are great choices to include in your container plantings. To maintain a steady population of these predators, make sure something is blooming in your container garden from the last frost in spring to the first frost in fall.

▲ Syrphid fly larvae are small maggots that prowl around plants, eating pests such as aphids, thrips, leafhoppers, and young caterpillars.

◀ Adult syrphid flies feed on nectar and pollen, and serve as important pollinators. Plant members of the daisy family to attract them to your garden.

Green Lacewings

These beautiful, slender insects are attracted to lights and are commonly found clinging to window screens on summer nights. The adults are light green with huge, transparent wings, threadlike antennae, and golden eyes. They measure up to an inch in length and consume pollen and nectar exclusively. Adult green lacewings lay eggs on the ends of long filaments, and several eggs lined up along a blade of grass look much like little lollipops in a row. The lacewing larvae that hatch from these eggs are fast-moving, flattened brown and white creatures with large, curved mandibles for grasping prey. They're only a ½-inch long but can consume up to 100 aphids per day—appropriately earning them the nickname "aphid lions." To lure them in, include angelica, caraway, coreopsis, goldenrod, yarrow, and tansy in your container garden.

▲ Lacewing larvae are predaceous and feed on many common pest insects, including aphids, caterpillar eggs, beetle larvae, corn earworms, spider mites, and others.

▼ Adult green lacewings are beautiful insects, with large, lace-like wings and bright gold eyes.

Ladybugs come in many different colors and with various spot patterns and other markings. This pink spotted ladybug is one of more than 480 different North American species.

Ladybug/Ladybird/Lady Beetle

With over 480 different species in North America, ladybugs may be the most recognizable of all beneficial insects. But not all ladybugs are red with black polka-dots. Ladybugs can be yellow, cream, brown, orange, black, gray, or pink, depending on the species. They can have lots of spots or no spots at all. They can be striped or mottled, or have bands of black running down their wing covers. But regardless of their coloration, ladybugs are great for the garden. These beetles measure between ⅙ and ½ in. long, but they're all dome-shaped with hard wing covers and six legs. Almost all ladybugs are predators, consuming such common pests as aphids, scale, mites, mealybugs, small caterpillars, whiteflies, mites, and psyllids. It's also important to note that larval ladybugs eat pest insects, too. Looking much like small, flattened, six-legged

alligators, ladybug larvae might look a little scary, but they're very good for the garden. Because adult ladybugs need to eat pollen and nectar to reproduce, planting their favorite nectar sources in your container garden can naturally support a healthy population of these important insects. Good plants are caraway, cilantro, dill, fennel, sunflowers, cosmos, daisies, and laceflower.

One important item to note: do not purchase ladybugs at your local nursery and release them into your garden. Most of the ladybugs you find for sale are a species called the convergent ladybug, which are wild-collected during their mass winter hibernation in some parts of the American West. They're then packaged and shipped around the country for sale. This is a dangerous practice because not only does it affect wild populations of this ladybug, it can also potentially spread diseases to other wild ladybug populations. If you purchase ladybugs for release, only buy insectary-reared insects.

Ladybug larvae are also voracious pest-munchers. They look much like tiny, six-legged alligators. This one is ready to chow down on some aphids.

Minute Pirate Bugs

These tiny insects are the smallest of the predatory true bugs commonly found in backyards across North America. Measuring a mere ⅛ in., the oval-shaped adult is black with white wing patches. The teardrop-shaped nymphs are even smaller and are orange or yellow in color. Both are surprisingly fast-moving, and both feed by piercing prey with their needle-like mouthpart. Minute pirate bugs feed on spider mites, thrips, aphids, insect eggs, small caterpillars, lace bugs, scale, whiteflies, and others. To attract them to your container garden, plant lots of spring-flowering plants. Since minute pirate bugs are often the first predators to emerge in the spring, before prey becomes readily available, they depend on early-season pollen and plant sap as a food source. Good plant choices for this beneficial insect include: basket of gold, oregano, sage, wallflower, sweet alyssum, crimson clover, and parsley.

Parasitic wasps can be as tiny as a gnat or as large as your pinky finger. They use hundreds of different pest insects to house and feed their developing young. This one is seeking out an aphid host.

Minute pirate bugs may be tiny, but they play a huge role in controlling pests. Their favorite lunch includes aphids, bean beetles, spider mites, leafhoppers, whiteflies, and many others.

Parasitic Wasps

There are over 6,000 different species of parasitic wasps in North America. These tiny, non-stinging wasps are some of the most beneficial insects in the garden and are known to parasitize over 300 species of pests. Most species of parasitic wasps measure between ⅟₃₂ and ½ in. long. Some species have pointed ovipositors that look a lot like an exaggerated stinger, but these are only used for laying eggs. Most female wasps lay eggs inside or on host insects. The eggs hatch and consume the prey, eventually killing it. Some species pupate in external cocoons, including the cotesia wasp that attacks tomato hornworms, while others pupate within the host's body (like the tiny *Aphidius* wasp that attacks aphid colonies). Depending on the wasp species, they can help control aphids, beetle larvae, bagworms, cabbage worms, potato beetles, corn ear worms, cucumber beetles, cutworms, caterpillars, Japanese beetles, leafminers, sawfly larvae, squash vine borers, and many other pests. Adult wasps consume nectar and pollen, and they're attracted to plants like allium, alyssum, cosmos, dill, fennel, thyme, yarrow, coneflowers, sunflowers, helianthus, and others.

Spiders

Though they aren't officially insects (they're arachnids), spiders are very beneficial to gardeners. There are 38,000 known species of spiders in the world. Some species are hairy, others are smooth. They range in color from drab brown to stark white, intense yellow, or various patterns of bright colors. They catch their prey and feed by liquefying an insect and "drinking" it. Which insects a particular spider feeds upon depends on its size and specialization, but all spiders are predators. They can help rid your garden of aphids, asparagus beetles, Colorado potato beetles, cutworms, various pest caterpillars, lace bugs, spider mites, squash bugs, and many others. Spiders find safe habitat in just about any sheltered area.

Tachinid Flies

This is North America's largest and most important group of parasitic flies, with 1,300 different species. Adults resemble small houseflies covered in dark, bristly hairs. They measure ⅓ to ¾ in. long. Adult flies are important pollinators, while their young are the pest eaters. They're parasitoids, because female tachinid flies deposit eggs or leave larvae directly onto the bodies of host insects, including various caterpillars, beetles squash bugs, sawfly larvae, four lined plant bugs, and many others. The eggs hatch, and the larvae tunnel into the host's body, consuming and eventually killing it. Some species also lay eggs on plants in hopes that they'll be ingested by a host as the plant is eaten. Most often, the fly larva then pupates within its host and emerges as an adult.

Despite their creepy appearance, spiders are incredibly good for the garden. Some species trap pests in their webs, while others, such as this wolf spider, crawl around the garden at night, consuming their prey.

A female tachinid fly has laid a tiny, white oval egg on this caterpillar. After hatching, the larva will tunnel into the caterpillar and eventually kill it.

Tachinid flies might look like common houseflies, but they aren't. These parasitic flies use many common garden pests as hosts for their developing young.

Since adult tachinid flies use nectar and pollen as a food source, they're attracted to gardens and containers rich in flowering herbs, particularly those in the dill (*Apiaceae*) family. Cilantro, dill, fennel, golden Alexander, and parsley are attractive to them, as are members of the daisy family, including aster, chamomile, feverfew, ox-eye daisy, coreopsis, and Shasta daisies.

One of the best ways to ensure there's an ample amount of "good" bugs in your container garden is to inter-plant vegetables with flowering annuals and herbs to provide these beneficial bugs with nectar and pollen. The following project is designed to include some of the best plants for attracting and supporting beneficial, pest-munching insects.

GOOD BUG WHEEL-BARROW GARDEN

If you have an old wheelbarrow sitting around, this is the perfect way to give it a new, meaningful life. In fact, if the wheelbarrow has holes rusted through, that's even better—there's no need to add drainage holes! Even flat or missing tires don't matter for this project—any old wheelbarrow will do.

MATERIALS NEEDED

Wheelbarrow

Enough 50/50 potting soil and compost blend to fill the wheelbarrow

10 to 15 plants selected from the list of beneficial insect-supporting annual plants (right)

TOOLS NEEDED

Scratch awl

Hammer

Eye protection

Plant List of Recommended Annuals:

- Signet marigolds (*Tagetes tenuifolia*)
- Cilantro
- Dill
- Basil
- Chamomile
- Feverfew
- Salvias
- Caraway (*Carum carvi*)
- Annual tickseed (*Coreopsis tinctoria*)
- Parsley
- Anise (*Pimpinella anisum*)
- Lemon balm (*Melissa officinalis*)
- Bachelor's buttons (*Centaurea cyanus*)
- Lacy phacelia
- Toothpick weed (*Ammi visnaga*)
- Borage (*Borago officinalis*)
- Calendula (*Calendula officinalis*)
- Chervil (*Anthriscus cerefolium*)
- Cosmos
- Sweet alyssum
- Sweet marjoram
- Dwarf sunflowers

HOW TO MAKE A GOOD BUG WHEELBARROW GARDEN

STEP 1 Flip the wheelbarrow upside down and use the hammer and scratch awl to create eight to ten ½-in. drainage holes in the bottom of the wheelbarrow, if there are no openings or holes already present. Turn the wheelbarrow upright and fill it with the potting soil blend to within 1 in. of the upper rim.

STEP 2 Choose a mixture of flowering plants chosen from the list above and add them to the wheelbarrow. You can also plant perennials in your wheelbarrow planter, just remember to pull them from the wheelbarrow and plant them somewhere in the ground before winter arrives, because many are not winter-hardy when grown in containers.

STEP 3 Water your newly planted wheelbarrow well and maintain it throughout the growing season. It's fine to harvest a few herb sprouts from time to time, but in order for these plants to support beneficial insects, they have to be allowed to come into flower. Don't overharvest the herbs you include, and encourage them to bloom.

NOTE: Feel free to move the wheelbarrow around your patio or garden, but make sure it receives a minimum of 6 hours of full sun per day.

PATHOGEN PROBLEMS

In addition to insect pests causing potential trouble in your container garden, there are a handful of plant pathogens that may appear from time to time. Though some are more common than others, most will not become regular issues in a container garden. Pathogens that live in the soil (soilborne) aren't typically problematic in containers, especially when the containers are filled with a fresh compost/potting soil blend every year. But pathogens that spread via wind, water, and insects can certainly prove problematic to container gardeners.

It's important to recognize that when it comes to these disease organisms, a little prevention goes a long, long way. Your first line of defense against these issues is this simple three-step plan:

1. Plant only resistant varieties. This all-important step essentially designs the pathogen out of the system. By choosing vegetable, herb, fruit, and flower varieties with natural resistance to a particular pathogen, you're reducing your chances of ever facing the disease to begin with. For example, if you've battled a fungal issue called powdery mildew on your bee balm plants in the past, plant only selections of bee balm with noted powdery mildew resistance in the future. For nearly all of the pathogens listed below, there are varieties of plants bred to be resistant to that particular disease organism. When you purchase seeds or plants from a local nursery or catalog, any disease resistance should be noted on the packet or tag. Do your homework and pay attention to this information. It can save you a lot of trouble down the line.

By selecting varieties with a natural resistance to pathogens such as powdery mildew, you'll save yourself a lot of trouble.

2. Maximize air circulation. Many disease organisms are fungal, and fungal spores thrive in wet and humid conditions. By spacing plants properly, and thereby increasing air movement around them, fungal issues can be slowed or stifled. Give your plants plenty of room; don't overstuff your containers.

3. Employ good cultural practices. From pruning and fertilizing to watering and harvesting, the care and maintenance tasks you perform in the garden play a huge role in promoting—or discouraging—diseases of all sorts.

- Water plants during the morning, whenever possible, to allow enough time for the foliage to completely dry before nightfall.
- Clean your pruning shears after working on a diseased plant. A simple application of a spray disinfectant or a quick dip in a 10% bleach solution is enough to kill most plant pathogens on pruning equipment.
- Don't overfertilize plants. Succulent, tender foliage is more susceptible to certain fungal attacks.
- Avoid working with wet foliage. Fungal spores spread easily from plant to plant on water droplets clinging to your skin or clothes.
- Regularly inspect container plants for signs of disease. Remove infected foliage and discard it in the trash or bury it to prevent further spread.

Common Plant Pathogens

Viral, bacterial, and fungal diseases are sometimes a problem in the garden, but they need to be properly identified in order to be treated effectively. Here are some of the common pathogens you might encounter in your container garden.

Septoria Leaf Spot (*Septoria lycopersici*)

Description: This fungal disease appears as tiny, round splotches on the leaves. The spots have dark brown edges and lighter centers. There are usually many spots on each leaf, and it typically occurs on the lower leaves first, just after the first green fruits appear. Leaves eventually turn yellow and then brown and fall off.

Plants affected: Tomatoes and ground cherries (another species of septoria leaf spot attacks 'Goldsturm' rudbeckia).

Solutions: Be sure to remove diseased plants at the end of the season to prevent the spores from overwintering on-site. Remove and destroy infected leaves as soon as you spot them and clean empty containers with a 10% bleach solution at the end of the season. Organic fungicides based on copper or *Bacillus subtilis* are effective, especially when used as a preventative measure.

The distinctive tiny round splotches on this leaf indicate an infection of septoria leaf spot. Often appearing on the lowest leaves first, this fungal disease is most common on tomatoes.

Early blight is a common fungal disease. It starts as bull's-eye-shaped spots that quickly progress to leaf shriveling and drop. The bottom leaves are always affected first.

Early Blight (*Alternaria solani*)

Description: This common fungus first appears as irregularly shaped, bulls-eyed brown spots on infected plants. Often, the leaf tissue around the spot turns yellow. Early blight always appears first on the lower leaves of the plant. If left untreated, the leaves turn yellow, develop dark irregular splotches of infected tissue, and fall off, but the fruit will continue to ripen. In severe cases, the fruit can also be affected.

Plants affected: Tomatoes, potatoes, eggplants, and peppers.

Solution: The pathogen lives in the soil, and once a garden has shown signs of the early blight fungus, it's there to stay because the organism easily overwinters in the soil. However, for container gardeners, early blight is far less problematic. Be sure to wash empty containers with a 10% bleach solution at the end of the year to prevent spores from spreading via infected plant debris. Fortunately, most tomatoes will continue to produce even with moderately severe cases of early blight. Organic fungicides based on *Bacillus subtilis*, potassium bicarbonate, or copper are effective in preventing and managing this disease.

Late Blight (*Phytophthora infestans*)

Description: Late blight is one of the most destructive diseases of tomatoes and potatoes, but it's not very common, particularly in the north where it doesn't survive the winter without a host plant. This pathogen causes irregularly shaped splotches that are slimy and water-soaked. They often occur on the top-most leaves and stems first. Eventually, the spots merge together and cause entire leaves to rot on the vine. There may also be masses of white spores on the leaf undersides, as well. In northern regions, this organism can only overwinter on infected potato tubers that survive underground. In the south, however, where freezing temperatures don't occur, it easily survives the winter. Come spring, the spores are readily blown north where cool, wet, spring weather conditions can cause it to thrive.

Plants affected: Tomatoes and potatoes.

Solution: The spores of this disease are fast-spreading, moving on the wind for miles. Planting only locally grown plants can help keep the pathogen out of your area. Once late blight strikes, there is little a gardener can do except tear up the plants, put them in a garbage bag, and throw them out to keep the disease from spreading. Organic fungicides based on *Bacillus subtilis* are somewhat effective.

Late blight is a devastatingly fatal disease that thankfully doesn't strike often. It affects tomatoes and potatoes.

Southern Bacterial Wilt (*Ralstonia solanacearum*)

Description: Plants infected by this bacterial disease are in big trouble. Though it is naturally found only in tropical regions and greenhouses, the disease often arrives to the garden via purchased plants grown in places where the disease is present. It is soilborne but can be transmitted by soil, water, plant matter, and even on clothes and tools. Initially only one or two leaves may wilt during the day, while the remaining leaves appear healthy. As the infection spreads, more leaves wilt and yellow until the entire plant succumbs, despite the stem remaining upright. Lower stems may develop dark brown splotches. Slimy, viscous ooze comes out of the stems when they are cut. When cut stems are placed in water, milky streams of bacteria are seen streaming out of the cut.

Plants affected: Southern wilt affects almost 200 different species of plants. In North America, it attacks geraniums, impatiens, mums, zinnia, salvia, petunias, eggplants, verbenas, and many other bedding and vegetable plants.

Solution: Bacterial wilt is soilborne and can survive for long periods in the soil on roots and plant debris. Like many other diseases, it favors high temperatures and high humidity. Sadly, there is no cure for this disease. Once confirmed, infected plants must be removed and discarded in the garbage. Keep them out of the compost pile.

Cercospora Leaf Spot (*Cercospora* spp.)

Description: The first sign of this fungal disease is small circular, yellow lesions on the lower foliage. Eventually the lesions develop a soft gray fuzz at the center with a dark brown ring around the exterior. Sometimes concentric rings appear. The disease is sometimes also called "frog eyes" because of this. In severe infestations, defoliation may occur and fruit size and production may be reduced.

Plants affected: There are many different species of this fungal pathogen, and each species affects a different species or group of plants. Common hosts include hydrangeas, beets, eggplants, okra, carrots, roses, beans, peppers, and figs.

Solution: Cercospora leaf spot survives the winter in plant debris, and when spring arrives the spores are spread by wind, rain, people, and animals. To keep spores off plants, clean up and dispose of infected leaves and fruits at the end of the season and wash all pots with a 10% bleach solution. Cercospora leaf spot is mostly an aesthetic issue for home gardeners and fungicide use often isn't necessary.

Fusarium Wilt (*Fusarium oxysporum*)

Description: Fusarium wilt symptoms often begin with drooping leaf petioles. Sometimes a single branch may wilt before the rest of the plant. Wilting often starts with the lower leaves, quickly progressing up the plant until the whole thing collapses. The entire plant may be killed, often before the plant reaches maturity. If you cut the main stem of an infected plant, there will be dark streaks running lengthwise through the stem. Dark brown, sunken, cankers may be seen at the base of the plant.

Plants affected: A broad range of plants can succumb to fusarium wilt, including tomatoes, eggplants, potatoes, daffodils, legumes, cucumbers, melons, as well as certain ornamental plants.

Solution: The fusarium fungus survives in the soil for several years and is spread by equipment, water, and plant debris. Like many other diseases, it favors warm soil and high moisture. Fusarium wilt is typically not problematic in container gardens, as long as the containers are disinfected with a 10% bleach solution at the start of the growing season and a fresh potting soil/compost blend is used to fill the container each year.

Verticillium Wilt (*Verticillium* spp.)

Description: Verticillium wilt is caused by a group of soilborne pathogens that block the vascular system of the plant, causing it to wilt. Symptoms progress slowly; often the foliage on one branch wilts suddenly. As the disease progresses, the plant turns yellow and withers, one branch at a time. Eventually, the entire plant dies. Cutting through the main stem of the plant will reveal dark brown discoloration inside. Symptoms are most likely to appear in July and August.

Plants affected: Verticillium wilt affects hundreds of species of vegetables, herbs, flowers, and woody trees and shrubs.

Solution: Verticillium fungi can survive for many years in the soil and on plants. They prefer slightly cooler summer temperatures (between 70 and 80°F). Because this organism resides in the soil, changing the potting soil/compost blend in your containers every year will suppress it. Also, clean containers with a 10% bleach solution before filling and planting them. Plant resistant varieties whenever possible, as there are no effective fungicides.

The first signs of a basil downy mildew infection look a lot like a spider mite infestation. Pale yellow mottling between leaf veins and tiny purplish-gray spores on the leaf undersides are identifying features.

Basil Downy Mildew (*Peronospora belbahrii*)

Description: Basil downy mildew is a recently introduced disease that's incredibly destructive to its namesake herb. First found in Florida in 2007, basil downy mildew has since spread across much of North America. The fungus is air-borne, seed-borne, and tissue-borne, making it extremely easy for the disease to spread via contaminated seed, plants, or air currents. Because this disease looks at first like a nutritional deficiency or a spider mite infestation, it's difficult to diagnose. Basil downy mildew first appears as pale yellow mottling between the veins on the upper leaf surface and miniscule purplish-gray spores splattered on the lower leaf surface. The disease eventually progresses to dark brown to black irregular splotches and mottling on the leaves. You'll also see the powdery, dark gray spore clusters on the leaf undersides. The disease does not live in the soil.

Plants affected: Basil.

Solution: Start battling this disease by planting only basil varieties with some resistance. Studies have shown that all sweet basil varieties are highly susceptible. Lemon, Thai, 'Red Rubin', 'Spice', and 'Red Leaf' basils were noted as being the least susceptible. Breeders are currently trying to breed resistance into new basil varieties. Be sure to properly space the plants, and remove and throw out any plants with a suspected infestation immediately. Organic fungicides are also an option, though they must be applied early and often, and as soon as symptoms are noticed. Potassium bicarbonate–based fungicides have been shown to be effective against the fungus.

Black Spot (*Diplocarpon rosae*)

Description: Black spot is a fungal disease that causes dark spots to appear on the leaves of rose plants, and once it takes hold the leaves eventually turn yellow and fall off. During particularly bad years, the plant may become completely defoliated. Black spot is a devastating disease for rose growers across most of North America.

Plants affected: Roses.

Solution: Aside from planting resistant varieties, be sure to remove infected leaves immediately and toss them into the garbage or burn them. Water roses only at ground level; avoid overhead sprinklers. Black spot easily overwinters on fallen foliage, so a good leaf clean-up in the autumn helps. Organic fungicides based on potassium bicarbonate or *Bacillus subtilis* serve to prevent and manage black spot infections.

Black spot is a common fungal infection on roses. It causes dark spots on the leaves that eventually cause the foliage to turn yellow and drop off.

Powdery mildew makes plant leaves look as if they've been dusted with baby powder. Though it's largely an aesthetic problem, a severe powdery mildew infection can affect photosynthesis and plant growth.

Powdery Mildew (many species)

Description: Powdery mildew is the result of several different species of fungal organisms that live on the leaves of certain plants. It is largely an aesthetic issue. Signs of a powdery mildew infection are quite distinctive. White powdery spots appear on the leaves and stems, most often on the lower leaves first.

Plants affected: Lilacs, phlox, bee balm, cucumbers, grapes, squash, melons, and many other common plants are susceptible.

Solution: Aside from choosing resistant varieties, keep the leaves as dry as possible. Since powdery mildew is largely an aesthetic issue, there's no need to go to extreme measures to save an infected plant. Organic fungicides, such as those based on *Bacillus subtilis* and potassium bicarbonate, help keep powdery mildew in check.

Bacterial Wilt (*Erwinia tracheiphila*)

Description: Bacterial wilt begins as wilting and drying of individual leaves. Because this bacterium is spread by cucumber beetles, wilted leaves may also show signs of cucumber beetle feeding damage. More leaves shrivel as the stems dry out. Soon, entire vines wilt, particularly during the day. Eventually, the entire plant dies. For confirmation, cut a wilted stem near its base and touch your fingertip to the cut. Slowly pull your finger away from the cut. If thin, white strands of ooze thread from your finger to the plant, bacterial wilt is probably to blame.

Plants affected: All members of the cucurbit family. Cucumbers and muskmelons are most susceptible with pumpkins and winter and summer squash showing occasional signs of infection. Watermelons rarely fall victim.

Solution: Plant only bacterial wilt-resistant or tolerant varieties. Good cucumber choices include, 'County Fair', 'Salad Bush', 'Saladin', and 'Marketmore 76'. Butternut and acorn squash are also resistant. The key to controlling bacterial wilt is controlling the cucumber beetle. Cover young plants with floating row cover and leave it in place until the plants come into flower to allow access to pollinators. Trap adult beetles by placing yellow sticky cards just above the plant tops.

Bacterial wilt is spread by cucumber beetles and affects cucumbers and other members of the melon and squash family. This plant has succumbed to bacterial wilt.

Botrytis or Gray Mold (*Botrytis* spp.)

Description: The botrytis fungus is probably the costliest disease in the greenhouse industry because it affects such a broad range of plants, and it can damage almost any part of the plant, including the leaves, stems, flowers, fruits, and buds. It is fast growing and spreads rapidly, and often enters through an injury site. Botrytis first appears as white to gray splotches on the leaves with fuzzy or dusty spores clearly visible. These spores spread via water, wind, and physical contact. Rot eventually forms on the infected tissue, leading to complete bud, leaf, stem, fruit, or flower rot.

Plants affected: Botrytis affects thousands of different plant species but is quite common on geraniums, strawberries, grapes, cyclamen, chrysanthemums, roses, dahlias, and peonies.

Solutions: Remove and dispose of any infected tissue. Make sure all your pruning equipment is sanitized after working on a plant with a botrytis infection. In addition to overwintering in the soil and on stem and leaf tissue, botrytis may also overwinter on infected fruit left clinging to branches and plants, so remove all infected berries and fruits at the end of the growing season. Copper-based organic fungicides, as well as those based on *Bacillus subtilis* and potassium bicarbonate, are effective controls. Botrytis, along with a handful of other fungal issues, is a common problem on ripening strawberries. One of the easiest ways to prevent these fungal diseases is to grow strawberries in containers. Sterile potting soil is pathogen-free and gives strawberry plants a good start. And, as long as you don't put your containers too close together, growing strawberries in pots helps improve air circulation around the plants as well, allowing the fruits to dry more quickly after rain and allowing you to have better control over plant spacing.

PHYSIOLOGICAL PROBLEMS

Occasionally a problem may crop up in your container garden that has nothing to do with an insect or pathogen, but instead is the result of something in the environment. Physiological disorders can be attributed to things like poor light levels, road salt exposure, hail or frost damage, herbicide injury, sunscald, drought, or a nutrient deficiency.

Here are a few physiological problems you may encounter occasionally in your container garden.

Cracked tomatoes. A problem tied to moisture levels, skin cracking most often occurs just after a period of heavy rainfall, primarily after a prolonged period of dry weather. The plant uptakes water from the soil, and it collects in the developing fruits. The skin can only expand to hold the excess moisture for so long before it cracks open. Some tomato varieties are more prone to cracking than others. Cracked fruits should be eaten within a day or two of harvest, and you may find they have a more diluted flavor.

Blossom-end rot. This disorder appears as a sunken, dark lesion on the bottom-end (or blossom-end) of the developing fruit. Tomatoes,

Blossom end rot is the result of inconsistent irrigation. It appears as a sunken, dark lesion at the bottom end of tomatoes, peppers, and eggplants.

peppers, and eggplants develop blossom-end rot when there is a lack of calcium in the growing fruit. The trouble is not necessarily that your soil is calcium-deficient, but rather that the calcium can't get into the plant. Calcium comes into a plant with water, and when plants are subjected to dry periods, the calcium cannot move into the fruits. This leads to a calcium deficiency and blossom-end rot. The key to staving off this disorder is proper mulching and watering. Do not allow your containers to completely dry out between waterings. Consistent soil moisture is key.

Hollow potatoes. If you slice open a homegrown potato and there's a hollow spot in the center, it's often due to environmental or nutritional stress. Periods of slow growth followed by periods of fast growth are often to blame. This growth pattern may be the result of heavy rains after a prolonged dry period or even a mid-season fertilizer application. To prevent "hollow heart" in container-grown potatoes, mulch the container well and use a fresh blend of potting soil and compost to fill the containers every year. Make sure the containers receive consistent moisture throughout the growing season.

Curled leaves. Leaf curl is a physiological problem often related to fluctuations in moisture levels. For many tomato varieties, curling up their lower leaves is a way to protect the plant from further moisture loss by protecting the pores on the leaf surface. Some varieties are more prone to leaf curl than others. If the leaves are blemish-free, leaf curl on the older leaves isn't anything to worry about. But curling leaves can also be a sign of root wilts such as fusarium and verticillium wilt, though when these wilts are involved, the entire plant is affected, with every leaf curling and drooping, not just a few. Mulch plants well at the beginning of the season to even out soil moisture levels, and make sure your containers are well watered.

No flowers. A complete lack of flowers on ornamental or vegetable plants could be due to too much nitrogen in the soil. Excessive nitrogen encourages green shoot growth at the expense of flower and fruit production. This typically isn't problematic in container gardens, as long as you're using a balanced fertilizer and a fresh potting soil/compost blend to fill your containers every season.

Deformed fruits and veggies, or none at all. In order to produce fruit, most flowers need to be pollinated, and if there aren't enough pollinating insects around, fruit and veggie production may not occur. Lack of pollination exhibits as the lack of fruit formation, blossom drop, or deformed fruits that are often puny and shriveled at one end. It takes multiple visits from a pollinating insect to form a cucumber or an eggplant, not just one. Do not use pesticides on your

Cracked tomatoes are the result of extreme fluctuations in soil moisture levels. Mulch plants well and keep them evenly watered to avoid this problem.

containers, and encourage pollinators by planting lots of flowering plants side by side with your veggies. Peppers, eggplants, and tomatoes are self-pollinating (meaning each flower pollinates itself), but they need the wind or a bumblebee to shake the flowers and knock the pollen loose inside. If your tomatoes, eggplants, and peppers aren't setting fruit, you can use an electric toothbrush to vibrate the pollen around and fertilize the flower by turning it on and placing it on the flower stem, just above the flower, for a few seconds every morning. Vegetables in the cucumber family, like melons, squash, cucumbers, and pumpkins, have separate male and female flowers and a pollinator is needed to move the pollen from the male flowers to the female flowers. If you aren't getting fruits on these crops, try using a paintbrush to move pollen from the male flowers (those with a straight stem) to the female flowers (those with a bulbous base) anytime between morning and mid-day.

Blossom drop or fruit drop. Young, developing fruits and/or blossoms are sometimes shed from a plant for several different reasons. It may occur due to a lack of proper pollination or because the plant is stressed. Some plants do not produce fruit when temperatures aren't ideal. For example, bell peppers will abort their blossoms or young fruits when daytime temperatures rise above 90°F and nights are warmer than 75°F. They may also drop their blooms if temperatures are too cool. Daytime temperatures over 90°F. or nighttime temps below 55°F will limit tomato production, too.

Deformed cucumbers, such as this one, may have contorted growth or a "stubby" malformed end. Such growth is the result of poor pollination.

All these troubleshooting tips make container gardening seem like a battle, but I assure you it isn't. This advice is meant to arm you with the knowledge to nip potential problems in the bud, before they become discouraging.

chapter 5

Harvesting and Seasonal Considerations

When planting a container garden at the start of the growing season, it's sometimes difficult to imagine what it will look like by the time the growing season comes to an end. Even after experience teaches you what to expect, any particular growing season can be unpredictable. For most gardeners, the outcome is a mixture of awe and exhilaration, with a little disappointment thrown in just to keep us humble. Most years you find yourself saying, "I can't believe I grew that!" But, occasionally you might also lament, "I can't believe I killed that." It's all part of gardening.

Although nature as a whole is unpredictable, there are many aspects of it that are not. Much of nature is cyclical: birth and death repeated over and over again. From the passage of the seasons and the movements of migrating animals to plant dormancy and the life cycle of a butterfly, these are parts of nature that *are* predictable. The biggest ones, of course, involve the life cycles of the plants we grow and the change of the seasons—cycles we can predict and use to our benefit. It might be something as simple as planting a pepper in the spring so you

get fruits in the summer before the plant is killed by frost, or adding a late-blooming perennial so there's nectar available for migrating monarchs. Gardeners think about the predictable, cyclical parts of nature all the time when making choices.

Planting cool-weather-loving crops, such as this bok choy (*Brassica rapa* subsp. *chinensis*), in the early spring or fall, results in better harvests.

◀ Trying new plants always feels like a risk, but you never know when you'll strike gold and find a new favorite.

We also consider the cycles of nature as we care for our gardens throughout the growing season. We plant flowering bulbs such as daffodils and tulips in the fall so they have time to grow roots before blooming the following spring, but we plant frost-sensitive basil in the late spring, after the danger of freezing temperatures has passed. We sow cool-weather-loving crops such as lettuce and radish very early or very late in the season, and harvest garlic when the plants begin to die back in high summer. Gardeners complete all sorts of tasks in a predictable fashion, using multiple cues from nature to time everything as perfectly as we can.

While Chapters 1 and 2 walked you through the early part of the container gardening process, and Chapters 3 and 4 honed in on cultural techniques and troubleshooting, this chapter takes the next step. In the first part of this chapter, we move another step forward through the cycle of the growing season and focus on the period of time when your plants reach maturity and need to be harvested. You'll learn valuable tips for optimizing the harvest, timing it properly, and improving the shelf-life of the fruits and veggies you've grown. The second part of this chapter is dedicated to what happens when autumn arrives and the season comes full circle. I'll offer some great ideas for freshening up late-season containers and using them as holiday decor. Also included are guidelines for overwintering plants and properly emptying and storing your containers throughout the winter months to prolong their life.

Radishes are one of the fastest growing vegetable crops. Knowing the days to maturity for a particular crop means you won't have to guess when it's ready to be picked.

HARVESTING

While autumn is often considered to be the season of harvest, the truth is that in a container garden where a variety of vegetables are growing, harvesting occurs off and on throughout most of the growing season. The timing of your harvests depends on which fruits and vegetables you're growing. Essentially, you'll be harvesting as necessary. Here are a few tips to help you maximize the yields and shelf-life of some of the more common crops you may be growing in your containerized veggie patch.

Pay attention to the "days to maturity" noted on the seed packet or nursery pot tag of each variety. This number reflects the amount of time that a specific plant requires to reach maturity. There is a great amount of variability among days to maturity for different crops. For example, radishes, one of the fastest growing vegetable crops, mature in as little as 30 to 45 days, while most sweet potato varieties take a good 110 days until they're ready for harvest. When planning your garden, pay attention to this important number and plan accordingly.

Continual harvests increase the yields of many different crops. For vegetables whose edible portion is a fruit or legume that develops from a flower, such as tomatoes, eggplants, peppers, cucumbers, beans, peas, and the like, the more frequently you harvest the ripe veggies, the more flowers the plant produces, extending the harvest and production of the plant. In other words, the more you pick most varieties of these plants, the more veggies they produce.

Root crops, such as carrots, turnips, beets, and radishes, don't get "ripe" per se, but rather they can be pulled from the soil and eaten at any point in their development. They can be harvested while still young as a "baby vegetable," or they can

The more frequently you harvest ripe peppers, the more fruits the plant will produce. The same goes for many other crops, including tomatoes, beans, and cucumbers.

be allowed to reach full maturity before harvest. It all depends on the flavor and texture you're aiming for. Unwashed root crops can be stored in a bag in the fridge or in a box in a root cellar or cool basement. You can also bury root crops in a bin of damp sand for the longest shelf life. Keep the sand-filled bin in a root cellar or basement that's cold but doesn't freeze. Beets are one of the easiest root crops to grow in containers. The next project features a very cool way to grow a beautiful combination of beets and Swiss chard in a unique raised planter.

BEET BOX

This raised planter is perfect for gardeners who want to remain upright while growing their own veggies, and its small size is a great fit for petite patios and balconies. This project combines a bar stool and a couple of old wooden wine crates or CD storage boxes to make a fun container for growing beets and Swiss chard. If these two veggies aren't your thing, you can use this raised planter to grow lettuce, mustard greens (*Brassica juncea*), radish, spinach, or any other small-statured crop instead. If you use an old CD storage box, each separate compartment is the perfect amount of space for one or two plants.

HOW TO MAKE A BEET BOX

STEP 1   Use a tape measure to find the exact center of the bar stool seat. Then use a marker or wax pencil to draw a line through the middle to separate the top of the stool into two equal hemispheres. If you'd like, you can paint the wooden boxes with spray paint before proceeding to the next step.

STEP 2   To attach the wooden crates to the top of the stool, begin by lining the long edge of one of the crates up with the marked center line. Use the cordless drill equipped with a driving bit to screw six to eight wood screws through the bottom surface of the wooden crate and into the top of the stool.

STEP 3   Line one of the long sides of the second box up with the long edge of the first and screw that one to the top of the stool seat with another six to eight screws. For increased stability, use wood screws to attach the two wooden boxes together along the length of their adjacent long sides. Use a ½ in. drill bit to make six drainage holes in the bottom of the wooden boxes, three down each side. Make sure the drainage holes are along the outer edge of the boxes' bottoms, so they aren't blocked by the stool seat.

STEP 4   Fill the boxes with the potting soil and compost blend to the upper rim. Plant the beet and chard plants or seeds, alternating them for added interest. If you use your beet box to grow lettuce or other greens, you can grow them in a dense mat and harvest them as baby greens, or you can space the plants out and allow them to mature into full-sized heads.

Leafy greens and lettuces are another group of fast-growing vegetables that can be harvested both in the "baby" stage or at full maturity. Many lettuces and garden greens, such as kale, collards, spinach, and mustard, much prefer the cooler weather of spring and fall, making them a great choice for early-season and late-season container gardening. The days to maturity indicated on the seed packet of these vegetables notes the amount of time it takes for them to fully develop, but almost all leafy greens can be harvested when they're just few weeks old. Unwashed, harvested greens will keep for several days when stored in a plastic bag in the fridge.

For tomatoes, ripeness isn't always tied to the color of the fruits. There are plenty of tomato varieties that are green, yellow, pink, white, orange, or even black at maturity. Instead of relying on color to determine ripeness, gently squeeze the fruit between your thumb and fingers or press a thumb into the blossom end. Ripe tomatoes are slightly soft and your thumb should make a slight imprint. Tomatoes should always be stored on the countertop and never in the fridge.

Melons are among the most difficult when it comes to determining the ripeness of the fruits, but here are some excellent guidelines you can use beyond noting the days to maturity for each variety. Harvested melons can be stored on the counter or in the fridge.

To pick watermelons at their peak flavor, check the curly tendril closest to the fruit every day. When it dries and turns brown, the melon is ready for harvest. There will also be a bright yellow spot on the bottom of the fruit. Remember, watermelons will not ripen once they're severed from the vine, so waiting until they're fully ripe is absolutely necessary for the sweetest flavor.

For cantaloupes, honeydews, and other muskmelons: types with netted skin turn yellowish and fall easily off the vine when ripe; and smooth-skinned types will lose their fine, peach-like hairs and feel waxy when ripe, but they'll have to be cut from the vine.

Smell is another good indicator of ripeness. All melons smell fruity and lush at the blossom end when ripe.

The ripeness of tomatoes isn't determined by their color. Instead, gently squeeze the fruit between your thumb and fingers. Ripe tomatoes are soft enough that your thumb makes a slight impression.

Potatoes can be grown in just about any deep container. Mature potatoes are ready to be dug 2 to 3 weeks after the plants die back.

Cucumber ripeness depends both on the specific variety and what you plan to use them for. For example, if you plan to make tiny pickles, you'll want to grow pickling cucumbers and harvest them when they reach the size of your thumb. But if you plan to cut them into dill pickle spears or bread and butter pickle rounds, wait until the fruits are 6 to 8 in. long before removing them from the vine. For fresh eating, harvest cucumbers before the seeds grow too large and the skin becomes tough. If you don't want any seeds at all, or want very small seeds, consider growing English, Armenian, or Mediterranean cucumbers. Cut the fruits from the vine when you harvest them, rather than pulling them, to avoid tears in the flesh that limit the shelf-life. Cucumbers keep best when stored in a plastic bag in the refrigerator. Thin-skinned varieties will last for about a week, while thicker-skinned types store for up to 3 weeks.

Potatoes are another crop that can be harvested before reaching maturity. Young tubers harvested from green plants are called "new" potatoes. These soft-skinned spuds can be dug up and eaten as soon as the plants come into flower. But for potatoes with the longest shelf life, hold off on harvesting until 2 to 3 weeks after the plants have died back completely. During this time, the tuber's skin cures while underground, toughening it up for months of storage. New potatoes are best eaten within a week or two of harvest, while mature cured potatoes last for months if stored in a dark, cool area. Potatoes are surprisingly easy to grow in containers if you follow a few guidelines. This project uses a wire bin and newspaper to grow a hearty potato crop. Plus, it includes lots of potato-growing tips for growing spuds in any kind of containers.

POTATO BIN

MATERIALS NEEDED

A roll of 3 to 4-ft. tall
  metal chicken wire or
  cattle fencing

Newspaper

3 to 5 pounds of seed
  potatoes

Enough 50/50 blend of
  compost and potting
  soil to fill the bin,
  or any mixture of
  compost, potting soil,
  shredded leaves,
  year-old composted
  manure, or any other
  organic matter

Straw

TOOLS NEEDED

Wire cutters

Knife

While you can harvest a good potato crop from just about any wide, deep container, this one is perfect for budget-savvy gardeners.

Because the edible portion of a potato plant are the underground tubers that form along the base of the stem, the more stem surface you have beneath the soil's surface, the more potatoes the plant produces. This potato bin uses a series of layers to continually bury the plant as it grows, leading to the production of many large, potassium-packed tubers. When done properly, the 3 to 5 pounds of seed potatoes planted in each bin yield 30 to 50 pounds of mature tubers.

HOW TO MAKE A POTATO BIN

STEP 1   If the seed potatoes are larger than a golf ball, use a sharp, clean knife to cut them into 1-in. chunks, making sure each piece has at least one "eye." Let any cut seed potato pieces rest on the kitchen counter for a day to callus over before building your potato bin. Do not plant grocery-store potatoes, as they're often treated with an anti-sprouting chemical that prevents them from growing. Purchase your seed potatoes from a reputable local nursery or online source.

STEP 2   Use a pair of wire cutters to cut a piece of the metal fencing. You can make the bin any size you'd like. For a bin with a 5-ft. diameter, use a 16-ft. foot piece of fencing. For a bin that's 4 ft. across, the fence should

be 12½ ft. long. A 3-ft. bin requires a fence piece that's 9½ ft. long. Bend the fencing into a cylindrical shape and wrap the loose ends of wire around each other to fasten it closed. Place your bin in an area that receives 6 to 8 hours of full sun per day.

STEP 3   Spread a layer of newspaper, 5 to 6 layers thick, around the inside of the bottom part of the wire bin. This will hold the soil inside the bin and form your first layer. At the end of the season, the newspaper will degrade. Fill the bottom of the bin up to the top of the newspapers with a 50/50 blend of compost and potting soil (or another mixture of organic matter as mentioned above).

Continued

3

5

6

STEP 4   Space the seed potato pieces 4 to 6 in. apart and plant them about 3 in. deep into the compost/potting soil blend. Once the seed potatoes are planted, water them well.

STEP 5   Cover this layer with 2 in. of straw. Make sure the bin stays well-watered during hot, dry weather. The potatoes should begin to sprout a week or so later. When your potato sprouts reach 4 to 5 in. in height, add another layer of newspaper around the inside of the bin. Fill this layer with the 50/50 compost/potting soil blend (or whatever mixture of organic matter you have on hand) and top with another layer of straw, covering the plants and leaving only the top-most leaves exposed.

STEP 6   As the plants continue to grow, add a third layer a few weeks later, filling the bin until the potato plants are spilling out the top. Continue to water the bin regularly throughout the growing season.

STEP 7   When the plants reach maturity, they'll start to turn yellow and die back. Your potatoes are ready to harvest 2 weeks after the plants are completely dead. This extra time in the ground allows the skin to cure before the spuds are harvested, increasing their shelf-life. To harvest, simply unfold the wire edges until the

7

bin pops open. Dig through the soil and pull out the potatoes. The same wire bin can be used for many years, though you'll have to replace the newspaper and use a fresh blend of potting soil and compost every season.

Ripe eggplants have firm, tight skin. The flesh should have a slight give when pressed with a finger.

Summer squash, such as zucchini, patty-pan, and crook-neck types, are harvested while the skin is still soft. For "baby" vegetables, cut the immature fruits from plants when they're just 1 to 2 in. long. But most elongated summer squash varieties are best picked when they're 4 to 8 in. long, before the skin grows tough and the seeds enlarge. For patty-pan and round summer squashes, harvest when the fruits are between baseball- and softball-sized for the best flavor and smallest seeds. Summer squash last for 2 to 3 weeks when stored in a plastic bag in the fridge.

Winter squash, on the other hand, is harvested when the rinds of the fruits are hard and thick and can't be easily pierced with a push of a fingernail. Acorn, Delicata, butternut, buttercup, Hubbard, Kabocha, turban, and other winter squashes aren't picked until the seeds are fully formed and the vines have almost died back completely. When harvesting, cut the fruits from

Eggplants come in a surprising array of shapes, sizes, and colors. The large, dark purple eggplants found in the grocery store are by far the most common, but smaller fruited types are better suited to container culture. But regardless of which eggplants you decide to grow, knowing when they're ripe can be a challenge. Ripe eggplants are firm and have shiny, taut skin. Pressing a finger into the skin is a great test for ripeness. If the flesh has a slight give but quickly bounces back, the eggplant is ready to harvest. The seeds of ripe eggplants should be soft and small. If they're large and hard, you've waited too long to harvest. Store harvested eggplants in the fridge or, if you plan to eat them within a few days, on the countertop.

When growing summer squash in containers, choose a pot that holds at least 8 to 10 gallons of the 50/50 potting soil and compost blend.

the vine, leaving 2 to 3 in. of stem attached to the squash to help prevent rot. Cure unwashed, harvested squash by putting them in a spot that's between 70° and 80°F for two weeks. Then, move them to a cool basement or storage area between 45° and 65°F, if possible, where they'll last up to 8 months.

Cole crops are members of the Brassica family. Some, such as cabbage, kale, and collards, have edible leaves, while others, such as Brussels sprouts and kohlrabi have edible stems or stem buds. Cole crops with edible flower buds include broccoli, rapini, and cauliflower. Most cole crops are cold-season vegetables, much preferring the cooler temperatures of spring and fall. Their flavor becomes sweeter after being touched by a few fall frosts. Harvest cole crops that were planted in fall or summer after they've been subjected to several fall frosts. Those planted in the early spring should be harvested before summer's heat arrives. Cole crops with edible flowers, such as broccoli and cauliflower, whether planted in the spring or fall, should be harvested before the flower buds begin to open. Store cole crops in a plastic bag in the crisper drawer of the fridge where they'll last for 2 to 3 weeks.

Peppers are best harvested soon after they reach their mature color. The days to maturity noted on the seed packet can help you know when to expect your first ripe fruits.

Sweet or hot peppers are best harvested soon after they reach their mature color. Check the plant tag or seed packet for the expected color of the mature fruits, and cut them from the plants as soon as they attain their full color. Though peppers are still edible in an immature state, their flavor won't be as well-rounded if harvested too early. The heat in many types of hot peppers is at its best when the fruits are at full color. Red, yellow, and orange bell peppers are almost always sweeter when the fruits are mature. Harvested peppers are best stored in a plastic bag in the fridge. If kept between 40° and 33°F, refrigerated peppers last up to 2 months.

Podded veggies, like beans and peas, are ready for harvest at various times, depending on the specific type you're growing.

- For snow peas, harvest when the pods are flat, before the peas inside of them start to swell and the pods grow tough.
- For English shell peas or edible-podded sugar snap peas, wait until the peas inside the pods are fat and sassy before plucking them from the vine.
- For snap, green, or string beans, where both the seeds and the pod are consumed, harvest when the pods are crisp but still tender, before they get stringy.
- For limas, whose pods are inedible, wait until the beans fatten up and then harvest them.
- Lastly, for dried beans such as cannellini, kidney, black, Great Northern, navy, pinto, and others, the pods should remain on the plants until they're completely dried and beginning to crack open.

Shell peas are harvested when the pods are swollen and the peas inside are fully formed. Don't wait too long to harvest them, though, or the peas won't be tender.

As for properly storing podded vegetables, if they're harvested in a fresh, green state, store them in an air-tight plastic container or bag in the fridge for up to 5 days. Dried beans should be spread in a single layer on a screen or baking sheet and placed in a dry room for 2 to 3 weeks before being packed in airtight, lidded glass or plastic containers and placed in a cool, dark room. If stored properly, dried beans last for years.

Time of Day for Harvesting

In addition to knowing when things are ripe, what time of day you make your harvest can also affect the storage-life of homegrown produce. Though it's always a good idea to pick fresh veggies right before you're ready to eat or cook them, sometimes it's necessary to harvest several days early. In these cases, picking produce at its peak is key to making sure it's still in good shape when you're ready to eat, prepare, or process it.

For the best results, harvest from your container garden in the morning, ideally before 10:00 a.m., when the weather is still cool and the water content within the plants is still high. If you wait until the afternoon to pick, the plants contain less water and may even be water-stressed, which can negatively affect their shelf-life. This is especially important when harvesting greens, such as lettuce, chard, and kale, as well as for fruiting vines such as cucumbers, melons, and squash. No matter what you're harvesting, it's important to move your freshly picked harvest indoors and out of the sun as quickly as possible. If the best storage technique is refrigeration, be sure to get your harvest in the refrigerator as soon as you can.

If your work (or play) schedule doesn't permit you to harvest in the morning, pick in the evening instead, when the plants are no longer heat- or water-stressed.

Root crops like these turnips, parsnips (*Pastinaca sativa*), carrots, and beets, aren't overly sensitive about when they're pulled from the ground, but put them in the fridge or cold cellar quickly to preserve their flavor and moisture content.

SUCCESSION PLANTING

Even the smallest container garden can produce big yields if you pay attention to the varieties you plant, care for your containers properly, and harvest them in a timely fashion. But, there's another technique you can employ to boost the yield of your container-grown vegetable garden: succession planting.

Succession planting is a simple system that allows you to make multiple harvests from a single container. It takes advantage of the fact that many plants prefer to grow during either a cool-season (spring and fall) or a warm-season (summer). Succession planting partners two or more crops based on their desired growing season and growth rates. Generally, a fast-maturing crop is partnered with one that takes a bit longer to mature. Or multiple fast-maturing crops are planted in succession, with one going into the container as soon as the previous crop is harvested.

There are three different ways you can use succession planting to your advantage in a container garden:

1. Plant a fast-maturing, cool-season crop in the early spring. Then, after it's harvested, plant a warm-season crop in its place.
2. Plant the warm-season crop first, as soon as the danger of frost has passed, then follow its harvest with an early autumn sowing of a fast-maturing, cool-weather choice.
3. Gardeners with a long growing season can harvest three seasonal crops from the same container by planting a fast-maturing, cold-weather crop in the early spring, a warm-season crop in early summer, and then another cool-season crop in the fall.

The timing, however, is critical. If subsequent plantings go into the container too late, they won't reach maturity before the end of the growing season arrives. But if they go in too early while the weather is too warm or too cold, the plant will also suffer. Succession plantings must be timed perfectly.

When you're planting a particular succession crop, look for the "days to maturity" on the seed packet or pot tag. Flip the calendar to the date of your first expected fall frost and count backwards by the number of "days to maturity" for the crop. Then, subtract 2 to 3 more weeks. That's when to sow your succession crop. Remember that many cool-season crops have improved flavor when they've been "kissed" by frost, so harvests can continue for weeks after these plants reach maturity, even after cold weather arrives.

Slow-maturing vegetables, like peppers, should be partnered only with a fast-growing crop in a succession plan. This ensures that both crops have enough time to reach maturity.

Carrots are a good crop to use for succession planting. Sow the seeds in early spring, and they'll be ready to harvest less than 2 months later, giving you plenty of time to plant bush beans or basil in their place.

These spring-planted carrots are now ready to harvest. They'll be replaced with another vegetable crop for a late summer and early fall harvest.

Here's a list of excellent, fast-maturing, cool-season crops that make great succession planting partners whether they're planted before or after a warm-season crop:

- Radishes
- Turnips
- Lettuce
- Spinach
- Kale
- Collard greens
- Swiss chard
- Kohlrabi
- Arugula
- Mustard greens
- Beets
- Carrots
- Cilantro

Even if a late sowing of these crops doesn't reach maturity before the season ends, they can still be harvested as mini-veggies or baby greens.

When succession planting, it's extra important to pay attention to your soil. Growing two or more crops in a single season in the same container quickly depletes soil nutrients. It's important to add a few tablespoons of granular organic fertilizer to the container's soil in between plantings. Using a liquid fertilizer every few weeks is another option.

The following project is an excellent way to utilize succession planting techniques by using a pocketed planter.

CROP POCKETS

MATERIALS NEEDED

A 6-, 8-, or 10-pocket fabric closet organizer

Enough 50/50 potting soil and compost blend to fill the pockets

Plants—a mixture of small- to medium-stature vegetables and herbs with different harvest times (see list of suggestions). Plan for two plants per pocket.

TOOLS NEEDED

Scissors

Some gardeners may be reluctant to employ succession planting techniques because they don't like the idea of their containers appearing empty in mid-season. One of the easiest ways to overcome this naked feeling is to grow your veggies in mixed plantings in a pocketed planter with multiple compartments, so that even when a few of the compartments are empty, or partially empty, the others help mask it.

This unique project uses a pocketed closet organizer as a container. I like to plant a mixture of crops in mine, so as one veggie or herb gets harvested, another quickly replaces it.

Good Plant Candidates Include:

- Kale
- Swiss chard
- Globe basil
- Small-statured hot peppers
- Miniature/dwarf eggplants
- Nasturtiums
- Beets
- Arugula
- Celery
- Miniature cabbage
- Radish
- Lettuce
- Salad greens
- Bush beans

HOW TO MAKE CROP POCKETS

STEP 1   Most closet organizers are packaged accordion-style, so begin by spreading the closet organizer out, opening each pocket fully. Use a scissors to cut two ½-in.-wide holes in the bottom of each pocket for drainage. Fill each pocket with the 50/50 potting soil and compost blend to within an inch of the top.

STEP 2   While they're still in their containers, position the plants in the pockets, organizing and reorganizing them until you have a creative mixture of plants. Try to intermingle fast-maturing crops with veggies that take longer to mature so as things are harvested, other plants will fill in the space.

STEP 3   Plant the plants, being sure to carefully loosen any pot-bound roots prior to planting. Water your new closet organizer planter well.

STEP 4   Harvest the veggies and herbs as necessary, removing plants from time to time as they finish producing. At the end of the season, when the peppers, basil, and other tender crops have been frosted, the kale, lettuce, and cabbage plants will continue to produce for weeks to come.

AT THE END OF THE SEASON

Just because regular frosts are on the horizon for cold climate gardeners and the gardening season is coming to an end, it doesn't necessarily mean you have to be done enjoying your containers. While some containers have to be emptied and properly stored for the winter in colder climates, others can stay outdoors year-round. But regardless of which types of containers you have, there are a few other tasks you may want complete at season's end.

Overwintering Hardy Perennials, Trees, and Shrubs

If your containers housed any perennials, trees, or shrubs, don't expect them to overwinter in the pot if the winters are cold. Often their roots will freeze out without the insulating properties of the earth to protect them. To safely see containerized perennials, trees, and shrubs through the winter, remove them from the pot and plant them in the ground. If you don't have a place for them in an in-ground garden, temporarily heel them into the compost pile for the winter and then repot them in the spring. If you don't have a compost pile or garden in which to overwinter them, you may be able to get perennials, trees, and shrubs to successfully overwinter in their containers by providing them with an extra layer of insulation

To do this, first make sure the perennial, tree, or shrub is planted in a frost-proof container (one that won't crack when exposed to freeze-thaw cycles). Then, surround the entire container with a cylinder of chicken wire or box wire fencing. This ring of fencing should be 1 to 2 ft. wider than the diameter of the pot and exactly as tall. Place the cylinder of fencing around the pot and

Depending on your climate, overwintering shrubs like this oakleaf hydrangea (*Hydrangea quercifolia*) that are grown in containers may require surrounding them with a bit of extra insulation.

pack autumn leaves, straw, or hay into the area between the pot and the wire ring. Fill it up to the top of the pot, being sure to pack it in densely by stepping it down with your foot. The outside of the pot should be fully surrounded by insulating materials, but the top should not be covered. Nor should the plant. Then, put 1 to 2 in. of shredded leaves or bark on the surface of the soil in the pot. Do not pile it up against, or on top of, the plant.

When insulating pots in this manner, you'll still need to water them throughout the winter months, making sure they receive adequate moisture if natural precipitation doesn't occur. When early spring arrives, gradually remove the insulation materials over the course of a week. Then, remove the wire fencing and cross your fingers that the plant survived.

Non-hardy tropical plants need to be overwintered safely. Many can be grown as houseplants during the winter months, while others are easier to overwinter in a dormant state.

Overwintering Prized Plants

When it's time to deconstruct your container plantings at the end of the growing season, it's also time to think about whether or not you'd like to try to overwinter any of the plants growing in them. Many popular ornamental and tropical container plants make wonderful houseplants, if you bring them indoors before they're frosted. Some container-grown vegetables, including peppers and tomatoes, can even be brought indoors for the winter where, with enough light, they may continue to produce for several more weeks. Some cold-sensitive plants are also easy to overwinter in a dormant state.

Just before fall's first frost is the best time to move any tropical plants indoors. Here's how to do it.

If the Plant Is in a State of Active Growth

1. Spray all the foliage with a sharp stream of water from the hose to dislodge all pests. Make sure the foliage has a chance to dry completely before continuing.
2. Choose an indoor location for the plant where it will receive a good amount of sun, but for best results keep it out of direct sunlight. Keep tropical plants away from drafty spots like next to doors and forced air ducts.
3. If you place a saucer beneath the plant to protect furniture and flooring, never allow water to sit in the saucer for longer than a few hours. Doing so could lead to root rot and prevent the roots from accessing the air they need to thrive.
4. To water, move the entire pot to a bathtub or sink, if possible, and allow at least 20% of the water you put in the top of the pot to drain out the bottom. This flushes out fertilizer salts and prevents the tips of the foliage from turning brown from fertilizer salt accumulation. Wait until the potting soil is dry before watering. In general, indoor plants should be watered every week to 10 days, depending on the humidity in your home and how warm you keep it during the winter months.
5. Don't be surprised if many of the leaves fall off your plant soon after you bring it indoors. This is particularly true of plants like tropical hibiscus and gardenias. Don't panic—just continue to care for the plant, and soon it will grow a whole new set of leaves. Some may even bloom.
6. Refrain from fertilizing overwintering tropical plants while they're indoors.

Fertilization encourages new growth and winter is not the best time to be encouraging new foliage. Instead, hold off on fertilizing the plants until early spring, when a period of active growth starts and the plants begin to make their way back outdoors.

7. Prune them only if you must. As you bring your tropical plants indoors for the winter, you may find that some of them hardly fit in the door! Fall is not the best time to prune these plants, but do it if you must. Otherwise wait until spring to do any pruning.
8. And lastly, keep a careful eye on your plants for any possible pest issues throughout the winter months. Aphids, mealybugs, scale, and other plant pests can quickly become problematic. Regularly inspect your tropical plants and treat them for any pests you happen to find by hand-crushing them or paying a visit to your local garden center for an appropriate organic pest control product.

If the Plant Is Dormant

Not all tropical plants can be overwintered in a dormant state, but these two groups can.

Non-hardy bulbs and tubers, such as elephant ears, caladiums, cannas, calla lilies, tuberous begonias, dahlias, and sweet potato vines are best overwintered as bare bulbs. Let the foliage get frosted once or twice, then dig up the bulbs or tubers, gently brush off any excess soil, label them, and place them in a cardboard box or plastic bin filled with slightly dampened peat moss or perlite. Put the box where temperatures range between 40° and 50°F. An attached, but unheated garage or basement is ideal. When spring arrives, replant them in your containers after the danger of frost has passed.

For non-hardy woody plants that can be overwintered in a dormant state, such as jasmine, brugmansia, plumaria, plumbago, and figs, move them indoors before frost arrives. Use a sharp stream of water to dislodge any pests and move them into a cool location with little or no light. Between 40° and 50°F is best. Soon after moving indoors, the plants will drop all their leaves and shift into dormancy. If there's any light coming in, cover the plants with a black trash bag. Water the plants sparingly once every 6 to 8 weeks. When spring arrives, repot the plants with new potting soil/compost blend and do any necessary pruning. Gradually increase the amount of light the plants receive, introducing them to full sun conditions slowly over the course of 4 to 6 weeks. Do not move them outdoors full-time until the danger of frost has passed.

Caladiums are quite easy to overwinter as bare bulbs. Once the foliage has been frosted, cut off the leaves and store the bulbs in a box of peat moss.

To Overwinter by Taking Stem Cuttings

If you can't bear to part with favorite container-grown annuals, take some stem cuttings to cultivate indoors. Sweet potato vines, lantana, verbena, fuchsia, geraniums, silver falls, coleus, plectranthus, heliotrope, some succulents, and many other specialty annuals are traditionally propagated by taking cuttings, so starting some of your own is an easy task.

1. Fill several 2 in. or 3 in. plastic nursery pots with sterile potting soil. Use new containers and new potting mix to ensure they're pathogen free.

2. Use a clean, sharp pair of scissors or pruners to cut off a terminal portion of stem containing two or three leaves and the growing point. Take multiple cuttings from each plant, as not all of them will take root. Each cutting should be 2 to 3 in. long.

3. Dip the bottom inch of each cutting into rooting hormone (available at most garden centers or online). Insert the base of each cutting into its own clean pot of fresh potting soil. Tamp the soil firmly around the plant stem.

4. Water the cutting in and let it drain, then cover the container (cutting and all) with a plastic baggie. Seal the baggie with a twist tie.

5. The baggie keeps the humidity high as the cutting forms new roots, so you won't have to water it very often. But if you notice the soil is dry, remove the pot from the baggie and water the cutting.

6 Place the pots in a bright location, but out of direct sunlight. A windowsill will work fine, but if you have grow lights, put the pots a few inches beneath them.

7. In 4 to 6 weeks, remove the pot from the baggie and gently tug on the plant. If it resists, roots have formed. You can also check for roots by flipping the plant out of the pot carefully and checking the soil for roots.

8. Once the cutting has rooted, remove it from the bag and treat it as a houseplant until the spring thaw. You may need to pinch the plant once or twice through the winter to help control the size.

MAKING SEASONAL CONTAINER PLANTINGS AND DECORATIONS

After the last few veggies have been harvested and the frost-nipped annuals are pulled from your containers, you can switch gears and use your containers for another purpose: decoration.

Many gardeners swap out their container plants upon autumn's arrival, pulling out spent annuals and summer veggies and replacing them with mums, ornamental flowering kale, asters, and other fall-themed plantings. Decorative gourds and pumpkins make great additions to late-season containers, as do cut branches of colorful oak, maple, and other leaves or berries inserted into the soil as accents.

Come winter, arrangements of evergreen boughs, berried branches, dried flowers, seed pods, and decorative accents spruce up empty containers for the holidays. One of my favorite things to do with the large ceramic container on my front porch is to swap the plants growing in it with a small Charlie Brown Christmas tree. I string the tree with small white lights, add a

Decorative gourds, pumpkins, and orange-berried winterberry branches make a beautiful container display after plants have been removed for the season.

few branches of rosehips and privet berries, and tuck in some dried ornamental grass fronds for a winter welcome to our guests.

There are a million different ways to use natural materials to fill empty containers for the holidays. Collect these materials from your own yard, the yard of a friend, or purchase them from flower or craft stores.

Some of my favorite cut branches, berries, and seedpods to use for decorative seasonal containers include:

- Evergreen holly
- Winterberry
- Rosehips
- Bittersweet vine
- Birch logs and twigs
- Red twig dogwood
- Beautyberries
- Crabapple branches with fruit
- Evergreen boughs
- Boxwood
- Dried hydrangeas
- Curly willow
- Ornamental grass flower fronds
- Privet berries
- Juniper boughs
- Pinecones
- Milkweed pods
- Perennial hibiscus seed pods

When using these materials to create a unique holiday decoration in a container, you can follow the design instructions discussed in Chapter 2 by using the filler, thriller, and spiller concept, the flat-backed style, or you can come up with your own creative designs, remembering to keep everything in balance by placing weightier items down low in the container.

If you're not interested in doing some type of design in your containers, but you still want to have something interesting in them, simply lay an evergreen wreath from your local nursery, floral shop, or hardware store down on the top of your empty container. Then, place a lantern or pumpkin in the center of the wreath, or insert a dozen twigs or sticks into the soil at the center of the wreath so it looks like a small deciduous shrub is growing there. You can even add lights if you'd like. It's a great way to introduce some interest without having to go to a lot of trouble with an official design.

EMPTYING AND STORING CONTAINERS

If your containers no longer contain live plants or house seasonal decorations, it's time to empty and store them for the colder months, if you live where freezing temperatures are the norm. While fiberglass, metal, and other frost-proof containers can stay outdoors year-round, many other containers cannot. Because attractive, quality containers can be expensive, I always recommend emptying pots and moving them to a sheltered area if you live in a colder climate.

Should you reuse potting soil? Potting soil is not cheap, and it's very tempting to use it for more than one season. But ideally you should use a fresh 50/50 blend of compost and potting soil to fill your containers every year. At the end of the growing season, the potting mix in your containers is largely devoid of nutrients, and the pots will likely be filled with many fibrous roots. There may also be certain disease organisms

Scrub out empty pots with a 10% bleach solution to ensure your containers don't harbor any fungal or bacterial diseases. This is especially important for containers used to grow vegetables.

present. So if your budget allows, I recommend replacing 100% of the potting soil and compost blend at the start each season. But if you can't afford to do so, save half of the used potting mix from year to year and top it off with new potting soil/compost blend before replanting your containers the following spring.

If you're feeling guilty about throwing your used potting soil blend into the compost heap, here are two great ways you can give it new life:

- Save your used potting soil in plastic garbage bags, buckets, or bins. In spring, you'll have it to pot up perennial divisions from the garden to share with friends.
- Add your used potting soil to the potato bin project featured earlier in this chapter by layering it with chopped leaves, compost, shredded newspaper, and aged horse manure, and using it to grow potatoes.

Once your containers have been emptied, it's time to store them for the winter. Ideally, all empty pots should be scrubbed inside and out with a diluted 10% bleach solution (9 parts water to 1 part bleach) and a stiff brush (a good quality toilet brush works great). This is important for pots that were used to grow tomatoes and other disease-prone vegetables, no matter what material they're made of.

After scrubbing, rinse the pots well and allow them to dry thoroughly. Stack your containers upside down in a garage, shed, or another protected site. If you don't have a storage area, place the pots upside down on a palette, bricks, or some other elevated surface, and cover them with a tarp or a sheet of plastic to keep water out.

Glazed and unglazed ceramic or terracotta pots will crack and/or flake if left outdoors during freezing weather. This happens because water

Most houseplants love being outdoors during the growing season. Just remember to move them back inside before the temperatures drop. This Dieffenbachia is quite at home in the low light conditions of a front porch.

makes its way into the material, and through the natural expansion and contraction of freeze-thaw cycles, the containers crack. Freezing temperatures weaken plastic containers, too, causing them to crack within a few seasons.

If you don't want to go through the effort of emptying, cleaning, and storing pots at the end of every season, consider growing your plants in fabric containers or growing your garden in disposable containers, such as feedbags, coffee-bean sacks, or canvas bags.

Follow nature's cues and the natural progression of the growing season to maximize the health and productivity of your container garden. From the start of the growing season until winter's arrival, let the life cycles of the plants you're growing take the lead.

chapter 6

More Container Concepts

The possibilities are nearly limitless when it comes to growing in containers, and there's no doubt that your own creativity is the best muse, but a little extra inspiration never hurts. Sometimes, the best container designs are an extension of a bright idea someone else had first, and there's nothing wrong with borrowing a little inspiration from another gardener who shares your style or whose style you can easily modify to fit your own. In fact, garden tours, public gardens, magazines, websites, and books like this one are the perfect places to get your creative juices flowing; they can help you craft some pretty wonderful stuff.

In this chapter, I'll introduce ten additional container gardening concepts easily tailored to many different gardening styles. All of these concepts are scalable and readily adapted to whatever plants you'd like to grow, provided they're the right physical size for the container.

◀ Public container plantings, such as this pot on a sidewalk in Quebec City, Canada, that uses cherry tomatoes as a "spiller," are great places to find inspiring ideas.

▶ Though these pots of basil will have to be moved when diners arrive, the ability to toss a few fresh basil leaves into their salads makes the effort well worth it.

TABLETOP PLANTERS

Greening up your outdoor living space can be as effortless as having a living centerpiece. Use pint-sized tabletop planters to adorn side tables, beverage carts, bistro tables, outdoor bars, and other small surfaces on your patio, deck, or balcony. Or group three or four petite tabletop planters together on a larger dining table or outdoor sofa table. A single large container filled with edible or flowering plants also makes a great centerpiece for a bigger outdoor dining table. For good design, select a round container for a round table and an oblong container for an oval or rectangular table.

More creative ideas for tabletop planters:

- If you're hosting a dinner party, consider creating a tiny individual planted container to place at each of your guest's seats. Write their name or an inspirational message on the pot and send them home with the planter at the end of the party as a remembrance of the evening.
- Containers of bonsai or tiny tree seedlings make lovely tabletop accents. Though they require regular maintenance and careful pruning if you want to maintain their size, these diminutive trees are always attention grabbers.
- Containerized culinary herbs are the perfect plant choices for living centerpieces, as they can be trimmed and added to salads and sandwiches as they're being served.
- For patio tables with umbrellas, use a bundt cake pan with a few drainage holes added to plant your centerpiece. Put the umbrella through the hole in the center of the pan and fill it with succulents, herbs, flowering annuals, or other interesting plants.

Large living centerpieces like this one make a bold statement in outdoor dining areas. Choose a unique container to really create an eye-catching focal point.

This collection of three small, succulent-filled containers helps green up an outdoor sofa table, adding interest and color to the space.

Choosing a foliage plant with colorful variegation is a fun way to accent a unique side table like this one.

A small maple seedling popping out of a pot of moss makes a clean, simple tabletop planter at Chanticleer Garden. The table itself is a surprise—it's a glass-topped garden pot with a collection of greenery growing inside.

Don't underestimate the power of simplicity. A single foliage plant does wonders to dress up a side table.

STRAWBERRY POTS

Strawberry pots are tall planters with staggered holes or pockets around their exterior. Traditionally they're used for growing strawberries, because they keep the ripening fruit off the ground, help improve air circulation, and allow you to grow lots of berry plants in a very small area. But strawberry pots have their downsides, too: they're notoriously difficult to water, they can be tough to plant, some styles dry out very quickly, and the plants often grow unevenly. But these faults are easy to overcome with just a few simple tweaks. In fact, strawberry pots are excellent containers for growing all sorts of plants, including vegetables, greens, herbs, and flowers, especially where space is an issue.

- Strawberry pots made from porous terracotta dry out very quickly. Choose one that's made from glazed ceramic or plastic instead, or seal the terracotta with two layers of sealant before planting.
- Look for strawberry pots with deep pockets instead of flat holes. The pockets are better at collecting irrigation water and they allow more room for root growth.
- When watering strawberry pots from the top, the water often runs out the side holes rather than soaking into the soil. One trick to ensure this doesn't happen is to insert a section of PVC pipe with ½-in. holes drilled down its length through the center of the pot at the time of planting. When irrigation water is added, it's poured into the hollow pipe where it will slowly soak into the surrounding soil through the holes.

One way to overcome the irrigation challenges of strawberry pots is to insert a perforated PVC pipe down the center of the pot to channel irrigation water directly to plant roots. Another is to fill the pot with drought-tolerant plants like these succulents.

Terracotta strawberry pots, such as this one filled with hot pepper plants, are notoriously difficult to water and can dry out very quickly. But these challenges are easy to overcome with a few small tweaks.

Strawberry pots with pockets instead of flat holes are far easier to water and allow for better root growth. This one also has no drainage hole in the bottom, making it a perfect fit for bog plants like these carnivorous pitcher plants.

Large strawberry pot-style planters are an excellent way to grow a lot of plants in a small space. This planter is unique in that it also serves as a worm composting system. Worms are added to the soil at planting time and kitchen scraps are tossed down the central tube on a regular basis to feed the worms whose castings then feed the plants.

- Do not fill your strawberry pot completely with soil and then try to push plants in through the holes. Instead, fill the pot up to the bottom rim of the lowest holes and then plant from the inside out by pushing the top of the plant out through the hole. It's far easier to gently jimmy the foliage out the hole than it is to cram a big root ball in from the outside. When those plants are in place, add more potting mix until you reach the bottom of the next set of holes and repeat the process until you reach the top of the pot.

- To prevent uneven growth, if possible turn your strawberry pot a quarter turn every few days to ensure all the plants receive ample sunlight.

FAIRY GARDENS AND MINIATURES

Fairy gardens are a very whimsical addition to your container garden, and children take great pride in helping to make and maintain them. Fairy gardens combine diminutive plants with tiny accents, such as fairy houses, dollhouse-sized furniture, and other wee adornments. It's great fun to design a container of miniatures for these imaginary garden creatures, and pint-sized garden guests will love playing with it.

Though fairy gardening is an art of its own with several books dedicated to the subject and entire plant collections selected, bred, and marketed specifically for them, here are a few easy ways to build a containerized fairy garden of your own.

- Wheelbarrows with a few added drainage holes make great fairy gardens. Easy to move from place to place, wheelbarrows sit at the perfect height for curious little eyes and hands. Simply fill the wheelbarrow with planting mix, select, arrange, and plant multiple dwarf or miniature plants in it, and then add a fairy house, some stepping stones, and other accents.

Use a favorite fairy tale, story, or movie to create a themed fairy garden in a container. This one includes Rapunzel's tower made from a section of PVC pipe covered in small stones.

Wheelbarrows make great fairy gardens because they sit at the perfect height for children's eyes and hands.

Containerized fairy gardens don't have to be large or elaborate to be appreciated by kids and adults alike.

- Create a themed fairy garden by choosing a favorite fairy tale, story, or movie and building the garden with that theme in mind. If *Hansel and Gretel* is a favorite, make a miniature gingerbread house out of small terracotta tiles and white caulking. Or, for mermaid lovers, build an underwater-themed fairy garden by topping the soil with sand, glass pebbles, and smooth sea glass, and including succulents with small, round, bubble-like leaves. Top it off with a small boat propped a few inches above the sand on a stack of rocks.

- Fairy gardens can be very elaborate or simple and sweet. Even a small pot by the back door will garner the attention of a child. Don't feel you have to go to the extreme to please the little gardener in your life. The key is to let them touch, feel, and rearrange the accents in your fairy garden as much as they'd like.

VERTICAL AND HANGING PLANTERS

Vertical gardens and hanging planters are a great way to grow up or down, instead of out. They save space, cover unused, empty walls, and add more growing area to almost any site. And a strategically placed, free-standing vertical planter can increase privacy, reduce noise, and provide shade for seating areas—not to mention its good looks.

There are hundreds of ways to grow vertically, each with its own merits and faults. Vertical planters are easily made from recycled or repurposed items such as wood pallets, plastic water jugs, picture frames, rain gutters, old buckets, hanging shoe organizers, plastic or metal pipes, and scrap lumber, to name just a few.

There are also scores of commercially made vertical planting systems, including free-standing planter "walls," wheeled, mobile gardens with multiple tiers, and fabric pouches to hang on a wall, fence, or other vertical structure.

Hanging planters are another effective way to save space and garner more room for your plants to grow. Hanging baskets and other types of hanging wall planters can be used to grow food or ornamentals, fill unused vertical space, or add a splash of color to an area otherwise devoid of interest.

A moss-lined wall planter flanks the front door and welcomes visitors with a combination of shade-loving foliage plants, including rex begonias, ivy, golden arrowhead vine (*Syngonium podophyllum* 'Maria Allusion'), and a staghorn fern (*Platycerium* spp.).

There are many ways to build a vertical planter out of a repurposed household item. This planter is made from pouches of chicken wire lined with moss and mounted in an old picture frame.

This wall planter at the Naples Botanic Garden in Florida is made from fabric pouches installed on a wood and wire frame. Filled with tropicals, herbs, and flowering annuals, a vertical planter like this one can increase privacy, reduce noise, and shade nearby seating areas.

Vertical planters such as this herb-filled pallet garden, are a great way to save space and add more growing area to almost any site.

Empty birdcages make great hanging planters. This one hosts a small potted vine and hangs next to a frequently used walkway.

CONTAINER WATER GARDENS

Easy to make and maintain, containerized water gardens hosting a small fountain or bubbler bring the sound of moving water to the landscape and create a small-scale habitat for birds, frogs, dragonflies, and other aquatic creatures. You can even put a few fish in your patio water garden—they'll eat the mosquito larvae and add another element of interest.

Containerized water gardens can be simple or complex, large or small. All you need is a container, a few plants, and water. The upcoming project takes building a patio water garden one step further and includes instructions for making a bamboo fountain to circulate the water in the pot.

At the end of the growing season, you have several options for seeing your water garden through the winter. The first is to completely drain the pot and overwinter the plants indoors. Most water plants can be placed in a tub of water in a cool basement or garage for the winter, where they'll shift into dormancy. Another option is to

Container water gardens can be made out of any type of container, including the kitchen sink! This one uses a re-circulating pump to send the water from the basin back out through the faucet.

keep the water garden outdoors all winter long. Hardy varieties of aquatic plants can be left in the pot during the colder months, though you'll need a birdbath heater to keep the water from freezing solid. If you plan to leave your container outdoors all winter long, stick to plastic, acrylic, or other frost-proof container materials for a longer life. Turn the fountain off and move the pump indoors until spring arrives.

Maintaining container water gardens is easy. There's no need to ever swap out the water in your container; just top it off with collected rainwater or de-chlorinated tap water as necessary throughout the season. Mosquitoes seldom become problematic as long as the water is being circulated, but if they do become an issue, float a round mosquito cake made from the biological pesticide Bti (*Bacillius thuringiensis* var. *israelensis*), called a "mosquito dunk," in the container. It will not harm plants, fish, or other aquatic life.

Even the smallest container water garden serves as excellent habitat for frogs and other creatures.

PATIO WATER GARDEN WITH BAMBOO

For this containerized water garden we used a glazed ceramic pot, but any water-tight container will do. Avoid porous pots, such as those made of unglazed terracotta, as the water will quickly seep out of them unless you take the time to apply a sealant. If you want to build a water garden in a half whiskey barrel or another container that may slowly leach water, line the interior with a double layer of pond liner at least 10 mm thick before filling the container with water.

There are many different aquatic plants that grow well in a containerized water garden. Select three to four plants from the following list for your water garden or head to your local nursery to see what they have in stock.

- Arrowhead (*Sagittaria latifolia*)
- Dwarf cattail (*Typha minima*)
- Dwarf papyrus (*Cyperus haspans*)
- Dwarf umbrella palm (*Cyperus alternifolius*)
- Water iris (*Iris louisiana*)
- Variegated sweetflag (*Acorus calamus variegatus*)
- Parrot's feather (*Myriophyllum aquatica*)
- Water lettuce (*Pistia stratiotes*)
- Water hyacinth (*Eichhornia crassipes*)
- Water lilies (many species)
- Lotus (*Nelumbo nucifera*, *N. lutea*, and hybrids)
- Floating heart (*Nymphoides peltata*)
- Taro root (*Colocasia* spp.)

MATERIALS NEEDED

1 large non-porous container; this one holds 30 gallons

1 tube silicone caulking

1 to 2-in. diameter bamboo stake; about 5 to 7 ft. long

2 plastic zip ties

1 roll jute twine

1 small submersible fountain or pond pump with adjustable flow control (100 to 140 GPH; pumping height of 3 to 4 ft.)

3 to 4 ft. of flexible, ½-in. clear poly tubing

Bricks or blocks to prop up plants

Rocks to weigh down pots

Decorative rocks for the container's edge (if desired)

3 to 4 aquatic plants from the list at left

TOOLS NEEDED

Caulk gun

Folding saw or bamboo saw

Continued

HOW TO MAKE A PATIO WATER GARDEN WITH BAMBOO

STEP 1   Begin by placing the empty container wherever you'd like your water garden to be, as it will be too heavy to move once filled with water. Select a location that receives at least 6 hours of direct sunlight per day. If your container has a drainage hole in the bottom, seal the drainage hole with silicone caulk. Let the caulk dry for at least 24 hours. Make sure the caulk is fully dry before proceeding to the next step.

STEP 2   Cut two pieces of bamboo to form the base for the fountain, using a sharp pruning saw. Each piece should be long enough to overhang the edge of the pot on either side by 1 to 2 in. Cut a third piece of bamboo to form the waterspout. The back end of this piece should be long enough to extend over the back edge of

the pot, while the front end should sit about 3 to 4 in. inside the front lip of the pot. If you want, you can cut the front edge of this piece of bamboo on an angle.

STEP 3   Fasten the two base pieces together, one above the waterspout and the other below it, using two plastic zip ties. Make sure the zip ties are about halfway between the waterspout and the pot's edge. Tighten the zip ties securely.

STEP 4   Wrap a long piece of jute twine over both of the zip ties multiple times to hide them. Wrap another length of twine in a figure 8 around both of the base pieces where the waterspout comes out. This holds the waterspout in place.

STEP 5   Slide one end of the clear poly tubing over the exit valve on the pump (making sure you have the ½-in. adaptor in place). Depending on the size pump you have, you may have to adjust the water flow in a later step. Place the pump in the bottom of the pot with the cord running up and out of the back of the pot.

STEP 6   Insert the other end of the clear poly tubing into the back end of the piece of bamboo that will be the waterspout. Pull the tubing through the bamboo waterspout. Cut any excess tubing off so the end of the tubing sits just inside the end of the bamboo spout.

STEP 7   Place rocks, blocks, or bricks in the bottom of the pot and begin arranging the containerized plants on them so the rims of the containers sit 1 to 3 in. below the rim of the large pot. Position the plants

so they hide the electric cord and plastic tubing. Add water to the pot until filled almost to the top. If any of the potted plants begin to float, weigh them down by putting a few rocks into the pot around the plant. Once the pot is full of water, add any floating plants, such as water hyacinth or water lettuce.

STEP 8   If desired, to soften the edge of the pot and help hold the fountain in place, put a few decorative rocks on the edge of the pot. Plug in the pump. If the flow rate is too heavy or too light, unplug the pump, lift it out of the water, and adjust the flow rate valve until the correct flow rate is achieved. Never run the pump when it's out of the water and never adjust the pump while it's plugged in. If you'd like to add fish to your water garden, wait 3 to 5 days before adding them.

SUCCULENT CONTAINERS

In addition to the cement bin succulent planter featured in Chapter 1, there are dozens of other great ways to utilize these versatile plants in your container garden. Succulents are plants with thick, water-filled foliage. They're drought and heat tolerant, and they require very little in regards to their maintenance and watering needs. Succulents can survive extended periods without water; they're a great choice for forgetful container gardeners!

Here are a handful of creative ways to use succulents in container plantings.

Use a single bold succulent, like a blue or variegated agave, in a featured specimen planting for a striking addition to your container garden.

▲ Succulents are excellent choices for vertical plantings, living walls, and living roofs. They're easy to propagate, and they don't mind living in tight quarters.

◀ Plant succulents in containers of any size, shape, or color to make a beautiful display of interesting textures and forms.

Pots of succulents placed on sunny window sills won't suffer from neglect like some other plants do. Hang a wire shelving unit under an exterior window and place potted succulents on it instead of installing a window box planter.

Top a birdhouse, mailbox, or chicken coop with a roof of succulents.

Make a succulent topiary by lining the inside of a wire frame with moss, filling it with succulent potting mix, and planting an assortment of mixed succulents.

Place bowls or small pots of succulents on top of just about any flat space to add texture and color to an otherwise blank slate.

PLANT FOUNTAINS

Plant fountains are among the most beautiful additions to a container garden. They add vertical flair and are an excellent way to showcase how creative container gardens can be, without requiring a lot of work to maintain them.

Plant fountains are made two different ways.

First, food, foliage, and flower fountains can be made by converting an existing tiered water fountain into a planter. This is a great way to repurpose a fountain with a broken pump system, one that was too difficult to maintain, or one that is simply no longer wanted. Once the fountain is in place, drill a few drainage holes into each tier (or open the drain plug in the base of the tier, if one is present), and fill the fountain with soil and plants. Keep in mind that the tiers of some fountains are deeper than others, so plant choices need to reflect that. Opt to include a mixture of plants in your fountain or stick with a single species, but be sure there are plenty of "spillers" in your fountain to mimic water cascading from tier to tier.

The top tier of your fountain typically needs to be watered more frequently than the lower tiers, which hold more soil. Also consider the height of your fountain when choosing what plants to add to it. Keep edible crops within easy reach on lower tiers.

Food fountains like this one are a great way to grow a wide variety of fruits, vegetables, and herbs in a small space. Plus, they're easy to build and harvest.

Surround the base of your plant fountain with more containers of plants to maximize space.

Plant fountains fashioned out of tiered garden fountains can be filled with edibles, flowers, or foliage plants such as sedum.

To further maximize production and beauty, surround the base of your fountain with more potted plants. Not only will it mask a potentially unattractive base, it's also a great use of space.

Food, foliage, and flower fountains can also be made by stacking graduated sizes of containers on top of each other to create a fountain effect. The containers can either have a matching style and color, or they can be a mixture of complimentary pots. Plant fountains made in this manner can house a single species of plant, or they can contain a mixture of plants.

Food fountains are a cool and clever way to grow a lot of herbs, veggies, and small fruits in a very compact area. Just select two or more containers of varying sizes and stack them on top of each other using an upturned clay pot or a few bricks to hold each layer on top of the one beneath. Once the pots are stacked, fill each container with soil and plants. Keep in mind that the north side of the fountain receives less sunlight than the other sides, so stick with plants that won't mind the slightly lower light level. The other alternative is to rotate the fountain every few days, if it's not too heavy to do so.

STOCK TANK PLANTERS

Large, galvanized stock tanks have always been familiar to ranchers and farmers who raise livestock, but now we gardeners are putting them to good use, too. Instead of filling them with drinking water, we're filling them with potting soil and plants, using them to grow all manner of wonderful plant combinations, from salsa gardens to cut flower combos.

I've seen stock tanks used as accessible planters in public gardens for people with disabilities, beds for colorful vegetables in school gardens, and as easy-to-harvest lettuce beds on an urban farm. Their versatility is pretty wide-ranging.

Another creative way to use a stock tank is as a water garden. Plug the drainage hole, fill the tank with a mixture of soil and water, and plant it with aquatic plants, making a raised mini pond. Because the tanks are galvanized and weather-proof, your stock tank water garden can stay outdoors year-round. Plant hardy aquatic plants in it if you want them to live from year to year.

In addition to using stock tanks as raised bed-like planters, there are many other items easily repurposed into similar garden beds. Large items such as old, metal wash tubs, water tanks, and even bathtubs, are readily converted into containers. Smaller items, such as baby pools and even empty dresser drawers make nice mini raised beds, too.

Use stock tanks to create raised garden ponds like this one. The horsetails (*Equisetum hyemal*) growing it in complement the modern style of the house and patio furniture.

This stock tank planter hosts a combination of flowering and foliage annuals and dresses up an otherwise barren area.

CARNIVOROUS-PLANT CONTAINERS

Carnivorous plants are surprisingly easy to grow in containers, if you provide them with conditions that mimic their natural habitat. Like other plants, carnivorous species use sunlight to make their own food, but they also digest small insects that get caught in their jaw-like leaves, trapped on their sticky surface, or fall into their water-filled, tubular leaves. The plants then digest their victims with the help of numerous enzymes.

Carnivorous plants do best in bright areas with high humidity, and they require wet, but not constantly saturated soil. Though not all species of carnivorous plants are winter hardy, some are. If you want your containerized carnivorous plants to survive the winter outdoors, make sure you choose varieties hardy to your area. Some species are fully hardy through much of the northern United States and Canada.

Carnivorous plants naturally grow in boggy areas, where the soil is lean and acidic. To accommodate their needs, the following project uses a casserole dish with no drainage holes as a planter, but you can grow carnivorous plants in any bowl-like container that lacks drainage.

At season's end, if you've selected winter-hardy plants, bury the container in the garden or compost pile so the top of the pot is level with the top of the soil and forget about it for the winter. Or if you've selected non-hardy varieties, move the pot indoors into a cold, but not freezing, basement or garage with a small window. The plants need to shift into winter dormancy for a few months, during which time the soil needs to remain damp, but not waterlogged. When spring arrives, the container should be moved outdoors again.

Carnivorous plants, such as these pitcher plants (*Sarracena* spp.), are surprisingly easy to grow in containers.

Hardy carnivorous plants can be overwintered by sinking the pot into the ground. Non-hardy varieties are best overwintered by moving the container into a cold basement or garage.

CARNIVOROUS CASSEROLE

Carnivorous plants are some of my favorite underused container gems. They garner a lot of attention and fascinate old and young visitors alike. As long as you're willing to care for them properly and choose the best varieties for your gardening zone, container-grown carnivorous plants will live for many years.

Note: Never collect carnivorous plants from the wild, even if it's on your own property. Instead, purchase only nursery-grown plants that have not been collected from the wild.

There is a sly comic irony to this project. Planted in a casserole container, this garden is not meant to be eaten, but to *do* the eating.

Types of Carnivorous Plants Suited to Container Culture

- Pitcher plants (*Sarracena* spp.)
- Sundews (*Drosera* spp.)
- Venus flytrap (*Dionaea muscipula*)
- Butterworts (*Pinguicula* spp.)

HOW TO MAKE A CARNIVOROUS CASSEROLE

STEP 1   Mix the peat moss or potting soil with the sand in a small bucket or bin, and fill the container with an inch or two of the mix. Carefully remove the plants from their containers and plant them one by one into the casserole dish. Loosen any pot-bound roots as you plant. After all the plants are in place, fill in around them with more of the peat moss/potting soil and sand blend until the container is filled to within an inch of its rim.

STEP 2   Cover the exposed planting mix with decorative reindeer moss or sphagnum sheet moss to aid in moisture retention and give the container a finished

look. When you water your carnivorous casserole planter, use rainwater or distilled water and fill the container until it's completely flooded. Then, over the period of a few days, let the water level drop, but never let it dry out completely. Add more water when the soil is merely damp.

STEP 3   Put your carnivorous casserole where it will receive 4 to 6 hours of full sun per day. Contrary to popular belief, do not feed your carnivorous plants raw hamburger. They're unable to digest the proteins in it. If you leave your carnivorous plants outdoors, the plants will trap plenty of insects on their own.

EVEN MORE IDEAS

There's really no end to what a creative gardener can do with containers. Here is a small sampling of some additional ideas.

Sometimes, plants themselves make great containers. This unique living basket hosts a collection of edibles and ornamentals, including kale, mustard greens, chard, hot peppers, and cosmos (*Cosmos sulphureus*).

Whether small or large, topiaries make gorgeous container specimens, even if your garden isn't overly formal. Here we see large topiaries growing in a collection of mixed containers.

Even empty pots serve as unique garden accents. This ivy-covered urn serves as a great focal point.

For apartment dwellers limited to gardening on balconies and fire escapes, hanging buckets and railing planters like these are a great way to grow.

This creative gardener built a tiered wooden planter box when a dead street tree was removed from a cavity in the sidewalk.

I will leave you with one final thought when it comes to creating a successful container garden. Don't be afraid to let your creativity take over. All the ideas, concepts, and projects featured throughout this book are merely a starting point that hopefully leads you to discover the infinite number of grand ideas already inside of your own head and heart. Find inspiration and happiness in your container garden and it will sing, no matter its style or size. As with all things gardening, take pleasure in the process as much as in the end results.

Enjoy your new container garden!

Resource Guide

Arbico Organics
PO Box 8910
Tucson, AZ 85738
800-827-2847
www.arbico-organics.com

Berries Unlimited
807 Cedar Lane
Prairie Grove, AR 72753
479-846-6030
www.berriesunlimited.com

Baker Creek Heirloom Seeds
2278 Baker Creek Road
Mansfield, MO 65704
417-924-8917
www.rareseeds.com

Bay Laurel Nursery
2500 El Camino Real
Atascadero, CA 93422
805-466-3449
www.baylaurelnursery.com

Bushel and Berry
800-457-1859
www.bushelandberry.com

Buglogical Control Systems
PO Box 32046
Tucson, AZ 85751
520-298-4400
www.buglogical.com

Burpee Seed Company
300 Park Avenue
Warminster, PA 18974
800-888-1447
www.burpee.com

EarthBox® by Novelty Manufacturing Co.
1330 Loop Road
Lancaster, PA 17601
800-442-7336
www.earthbox.com

Fedco Seeds
PO Box 520
Clinton, ME 04927
207-426-9900
www.fedcoseeds.com

Gardener's Supply Company
128 Intervale Road
Burlington, VT 05401
800-876-5520
www.gardeners.com

Garden Dreams Urban Farm and Nursery
806 Holland Avenue
Pittsburgh, PA 15221
412-501-FARM
www.mygardendreams.com

Gardens Alive!
5100 Schenley Place
Lawrenceburg, IN 47025
513-354-1483
www.gardensalive.com

Heirloom Seeds
287 E. Finley Dr.
West Finley, PA 15377
724-663-5356
www.heirloomseeds.com

High Country Gardens
2438 Shelburne Road, Suite 1
Shelburne, VT 05482
800-925-9387
www.highcountrygardens.com

High Mowing Seeds
76 Quarry Road
Wolcott, VT 05680
866-735-4454
www.highmowingseeds.com

Johnny's Selected Seeds
PO Box 299
Waterville, ME 04903
877-564-6697
www.johnnyseeds.com

Logee's Plants
141 North Street
Danielson, CT 06239
888-330-8038
www.logees.com

Nature Hills Nursery
9910 North 48th Street, Suite 200
Omaha, NE 68152
888-864-7663
www.naturehills.com

Ohio Heirloom Seeds
4054 Reed Road
Columbus, OH 43220
614-554-4657
www.ohioheirloomseeds.com

One Green World Nursery
6469 SE 134th Ave
Portland, OR 97236
877-353-4028
www.onegreenworld.com

Orange Pippin Fruit Trees
Ithaca, NY
607-330-6015
www.orangepippintrees.com

Patio Edibles
www.patio-edibles.com

Raintree Nursery
391 Butts Road
Morton, WA 98356
800-391-8892
www.raintreenursery.com

Renee's Garden Seeds
6060 Graham Hill Road
Felton, CA 95018
888-880-7228
www.reneesgarden.com

Seeds of Change
PO Box 4908
Rancho Dominguez, CA 90220
888-762-7333
www.seedsofchange.com

Seed Savers Exchange
3094 North Winn Road
Decorah, IA 52101
563-382-5990
www.seedsavers.org

Southern Exposure Seed Exchange
PO Box 460
Mineral, VA 23117
540-894-9480
www.southernexposure.com

Stark Bro's Nursery
PO Box 1800
Louisiana, MO 63353
800-325-4180
www.starkbros.com

Territorial Seed Company
PO Box 158
Cottage Grove, OR 97424
800-626-0866
www.territorialseed.com

Tomato Growers Supply Company
PO Box 60015
Fort Myers, FL 33906
888-478-7333
www.tomatogrowers.com

2B Seeds
280 E. 1st Avenue #1055
Broomfield, CO 80038
303-465-3395
www.2bseeds.com

Index

Capitalized entries refer to container-gardening projects. Page numbers in *italics* refer to figure captions. Page numbers in **bold** refer to tables.

About the Author

Horticulturist Jessica Walliser cohosts *The Organic Gardeners*, an award-winning program on KDKA Radio in Pittsburgh, Pennsylvania. She is a former contributing editor for *Organic Gardening* magazine and a regular contributor to many regional and national magazines, including *Fine Gardening* and *Hobby Farms*. Jessica also serves on the Editorial Advisory Board of the American Horticultural Society.

Her two weekly gardening columns for the *Pittsburgh Tribune-Review* have been enjoyed by readers for more than ten years. Jessica's fourth book, *Attracting Beneficial Bugs to the Garden: A Natural Approach to Pest Control*, was awarded the American Horticultural Society's 2014 Book Award. She is also a cofounder of the gardening website, SavvyGardening.com, and owner of Ironweed Apparel, a company that creates unique, hand-printed shirts for gardeners and urban farmers.

To follow Jessica and her gardening adventures online:

Websites: jessicawalliser.com and
   savvygardening.com
Facebook: Jessica Walliser
   (www.facebook.com/jessica.walliser)
Twitter: @jessicawalliser
   (https://twitter.com/jessicawalliser)
Instagram: @jessicawalliser
Pinterest: Savvy Gardening
   (www.pinterest.com/savvygardening/)
Blogs: Savvy Gardening
   (www.savvygardening.com) and
   The Dirt on Gardening for Hobby Farms
   (www.hobbyfarms.com/author/jessica-walliser/)